What Colo

Is Your

Slipcover?

What Color Is Your Slipcover?

How Discovering Your Design Personality Can Help You Create the Home of Your Dreams

Denny Daikeler

Foreword by Kate White

RODALE

Printed in the United States of America
Rodale Inc. makes every effort to use acid-free (∞), recycled paper (♻).

Book design by Christopher Rhoads
Illustrations © 2004 Cornel Rubino
Photographs on pages 2 and 26 © Janis Christie/Getty Images, page 34 © Junshi Nakamichi/Getty Images, page 50 and 94 © Digital Vision/Getty Images, pages 66, 132, 144, 178, and 198 © Royalty-Free/CORBIS, page 80 and 116 © Ryan McVay/Getty Images, pages 220 and 266 © Digital Vision/Creatas, and page 242 © Brand X/Creatas

Library of Congress Cataloging-in-Publication Data

Daikeler, Denny.
    What color is your slipcover? : how discovering your design personality can help you create the home of your dreams / Denny Daikeler ; foreword by Kate White.
       p.   cm.
    Includes index.
    ISBN 1–57954–949–7 paperback
    1. Interior decoration—Psychological aspects.   I. Title: How discovering your design personality can help you create the home of your dreams.   II. Title.
NK2113.D35   2004
747'.94—dc22
               2004013411

Distributed to the trade by Holtzbrinck Publishers

2   4   6   8   10   9   7   5   3   1   paperback

RODALE

WE **INSPIRE** AND **ENABLE** PEOPLE TO IMPROVE
THEIR LIVES AND THE WORLD AROUND THEM

FOR **MORE** OF OUR **PRODUCTS**
WWW.RODALESTORE.COM
(800) 848-4735

Dedicated with great gratitude to my children, Robin, Carl, and David Daikeler, and to all the wonderful people who were my students or clients, willing to trust and use this process.

Contents

3 CLEARING THE CLUTTER

Foreword

BY KATE WHITE

There's a very good chance that you and I have something in common. Because you purchased this book (or you're looking through it deciding whether or not to buy it), your home must be important to you, and you obviously want it to be beautiful. Well, my home is incredibly important to me, and I want mine to be attractive and welcoming, plus a wonderful spot for me.

Perhaps there's something else we have in common. If you're buying a book on how to decorate your home, you may have felt that you're not *there* yet, that you've tried to create a beautiful space but haven't been successful. Maybe you attempted to decorate on your own and the results were just not right—or worse, disastrous. You may have even hired a decorator but still don't feel that you got what you craved. That's pretty much what happened to me. I tried—I really, really tried—to make my home look great. But the results just didn't hit the mark.

Well, you've come to the perfect place. Denny Daikeler is a fabulous designer who helped me create the kind of home I'd fantasized about.

It's actually a *weekend* home in Bucks County, Pennsylvania, a place that my husband and I had purchased just after our first child was born. We were working in New York City and loved urban life, but we also wanted to have a little getaway. When we found this small farmhouse on a quiet road, we fell in love with it at first sight.

Admittedly, it was something of a dump when we found it, thanks to the renters who had been ensconced there for several years. But architecturally it was in great shape—and thus we didn't need to do a serious renovation. The dining room, for instance, had a huge brick fireplace and old beams across the ceiling. Over the first year, we painted, sanded floors, removed the tacky tiles from the living room fireplace, and spent a lot of time hacking away at the yard and garden, which were seriously overgrown.

By the end of the year, we'd made a lot of progress, and yet I wouldn't say our home looked very comfortable or special. I attempted decorating myself, on a limited budget. I found some reasonably priced fabrics in green floral and stripes, which I used on most of the furniture for the living room and sunroom, and then painted some of the walls the same shade of green. But I just don't have a knack for turning the proverbial sow's ear into a silk purse—and you would never have walked into my house and said "Wow!"

A few years down the road, I was able to afford a decorator on a consultant basis, and I was thrilled at the idea that now everything would come together. She spent a full day with me at the house and made lots of suggestions. She didn't think the green walls in several of the rooms worked and suggested I paint them various shades of off-white: cameo

and coffee. She was a big believer in clean, spare walls and told me I needed less on the walls and less in the corners of the rooms. I was unhappy with my new kitchen cabinets because, though they were supposed to be whitewashed, a rose tint from the wood showed through, giving them a "blush" color. She suggested I fight this by painting the walls beige and the wood floor "antelope."

I followed every one of her suggestions and was relieved when, after six months, I was done. But though the rooms seemed more pulled together and "decorated," I slowly began to realize that I hated them. All that beige and off-white seemed not only dull and boring but not at all a reflection of my desires. My husband glanced around the rooms one day and announced that that our house looked like a giant pair of chinos.

For the next two years, I did nothing. My husband would have had a heart attack if I'd suggested painting again. But I was miserable. And I knew my concerns weren't just in my imagination. When new people came to my home, they always told me how much they liked the gardens, never the house.

Then I heard about Denny through a friend in the area. She referred to her as a "decorating doctor," someone who came in and saved you from bad decisions. It sounded like just what I needed. Plus, I saw some of the things that she had done in my friend's home, and I knew intuitively that she could help me.

I loved her from the moment I met her. The most remarkable thing was that she made no suggestions or comments on her first visit. She simply asked me questions about what I liked and what I hated. Then she told me she wanted me to keep a decorating journal. I had to cut pages from magazines, tape them into a big artist's sketchbook and, if I wished, make comments. She would analyze the book, and from there we would come up with a plan.

I enjoyed the process, but I felt there was no way Denny could make sense out of it. I didn't see any unifying themes. And yet Denny did. She told me first and foremost that I didn't like green. And I didn't like white walls. And I didn't like florals or spare-looking rooms. Rather, I loved bold colors: reds and yellows and purples. I loved walls painted those colors and then accented with white trim. I loved *checks*. I loved clutter and unmatched things and old wood and lots of books thrown around. As she said all these things, I knew instantly they were true. So that was the basis of everything we did.

And you should see my house now. My living room is painted apple green with white trim, and there's a red couch with gold animals in it. And there are checks all over the window seats. My dining room is bold yellow, with red and purple fabrics on the chairs. My little library is purple, with faux peach valances.

OK, it may sound a little zany, but it's

me and I love it. Here's the interesting point: If Denny worked in your home, she'd do something totally *different*. She's the kind of designer who wants to know what makes *you* tick, what makes *you* feel fabulous.

Since she can't come to your home, this book is the next best thing. When you're done reading it, when you've learned about her philosophy and her strategies and then tried them yourself, you'll probably be as thrilled as I am. Good luck!

Kate White is editor in chief of *Cosmopolitan* magazine and author of the Bailey Weggins mystery series, including *If Looks Could Kill* and *A Body to Die For*.

Acknowledgments

This moment of publishing seems strangely like all those moments I've watched annually of celebrities receiving their Oscars at the Academy Awards. I can't believe the moment is here. I can't believe that I did it. And yet the occasion is not me being chosen as the best but instead being chosen because in someone else's eyes, I had something important to say. That is the best.

For years, a writer self was not running the marathon within me alongside the designer, the teacher, the mother, the friend, the servant, the minister, the dancer (puff, puff)—not until I met and began working with Rev. Gordon R. Dragt, now pastor of Middle Collegiate Church in Manhattan. Our time working together was at Pebble Hill Church in Doylestown, Pennsylvania, where Gordon was founder, pastor, and friend. Gordon told me I could write, and he proceeded to give me assignment upon assignment where I composed, on paper,

my personal theology to present to the community.

And so a writer self began to run the race of meaning with all those other selves alive and passionate within me. Thank you, Gordon. This marriage between writing and designing has been the best. I also am so grateful for the encouragement from my dear children, Robin, Carl, and David; my ex-husband and lifetime friend, Raymond Daikeler; and my dear friends Kacey and Jonothan Daly.

Kate White, my long-time client and friend, offered tremendous advice and support and wrote the brilliant foreword. Thanks, Kate! Also, huge thanks to Marcia Yudkin for her help in editing; Barbara Hoberman Levine, Susan Caba, and Susan Schulman for powerful encouragement; my wonderful agent, Jessica Faust, for further editing and finding Rodale as the perfect home for the book; and Ellen Phillips, my first editor at Rodale, whose support and touches were the best. Thanks to Jennifer Kushnier, my brand new editor; Tom Mulderick, my Rodale publicist; Chris Rhoads, the designer; Lisa Dolin; and Jessica Titel.

Walking with me along the important friendship side of my life were especially Janice Beymer, Jim Fallen, Jean Daikeler, Jan Murray, Bill Arnold, Marie Woody, Liz Theodore, Jayson Stover, Tom Christian, Timothy Early, Marianne Heidelbaugh, Linda Timpone, Stephanie Noonan, Marilyn Phister, Paul Hilt, Paul Midiri, Gayle Dragt, Joe and Claire Billingham, Rev. Gary and Jennifer Culp, Rev. Rosemary and Rev. Richard Bredeson. And special thanks to my dear friends Barbara Reid, Fran Grabowski, Bill Ehrich, and Jennifer Thomas.

The acknowledgments must include all my students and clients who fed me meaningful stories about creating home. Their desire, openness, and willingness to experiment with home being personal were what kept me going. Thanks especially to Cathy Cushmore, Julie Berger, Eileen Kohlhepp, Lucy Schwartz, Marion McGowen, Doren O'Conner, and Susan Hugo.

Thank you all. I have been truly blessed.

contains the most amazing and finite details of what you love and need. It's your lifetime of accumulated visuals, joys, laughter, observations, and values. You've collected them, even though you've not respected them. When you "remember" this design personality, take back your own identity and start to live it, you will be happy, confident, enlightened, and safe. And in my opinion, that's an enviable way to be.

This book contains the process to do that—for yourself and for your home— story by story, chapter by chapter. There are exercises in each chapter that ask you the questions to open up your "files." As you work through them, what matters to you, what makes you happy—even who you really are—will emerge. Bit by bit, you'll find the pattern for your design personality.

Once you've found your design personality, the book will help you use it to design a home that is personal and meaningful—one that is created just for you and no one else. This home will present the real you to your friends and family, and it will become your sanctuary in the world.

It will also be beautiful. Homes that are created from very deep loves have a charm that goes beyond stereotypes and trends. There seem to be more nuances, more thought, more excitement. I tell you this because we often fear that sacrificing the image is a giving up of the bigger design potential. In this book, you will read many stories that disprove this belief.

This book also addresses how your sanctuary will sustain and support you, your relationships, your growth, and your well-being. You'll learn how much of a friend your home can be if you court it with love just like any relationship. You'll create spaces for hobbies you've dreamed of doing. You'll discover what's been missing from your life and restore it with support from your environment. I've had students who've suddenly sold their homes to move to the city, chucked floor plans and moved on to exciting new ideas, downsized, started traveling, or moved

Introduction

Creating pleasing surroundings often seems like an impossible dream—the more you try to achieve it, the farther away it gets. This is often true even when we call in professional help. And the reason is that the person we're trying to please isn't the person we really are: It's the image we've created to please society.

This personal image is something we've told each other is of prime importance. We've schooled ourselves forever in it and believed that image is our best foot forward. This has focused us completely on pleasing others. We've developed codes of behavior about how we should dress, act, and talk. We've said it will get us the right job, the right friends, the right life. It's really been our "lifestyle." We've taught ourselves, "act the way you *want* to be" instead of "be who you are."

Our image making has been so thorough that we're convinced that who we really are, our natural self, isn't worth a plug nickel. It won't sell, and it won't please. So we just forget that worthless self. We disconnect. We camouflage, and we do it so well that we even fool ourselves. We put the mask to work and numb our feelings forever. Thus we lose our identity and all self-love.

Since you grew up where I did—in this society—you've surely gotten this routine down well. But I'll tell you a secret: None of us will ever be happy until we reconnect with who we really are. All of the stuff that we disconnected from is the stuff that we need the most. It's even what we truly want. We just don't know it. Our spirits, yours and mine, are in anguish. We have got to get it. We have got to start pleasing ourselves.

I now believe that nothing will serve you and me more than giving up the image. It's time. In fact, it's past time. So here's the scoop: Deep inside of you and everyone else is a home design personality. It's all the stuff you've stuffed! It

into whole new careers. This process is life changing and life enhancing. It's exciting!

Our patterns of living seem to move in a sequence of chaos, then order; chaos, then order. Chaos is a place we can get stuck in if we don't intentionally resolve it. How *you* need to resolve your chaos is a part of your design personality. Each exercise gives clear problem-solving questions to lead *you* to *your* resolutions. You will get better at letting go of stuff that's not vital anymore and finding peace and ease.

Once you've looked at your design personality head-on, you will begin to trust yourself in choosing everything: colors, patterns, even lifestyle. You will use this skill whether you're creating your own design or designing with a professional.

If you are a designer reading this book, I suggest as you read that you do the process for yourself. As you see and feel its impact, you will be able to create your own ways of bringing personal design information from your clients to the surface. I promise you new rewards and insight into your awesome work as a designer.

I believe that this is soul work. By discovering your home design personality, you'll get to know yourself, you'll apply it to making your home sweet, and you will become happy and free. I encourage you to move ahead, turn the page, and enjoy your journey. When you reach the end, you'll have more than a new design sense. You'll discover a very rich interior life—and how to reconnect with it. What color *is* your slipcover?

STARTING OUT

1

The IMPORTANCE
of HOME

This is a book about your home. It is also a book about your life and securing your happiness. It is a process that links your home and your heart, so what you choose in terms of the plan, the space orientation, and the furniture—right down to the smallest accessory—is the best choice for you. It helps you understand the importance of your home environment: how it feels, how it looks, how it functions, and, most important, how it identifies with you.

Through my years of designing, I have witnessed powerful changes in my clients' lives as they've used this process. I have seen it assist them in moving from day to day or job to job, approaching change and building life and family. I've seen it make a difference in how they feel and how easy life becomes for them because of it. I've seen people become happier. I now know that when the essence of space relates to the essence of its inhabitants, the right home environment can soothe, assist, support, and provide energy. As people begin to feel really good all the time, they attract new opportunities into their lives that move them and expand them.

For this to happen, you have to know what you need. You must know who you are and how you want to live. That is why this book works from the inside out: I believe it is imperative to do an in-depth study of yourself before you design, so when you begin planning, you find what you love now, then work with those things and add them to your life. It is the way for your home to become truly what you need and want. If I succeed only in connecting you to what you love, so that your design decisions are made from your heart, I will have accomplished a great deal. If I also convince you of the concept of making your home a true reflection of you, I will have fulfilled my goal in writing this book.

Two of my favorite authors, Lynn Grabhorn in *Excuse Me, Your Life Is Waiting* and Gregg Bradden in *The Isaiah Effect*, go deeply into a philosophy of how positive feelings can truly change our lives for the better. Each proposes that we can create more positive lives if our thoughts and our moments are filled with positive feelings. They note that we need to start with thoughts of what we want, rather than what we don't want. They remind us that we need to *know* what we want and what we don't want, and we need to hold on to the positive feelings around what we want. Then we will become magnets that attract the best that's possible in life.

I believe these concepts present powerful truths. And I believe that our homes can serve as tools to help us maintain good feelings about ourselves, about life, and about change. This is why I present the notion that we must not design from trends or for other people's approval or taste. We must design from our own feelings, from our own memories of the past and dreams of the future, from our own needs and wants.

a PASSION for FAVORITE THINGS

Mark Helprin's novel *Winter's Tale*, and his character Pearly Soames, are a great place for me to start. Pearly was a thief, a thief who was wild about color. He loved color so much that he stopped dead still in the middle of a "job" when he encountered a painter applying a "heavenly coat of apple green." His infuriated thieving buddies called it his "color gravity," because the color made him go bonkers. In that moment, he didn't care if he messed up the job, for it was the feeling the color gave him that mattered, that transfixed him. Color was a huge love in his life, and he could not resist it. It made him feel fabulous!

Pearly reminds me of my father, who would go "bonkers" when he held in his hand a sterling silver spoon that was perfectly balanced. And of my friend Linda,

HOME *as* SELF-EXPRESSION

*t*HE AUTHOR G. K. CHESTERTON wrote about home as the one place in life where we can experience ourselves most authentically, without the interference of any other authority. Very few of us look at our homes as tools of powerful self-expression. That's why we listen to the trends. I hope that after reading this book, you will never ask the question, "What sofa is best for this room?" You won't spend a cent until you know what is best for *you:* how you want to create the stage on which you play out your life.

who coos with comfort as she sinks into her down bed. Another friend, Barbara, loves a high sense of order and beauty, while my friend Maria craves romance and softness. Me? An extremely creative concept or a fabulous combination of colors is what brings me to my knees. I, too, can identify with Pearly.

Responses to "favorite things" are very deep, and they're as individual as each one of our faces. Loves like these, if forgotten or ignored, rob us of excitement and pleasure. The moments of ecstasy that Pearly felt when he saw apple green just plain make life feel good. I believe one of the reasons we're in a human body is to feel and experience. It's wonderful to be in the middle of a moment of aliveness, and we can build the potential for more of these moments into our homes.

Getting Back in Touch

Unfortunately, being in touch with our feelings has not always been a priority, let alone being in touch with what makes us feel alive. We rush around, we pick up, we deliver, we work, and we prepare constantly. It's repetitive, and it's boring. It's painful to our spirits. We throw down our cups of tea or coffee; jog hardly breathing; chauffeur the kids; do our jobs; eat in jammed, noisy restaurants; come back to the brain-starving Internet experience; and fall into bed. We never feel the spoon, the down, or the warmth of a fire. Too brutal? I'm not so sure. I think it's pretty right on, and a form of self-betrayal. Remember that we evolved from ancestors who knew exactly when the moon was full and when it was new.

We don't know what we hold dear because it isn't a priority. And not knowing, we definitely do not gift ourselves or our homes with *our* form of beauty or function. And so we feel numb when we're at home. We need to change this. We need to come from our inner loves as we design, instead of coming from outer responses to looks, trends, and other people's approval.

Don't get me wrong. There are important principles of design that help a room or a home become beautiful. But right now it's the objects, patterns, colors, materials, shapes, and textures you choose relative to who you are that I'm addressing. It's your level of drama, mystery, opulence, simplicity, or complexity that I want you to consider, so that your home is *you*.

a DESIGN EVOLUTION

Describing my history may help you understand what I'm saying. In the beginning years of my career as a designer, I didn't consider feelings important. The visual was everything. I knew I had a good sense of design and a good education. Now I know that I had only the basics. I didn't have a clue where I was going!

Those beginning days would go like this: A client would call. We'd set up an appointment. I would go to the home and immediately move into the picture of the "great design" unfolding. The problems of the space and how they could be solved, the axis of the room, and the flow of the traffic pattern were my starting points. Designs and ideas would stampede through my veins, and I'd chomp at the bit to begin.

At first, constantly coming up with new ideas was easy, but it slowly became more difficult. Tract homes were abundant, and you remember how they were all the same. So I had to do something. Listening to the lives of my clients brought me new input toward the design. My designs improved and became more personal. Identical houses on the same street became extremely different and exciting. I began to feel more of a partnership with my clients. They seemed happier, and they seemed to fit into their homes more easily.

As I became aware of all of this, the way that I approached interior design changed. My philosophy altered. The only roadblocks to this new approach seemed to happen when I was designing with someone who didn't know what gave them feelings of ecstasy, who didn't know how they wanted to live or what they loved, who didn't have a strong connection to those special parts of themselves. These people were inevitably headed toward some stereotypical version of design dependent on trends or my tastes instead of theirs.

Luckily, I began to pull in some clients whom I called "feelers." They were easy to design for because they could communicate. I began to listen to them to find out how I could help others know what they wanted. They became my teachers.

A significant factor about these "feelers" was that they seemed to accept their homes as significant parts of their lives. They knew that if they got their spaces to be connected to their hearts, their

PUTTING PRINCIPLES *into* PRACTICE

*J*ONATHAN IS a playwright. He got very stuck in Act II of a play he was writing and couldn't get the story line to move along no matter how hard he tried. He is a great friend, and we would talk forever about what I was discovering in environmental influences. He loved my concepts and decided that, if he believed me that environment affected life, maybe he should apply the idea to himself.

He began examining his feelings about where he did his writing. It never seemed to bother him before, never had any effect—or so he thought. But he decided that perhaps, if he examined the dynamic of his workspace, it would jar him out of this mental block and shift his energy. He began to dream about how he wanted to feel when he was sitting at his desk, what he loved having around him that spurred his creativity, what he wanted most for himself each time he wrote. It's exactly the process you'll be following in this book. Here are his steps.

• Jonathan had done most of his writing in a back corner away from windows and natural light. This was crazy. He loved having a view, and he often wrote during the day. No wonder he was stuck. He was stuck in a corner he didn't like! He brought his writing space to the front of the apartment, where there was a window and an inspiring view.

lives would become fuller, and they would move on to other dreams and projects to enhance their joy and fulfill their life goals. If their homes were done really well, they would be places to rest, to make love, to contemplate, to create, to entertain, and to fill up their senses. They would become islands where the owners could lick their wounds, restore their spirits, and get back in touch with their true selves. Then they could go back out into the world all filled up and ready for action.

Changing the Process

I wanted this sense of a home retreat for everybody, and I wanted to make it my work to get design to this higher

- He knew his comfort level was low while writing, and he thought perhaps it was his desk. He went out and bought a small secretary, an antique that really caught his attention.

- He'd always been annoyed by his lighting, so he shopped for a lamp that was attractive and would give him better illumination.

- Jonathan always handwrote everything before putting it into the computer. His writing tools were not organized, so he found a holder for his pencils, and he set up his middle drawer to serve him better. These are simple things, but sometimes we never address them to resolve small space issues.

- I suggested that Jonathan think of what he loves and use those things as cues about what to have around him for inspiration. One of his loves is London. He had lived there for a time and adored its sense of history. He found an oil painting of a London street scene and hung it on the wall near his desk. And he brought in pictures of his children and grandchildren.

Almost immediately, Act II was on its way. Jonathan's change in environment got his energy shifted—and the plot thickened!

level. I began to encourage my customers to really think through what they loved so that I could do their design work more personally. If I walked into a new client's home and they asked me what I thought was right for the room, I would explain that knowing them first was paramount before I addressed the creation. We really needed to talk first.

Sometimes, clients were disappointed that my professional eye did not immediately give me answers for them. But explaining my process and what I had discovered helped them understand. I shared how allowing me to work *only* with a professional eye was a huge giveaway on their part and handed me total authority over the most important spaces in their lives.

I didn't deserve that authority, and it meant we hadn't shared the beautiful landscape of their histories, their loves, their relationships and priorities. I tried to help them understand how my getting more in touch with them and helping them see themselves

would be the appropriate path to an incredibly designed home. Enjoying a time of talking and questioning would be so beneficial to successful interior design.

Working carefully on each job to establish this new "step before design" was difficult, because everybody wanted fast answers. The minutes of our time together were ticking away, and they knew it. They wanted to move to the process of planning and buying. But they began to see that, in the long run, the moments we spent talking saved both of us time and money and, most important, prevented mistakes.

I worked to convince clients that their homes were their pleasure and their medicine. This language didn't always turn them on. They had their money saved and wanted to spend it wisely. What did that have to do with them telling me their pleasure? Their pleasure was to have a beautiful sofa to sit on. Medicine? You take that by the spoonful when you don't feel well. But slowly, as I said it better each time and they started to crave a truly personal home, we made headway.

Principles, Not Rules

I was teaching at the time, so I developed classes in the home instead of the lecture hall so people could put their hands on objects, move them around, and drop the limitation of recipes for a "good room." In these classes, I suggested that everyone explore new ways of approaching design, discarding fashion dictates, rules, and peer pressure. I asked them to wipe the slate clean that contained the trends, the childhood memories, and the preferences of friends, family, neighbors, mentors, and celebrities. And I urged them to drop the "shoulds"—the perfect pictures in the magazines. I began asking questions that nobody had ever entertained in relationship to designing a room. This created many weird and funny moments.

The more I studied the concept and put it into practice, the more convinced I became that this path was important. I

began to see how the inner person, that part inside each one of us, really had strong preferences for particular forms, colors, and shapes. Also, I began to see that certain people loved views, while others needed to feel like they were in a cave. Some loved no window treatment, while some wanted three layers pulled across the glass. Some wanted to feel like they were floating on air, and others wanted the grounding influence of large furniture, deeper colors, and lots of both. These preferences were serving definite needs in them emotionally, physically, and spiritually.

Also, I could see that the principles of design—the information that tells you what will happen as you use line, color, and space in particular ways—were much more creative than the rules that were so specific and limiting. The rules said things such as, "When you have a long, narrow room, you always put the sofa on the narrow wall to widen it." It seemed that as long as I counted on the principles of design, such as, "A horizontal line widens, a vertical line creates height" (see the difference?) and dropped the rules of what was "right" in particular situations, we moved further and further away from any stereotyped room. And the design results were excellent.

As a way to unveil a person's deeper yearnings and feelings, I also began offering classes in what I called Surfacing Your Style. It was fulfilling to be supporting and encouraging personal freedom along with beauty and a high sense of living. It was exciting to see that as a part of design.

Well, now I design mainly for clients who are willing to do this upfront work so the end results are true to who they are. Sometimes, my only work with clients is to help them decide who they are in design, and then they go on their own way designing. Sometimes, I move in with a family to begin this process of self-discovery. There have been times where we have redesigned the entire plan of a home and not moved a wall. I do all of this because I can't do it any other way. If I do fall back on the old be-havior of doing visual design from my own perspective, it makes me feel like I'm not acting with integrity. This new way has made my work more significant and more fulfilling, both of which are very important to me.

I now believe that design is about creating space using objects, colors, patterns, lighting, art, sounds, and a personal form of order and beauty that is relevant to the inner landscape of these beautiful clients. And I now know that the right design for my clients can deepen their relationships, move them, comfort them, inspire them, support them, and on and on and on.

MAKING your own MEANING

Please understand that in convincing you that your objects need to be significant to you, I am not suggesting that you acquire a vast amount of stuff. I am suggesting that you have around you only those things you need or want—

only what makes you feel good. Gandhi had only a few possessions. His life was one of contemplation, intentional living, and simplicity. He needed certain objects that were pertinent to him: his loincloth, his sandals, his book, his glasses, his bowl, and a trinket. (The trinket was the three monkeys—hear no evil, see no evil, speak no evil.) His possessions were deliberate, and they were chosen from knowing who he was and how he wanted to live. And that's what I'm saying to you. I want you to know who you are, what you want, and how you want to live based on *your* feelings.

As you continue, I will share with you some wonderful stories that reflect changes in the lives of my clients. I now believe that our home environment can affect our lives on every level—the emotional, physical, spiritual, functional, and romantic. This potential is possible when the inner loves, feelings, and yearnings of a person have been brought to the surface and understood. The Pawnee Indians claimed that if you feel at home in your home, you feel at home in the universe.

Clearing House

An example of this concept is Nancy's story. I was giving a lecture in a local furniture store when a woman wanting my services approached me. She had a problem. She and her husband had held onto everything they had ever bought, or ever been given, since their wedding. They were now in their fifties. This is a lot of stuff!

Nancy wanted to work with me. I told her I would meet with her and discuss our possibilities. We did this in her home, where I found rooms with more than one television, crafts that she had lovingly made and not known where to place, and fabrics that were faded. The house was crowded, and she was obviously not a happy woman. I wanted to work with her, but first we needed to make some agreements.

I felt we would work best room by room. She agreed to that. I felt the family needed to be sure they were ready to let go of a lot of this accumulation. They talked. She said the family supported our work. I was ready.

My method of beginning was based on a format of questioning where their lives were now, what they loved now, what brought them significant happiness now. It flowed nicely, and we made huge decisions, letting go of things that no longer served her or them. She got stronger and stronger at making decisions, choices that served their current life instead of their past. The opening up of space allowed me to arrange things in more attractive ways. The home became much lovelier and far less cluttered.

We worked together for quite a few years, finally adding on a new kitchen and sunroom, but as the basic work of letting go happened, Nancy began to change. When I first met her, she did not have a lot of color. She was wrinkled, and her hair was pulled back tightly. Her husband traveled a great deal and yearned for her to join him, but it did not appeal to her. Well, the wonder is that this all changed. She regained facial color and liveliness. Her face relaxed, and she began wearing her hair loosely curled, and yes, she began traveling with her husband and enjoying it. It was a healing. This woman had pulled me into her life, responded to what I had to offer, allowed herself to let go, and therefore brought about a beautiful change to her space, her person, and her life. She had healed herself!

You see, when your home has not evolved along with the cycles in your life, it gets clogged. Nancy and her family had the stuff of many decades surrounding them. They did not have their home set up so that their present lifestyle was supported. They didn't know who they were now.

Clutter confuses you and gets you stuck. (We'll talk more about this and what to do about it in part 3.) The environment is a mirror, and if it's mirroring decades of life, then you are not inspired to go, to do, to be. You're always deliberating, wondering what you *should* be doing. As Nancy broke through her "stuckness," she became more focused and open. This gave her the feeling of freedom: freedom to travel, enjoy herself, and begin new projects with the support of the changes she had finally made.

the ELEMENTS of HOME

Where my first goal, early on, was to give my clients the satisfaction of visual

DESIGNING *toward* FREEDOM

SUSAN CABA, a reporter for the *Philadelphia Inquirer*, shared with me a story about Carl Jung, one of the grandfathers of psychiatry. She said he recognized that our homes provide us with enormous amounts of psychic support. Jung built his own home in Bollingen, Switzerland, in four stages over a period of 40 years, and he wrote about the experience in his autobiography, *Memories, Dreams, Reflections*. The house, which he called the Tower, had become his symbol of psychic wholeness.

At Bollingen, Jung felt that he lived what he called his true life: In his home, he was most truly himself. He wrote that there was nothing in the Tower that had not "grown into its own form" as time passed and that he was linked to every object there.

If you want to live in a quality way, with your home as your tool and your medicine, then this process will help you get what Jung got. It is what this book is about. I will attempt to lead you to yourself and to the home life your soul desires. I will assist you in discovering your level of order and how to reach it, your level of beauty and where to find it, your level of passion and comfort and what they look like.

We will look at your sense of order and help you organize according to how you move in your space. You'll begin to place things in a way that makes it a joy to work, to cook, to dress, and to relate. Hopefully, you will never have to search for your car keys again.

This will be a fabulous journey filled with wonder—one that will make you *feel* great!

beauty, I now know that the environment holds far more potential than just the visual. It provides you with so many of your needs. Many of our needs are filled by the elements of joy from sound, sensuality, sexuality, comfort, intellect, exploration, stimulation, relationship, identity, community, privacy, safety, ease, history, and wholeness. Let's take a few of those elements and talk about them as possibilities for you.

The joy of sound. So many of us are sparked or soothed by the sounds of life, like the sound of a gurgling brook or a waterfall. Some of us hear birdsongs and are inspired or feel joy. So we prefer resonating surroundings created by hardwood floors, crackling fireplaces, and rain on the roof rather than soft, quiet rooms with wall-to-wall carpeting and totally upholstered furniture. If you are a person who loves those resonating sounds, and your designer says the space would look best with wall-to-wall, you'll be in trouble if you agree. You will miss the essence of sound as you like it around you—probably without even knowing it.

The life of the mind. Is stimulation of the intellect important to you? Are you always listening for new ideas, or do you find yourself drawn to quotes or poetry? If so, you might like quotes of an intellectual or inspirational nature stenciled on your walls, or lots of bookshelves and technology. Depending on your focus, you could build a world of intellectual stimulation that is supportive and beautiful. This idea certainly goes beyond the simple focus of the right sofa, table, and window treatment.

Creating numerous workstations—one for writing, one for reading, one for studying the ways of the Mayan culture, any and all that support your interests— could offer you an environment that expands you constantly. Each space would be set up for whatever you're going to do in it, like Jonathan's writing space, and each would be there for you to slip into at a given moment and wander off (mentally, that is). Even the sight of these stations would be a comfort for you. You would be reminded of their possibilities and your enjoyment.

Much has been written about mental stimulation in the environment where the elderly are concerned. So often, the small spaces that house senior citizens are devoid of possibilities that bring the mind into action. This is known to bring dementia and other mental disorders into our lives. Our minds and memories need to be maintained, and our home environment can help by providing spaces and activities (equipment) that stimulate us to think and discover. Of course, the reality is that we *all* need mental stimulation—it's good for all of us at all ages.

The pleasure of company. Is your focus community or relationships? You're a people person and friends stop in often, or yours is the house most used for meetings or social gatherings. You'll want to put special care into creating areas for being with others, one on one or in groups. The focus in these areas needs to be on spaces that allow good conversations, with chairs close, lamps out of the way, and comfortable seating. If you love tea for two, make a won-

derful space for it to happen. Think of a place for lovemaking other than the bedroom, a place for playing with the kids, a place for consulting, or any other relationship needs.

I hope these examples have given you a starting place as you think about the elements that matter most to you. What do you need to make a house (or any space) your home?

DISCOVERING your DESIGN PERSONALITY

So how do you start discovering your design personality? To state this process clearly, first we dig out your personal information and get *you* in touch with you, and then we take this design personality profile and help you use it in your home. We'll go into figuring how to fulfill your needs once we know what they are. In upcoming chapters, I'll be challenging you to explore everything from how you want to wake up in the morning to how you want to move around, eat your meals, take your naps, play your games, even enter your house. First you'll find out what feels right, then you'll figure out how to create it. In the discovery process, you'll end up expanding your vision of how you want your life to be and how much your home can help you.

I have used this process to move people through grief, change, illness, divorce, chaos, and depression, as well as simply creating a wonderful home. In all of these cases, we used their home environment as one of their instruments of healing. And in each situation, we followed the basic process of discovering their own design personality, which helped them see what they really needed. Then we worked with their home environment, changing it to help them heal.

I have also used this process to transform myself. I've learned how to fulfill my priorities through my environment—priorities of my current life as well as those for my future. In fact, I discovered the benefits of the process as I accomplished my own self-discovery and applied it to the interior spaces of my own four walls.

My surroundings now offer me compassion, comfort, relief, and a feeling of newness through their transformational capabilities. I have a very diverse life, so I need many different kinds of work and play stations. When I do my yoga, for example, I have permanent open space, a source of music, and a good supply of candles *and* matches. This is true when I write, when I dance, when I read, and on and on.

I will tell you story upon story about how this magic worked for others, too. The process is for everyone: It is for do-it-yourselfers who wish to design their own living spaces, and it is for people who love a new perspective and a new way to expand and grow. It is for designers who wish to include this step with their clients and for clients who wish to work with designers and end up with meaningful space.

The process is a jewel. It has come to me in stages. When you use it, you, like me, will benefit from your journey of discovery and experimentation. You'll certainly have fun, and you'll bring a depth to your passion for home and beauty that you hadn't dreamed possible.

Process, Then Plan

You may be wondering what happened to the plan—the typical sketch of what goes where in the new design. Interior design up to this time has always begun with the plan. This consisted of looking at the space and deciding if the walls, windows, ceiling, floors, and so on were going to stay the same or be changed. Certainly a lot of this came from personal preferences.

Once decisions were made, we contemplated how the spaces were going to be filled, what the budget was, and what fabrics would be used and how. But starting the plan that way is starting with all the externals. It comes from visual preferences, not from inner knowledge or a focus on living and self, and it certainly does not come from your heart. So my process insists that we first contemplate our living and being.

When a room is well planned, staying within the plan's solutions assures a success visually and functionally. Thinking out the plan in careful detail offers a clearer picture and process to the designer and/or homeowner. So, a plan is genuinely good and important. It allows roots to grow in the project. It offers sound judgments and the feeling of control, and it needs to be complete before anything is purchased.

Think of my process as the step *before* designing the plan, a most important step. I'm suggesting that you now enter a world of design that begins with you, not with your space. It's the world where there are no limits, no rights or wrongs, no rules, no prescriptions. It is truly an exciting world, which offers you a deep connection with yourself, a possibility of creating a world of beauty, order, and feelings that you've never entertained or experienced before. It also offers you a chance to truly experience who you are—maybe for the first time in your life. The Pawnee Indians believed this, too. They said, "Plan emerges from feelings," and they took this belief into every area of life.

SUCCESS STORIES of STUDENTS

As I've facilitated the seminars that help people delve into who they are, I have been impressed by the efforts of many of the seminar participants. Here are some of their stories, so you can see the outcomes for yourself. Remember, you can do what they did!

Two Sisters, Two Design Styles

When I think of my students, Bernadette and her sister, Jean, come immediately to mind. Bernadette did the exercises with great intensity. When she felt in touch with herself, she went on to design her spaces on her own. The result, she reports, is the best she and her husband could have imagined.

Bernadette's priority for comfort was a huge discovery. She would visualize herself curled up here and there in little nests. She kept cutting out pictures of cozy, comfortable places for reading, relating, and sleeping. Once she was in touch with what she was doing, she had to find out how her desire for comfort could play out in her home. But what's most impressive is how comfortable and happy she and her husband are in their home. Her friends now exclaim over the fabulous connection between her home's design and the couple's identity.

I asked Bernadette what she felt about

it all. She had many things to say, but this stands out: She said that the process focused her completely, so she could move forward with clarity and confidence. She made decisions easily, and she always seemed to know what she was looking for in fabrics, furniture, wallpapers, and colors.

By contrast, Jean discovered in all of her exercises her love of sports: doing them, watching them, and reading about them. Her picture journal was full of organized closets and very functional space. We designed her environment as a place, a station, that could serve her coming and going; a place where her equipment for the sport of the moment was at hand and easily accessible, her apparel always available and clean. We placed Jean's exercise equipment where its use was fun and effective. Bernadette's nests would have been in her sister's way. Jean wanted an open, easy, active life and therefore an open, easy home.

The focusing aspect of this process that Bern spoke of is interesting, for in doing the process, you explore parts of yourself and your life that you didn't know could affect the design or—even better—be provided by the design. Focusing allows you to funnel the information into each project you're exploring.

Mary Jo's Style Solutions

Mary Jo, a past student, is a highly intense and energetic person. She yearns for culture all the time. Her fulfillment usually comes through reading, going to art shows and the theater, and travel. These are quite external to the home and involve planning and time. When time was not available, Mary Jo became frustrated by her lack of exposure to new ideas. "Nothing's happening," she'd say.

Being extremely creative, she figured out one antidote. She purchased a beautiful old book rack that stood about 33 inches tall. She placed it in an archway where there was always light, either natural or electric. On this rack she placed an open book of paintings, photographs, poetry, or history. She turned the pages periodically to some new illustration or passage. When a book had been totally enjoyed, she had the great moment of deciding what the next book would be.

Since the rack stood in a passageway, it allowed her enjoyment to happen within her margins of time. It looked stunning, and as the pages were turned, there might be a Georgia O'Keeffe flower or a Wordsworth poem. Since she

HOME *as* MEDICINE

*M*Y STUDENT JUDY is another success story. Her home was nice, but again, it had not been thought out or designed through the depth of who Judy was or what she loved. An abundance of quilts of all types came up as beloved objects in her process. (You'll be working on your own process in chapter 3.) Even pictures of quilts were a great source of enjoyment. We slowly collected her quilts and hung them on the walls, folded them in cupboards, draped them over racks, made pillows, and framed them as pictures. I helped her use good design principles, so each was successful in its placement but the theme was not overdone.

A few years later, Judy's father became seriously ill. His illness took a long, agonizing toll on the family. I received a note from her in the midst of his illness. She shared how grateful she was that she'd gone so deeply into herself to create her home. "It literally holds me when I come from the hospital," she said. "It makes all the difference as I deal with my pain and energy during this hard time."

That's so significant. Not only did Judy discover her medicine—what would help her feel good—but she also discovered what worked for her in setting up a healing environment. Then, when she needed that dynamic (and when don't we?), it was there to assist her. This is the message. This is my goal for all of us. It's not about money, it's not about what's right; it's about *learning* about yourself and then creating yourself in the surroundings of your home. You will have an enriched environment. Like vitamins, a supportive environment will deliver energy to you through everything you create.

knew her own needs, she was able to create this source of joy. She also used important accessories: ethnic art on her walls and tables, period furniture in as pure a form as possible. She surrounded herself with culture. But first she had to know this need, and then she had to do the creating.

Here's another example of Mary Jo's home design personality. She loved flowers: their scents, growing them, and getting them as gifts. But she hated throwing them away, especially the ones that were gifts. When accessorizing a sideboard in her dining room, she bought a large, round glass vase; pulled apart some wilted flowers; and accumulated their petals in the shiny, clear glass. As new bouquets wilted, she'd throw them in. They would dry, intensify in color, and look great. Then she began adding other things to the vase to enhance the colors and textures, such as orange rinds, cinnamon sticks, and nutshells. It was exquisite, and a great reminder of life's moments. Instead of a meaningless object to fill the space, she invented an object of meaning.

A High School Gets Smart

Once, I used this concept commercially at a local high school. The school board wanted to paint the faculty dining room and asked for a color suggestion. We made an appointment. The room had the basics: tables, chairs, commercial-grade carpeting, and appliances, all done in neutrals. This meant that they could really choose any color. There was no limitation. There would be no conflicts.

I suggested that the school board talk with some of the faculty and get their feelings about color. I picked several colors as suggestions. I also explored with some faculty members how they felt at midday and found out what they needed to happen in that "off" time. I wondered what they enjoyed most when they used the room and what they needed that time to provide. I asked whether they yearned for some excitement in design.

Out of that process evolved a project for the whole school. They'd been considering renovating and adding a library and more classrooms. I pulled in a coworker who was great at organizing thoughts, and we began to talk to the faculty, parents, students, and office staff to see how education was achieved in this particular school. We searched out frustrations, ideas, patterns of behavior, and decision-making priorities. The outcome was interesting: It turned out that whether they knew it or not, at this school, education was achieved through relationship. The emphasis was on teacher-student relations, parent-teacher relations, and student-student relations. Our designs from that point were all biased toward the question: Do they support relationship?

The library ended up with a fireplace and sofas, the halls with benches to stop and talk or, in the spring, to watch a mother duck and her ducklings on the other side of the window. Colors and graphics were used to stimulate conversation and fun, and photographs of the students became the artwork, photographs that mirrored the relationships of the students, teachers, and parents in their life at the school.

your ACTION PLAN

I now invite you to move into the process, which will be the discovery of your inner preferences. Consider this process important and user friendly. It has worked for many over the years and promises to engage you as it changes and supports your life. If you are a designer, it will assist you in your work with your design clients.

All of the exercises in the chapters to come are quite simple. It's their interpretation that can be tricky. But don't worry: Interpretation and metaphor are fun and can be fascinating. They'll give you tons of information on who you are and what you love, all of which you can use in your home design.

At this point, you should be convinced of two things. One is that you have your own individual and very personal home design personality, which is an accumulation of all the moments in your life. This personality knows what you love and need today. It is available if you do the work of uncovering well. (I'll cover this in the next few chapters.) Two, your home can be a powerful tool in your life if you apply the information you discover about yourself, your design personality, to its design. Then you will be centered, nourished, and organized as you go out into the world.

In chapter 2, you'll find out how to get ready to begin your process and dig into the exercises that will help you design the home of your dreams. You'll find those dreams along the way. Let's get started!

2

PREPARING *to* FIND *Your* HOME DESIGN PERSONALITY

My mother always used to say, "A job worth doing is worth doing well." I think she was right. I've watched so many people begin projects, and the people who had the most successful outcomes seemed to be the ones who brought the tools for the job together in a specific space before they began.

There are women who can sew magnificent outfits that fit perfectly and look as good inside as they do outside. And these women always seem to have a perfect sewing room that holds a sewing machine, an iron, a large collection of colorful spools of thread, scissors, thimbles, tape measures, pictures of enviable fashions, and whatever else supports them.

I've seen parallels with a well-organized woodworking space, an artist's studio, or a well-equipped kitchen. The creators who work in these spaces produce powerful products, and they seem to emerge unshackled, wearing smiles of fulfillment.

This book and its self-discovery and design process also create a product. The product is more than a wonderful home—it's a picture of you, *your* magic. This picture will replace a cloud of "shoulds" and right and wrong ideas that society has put into your head, which have kept you from your authentic self.

How do you create your picture, your home design personality? How do you get your marvelous life force moving and re-vealing your magic—the magic of who you are, where you're going, what you want, what turns you on now, what you love?

First you need space, time, and tools, just like all creators, in order to make it happen. The process will require you to sit and ponder, to let visuals pass before you, to shower yourself with details. You'll be looking within.

Doing all that involves more than just reading the book. There are exercises with each chapter that require relaxed time and thought. They will bring up important information, which you will then apply to the design of your home. To get the greatest results, you need to set up a space to do the exercises carefully. And you need to gather the tools that will help you do the work.

The process works best if you do it before you plan your design or buy new furnishings. But don't fret if you're already into or past those steps. It's never too late to discover how to be more alive, focused, or happy—or more *you*. Shifting the home toward your design personality can happen at any time.

STARTING the PROCESS

To get from where you are now to a beautifully designed home, you'll need to first read each chapter, then do the exercises at the end of the chapter. The exercises are based on the concepts presented in each chapter. The reading is important.

The exercises are important. I'll take you step by step through the process of actually making your personality a part of your design and, finally, part of your home.

Alone or Together?

One decision you can make now is whether you are going to do the process

*t*HERE ARE many rewards to completing this process of discovery. Here are some of my favorites. I hope they help you muster the enthusiasm to start your preparation.

• You will discover who you are in design and preference.

• You will learn the extreme importance and relationship home has to life.

• You will be shown the support that your home environment can give to relationships, work, and play.

• You will become focused in your design process.

• You will be shown how to set up work spaces, play spaces, relationship spaces, and any other spaces that are pertinent to your current life.

• You will be opened to the concept of how a carefully thought-out space can heal you emotionally and physically.

• You will learn how to relate your design personality to your present home or new home.

• You will be empowered.

• You will truly have fun!

alone, at your own pace, or with your spouse or partner, your entire family, or a group of friends or colleagues. In all situations, the sequence of the chapters will guide you nicely.

If you're working with others, it can be lots of fun and very valuable. I would suggest that you all read and do the exercises individually, then come together to share your results. Allowing others to hear your interpretations and add their input brings another dimension to this work. The objectivity of other people's observations will extend what you've discovered. It's also very affirming when others agree with your observations of yourself. But remember, you're not looking for approval. Create your own format. You might want to meet regularly, perhaps biweekly.

TWO ESSENTIAL STEPS

Now it's time to get ready to do the necessary discovery work. There are two

steps of preparation. They represent my perspective of what you need. Perhaps you will think of even more ways to support yourself in the process.

The two steps are:

1. Creating the space where you're going to do most of this work (your workstation).

2. Gathering the supplies you will need beforehand so that they're available when an exercise calls for them.

Creating a Workstation

One of the lessons this book has to offer is helping you organize and create spaces for designated activities. You might as well begin that learning process now!

Start by choosing and preparing a space in your home where you can have all your supplies stored, where you can spread out with the pictures you accumulate, and where you're comfortable and at ease working. You will need good lighting, and you might consider having music nearby. Also, think about whether you like working on the floor, at a desk,

or at a kitchen table; what kinds of containers you need to hold the tools; and how it all can be stored in the most accessible way.

The most important thing is that this space be right for you, so choose it carefully. Make sure it's comfortable for you and that you'll enjoy working there. Some people have open space on the floor near a bed, and that works for them. All the supplies can be stored under the bed and pulled out quickly. Reading can be done nearby or on the bed.

If you're doing the process with a group, the personal workstation is still important for your own process. Once you've chosen your own space, you can think of where the group will meet. Moving from house to house is excellent. Have fun, serve refreshments, and have comfortable seating and good lighting. And make sure you set up a schedule of times together.

Gathering Your Supplies

You'll need certain supplies to help you select and record your home design personality and preferences. I suggest these:

Magazines

For the picture journal exercise in chapter 7, you will want a lot of magazines. That way, you can select hundreds of pictures to help you focus on the elements that give you pleasure and to think about why they do. All the pictures you choose will tell you something about yourself and begin to give you a blueprint for your best design decisions.

You will need lots of pictorial magazines (I suggest at least 10 to 30) that resonate with you. You can use periodicals that are focused on interior design, travel, photography, food, or fashion. Mail-order catalogs can be used, but I find that they're sometimes limited in their visual excitement and inspiration. They also focus on objects instead of an overall combination or feeling, so they don't offer you as much assistance.

A Large Spiral Sketchbook

You can buy a sketchbook at any art supply store. A good size is 11" × 14", but it can be larger. This is where you'll paste the pictures you choose from the maga-

zines and begin to see similarities in your choices.

Fasteners

You will need to fasten your pictures in the sketchbook. Decide what type of fasteners you will use, and have an ample supply on hand. Glue sticks, liquid glue, and transparent tape work well. If you're unsure, test each type with a photo you don't care about and compare results and ease of use.

Scissors, an X-Acto Knife, or a Razor

Find the easiest, fastest way to cleanly remove your pictures from the magazines.

A Small Spiral Notebook

In most of the exercises, I recommend journaling. Using a separate spiral notebook for thoughts and feelings, as well as the design work, is efficient. Journaling anytime something occurs to you relative to this process will deepen the work. I'll also let you know when to do specific kinds of journaling. Some students actually do the exercises in the back of the large sketchbook that becomes the picture journal. The choice is yours—do what works for you.

your ACTION PLAN

After reading this chapter, you should have decided on and created your workstation and gathered your materials. You are now ready to begin!

2

GETTING IN TOUCH WITH YOURSELF

3

BEGINNING *the* DIG

All new undertakings require learning and understanding.
Wouldn't it be great to just look at a picture and slip into a yoga pose,
or decide to play "Clair de lune" on the piano and do it at the drop of
a hat? But any new discipline just doesn't work that way. A book or
class gets us greased up for the new process. Then we come to it
slowly, without injury or immediate loss of interest because of
failure at performance. The learning stage of any new undertaking
allows you to feel what the new discipline is. You learn how to do it
correctly, and then, as time passes, you test your continued interest and
development by feeling whether it's still working the way it did at first.

In fact, usually it begins to feel better, and your inner response deepens. You grow in the trust that you're doing it correctly.

Yoga is a favorite practice of mine. It took quite a while to get the correct breathing and stance for each posture. But as I mastered each one and found that it opened me up, I wanted more. As yoga opens the body, we have to open up our psyche, our feelings, to this process to find our design personality. We haven't done this before, so we have to exercise the muscle, open up the flow, get the heart and the mind connecting and moving together. We have to get them talking to us and to each other.

In the first chapter, I shared my sense of the central role of your home and your design personality in creating a quality life. I hope by now you're convinced! This chapter offers you three exercises to help you *feel* what the experience is about. They will help you generate a dialogue between your everyday self and your inner feelings, your conscious mind and your subconscious mind. Have fun with them, and know that they're moving you forward in ways that will guarantee

that you get the most benefit from this process.

The first exercise will zoom in on your feelings right at this moment. Your answer to this exercise may be entirely different tomorrow. That's okay. All the exercise intends to show you is how inner feelings can be represented in the world around you. Actually, it's the whole concept of this process in a nutshell: Figure out what you feel strongly about, then put it in your environment. You create your world to suit the real, inner you.

Getting the conversation going with your inner being so you can see the design personality is your first challenge. Once you've learned it, you'll use this practice of listening to your inner self in all aspects of your life, for the rest of your life.

The second exercise is the next logical step in the process of self-discovery. It will expand your perception of your needs and, at the same time, clue you in to what's meaningful in your life now.

As for the third exercise—sit back and strap on your seatbelt! It's going to be a wild ride. Let's go!

exercise 1
Select a Household Object That Represents You

What you'll need: your favorite pen or pencil and your small spiral notebook.

Exercise 1 is short and sweet. You are going to find one object in your home that you feel represents who you are today. In other words, if asked what object is most like your feelings at this moment, this is the object you would choose. It's best to do this exercise at home, since you'll be surrounded by your things.

First, I want you to check in with yourself. Sit in a chair, close your eyes, and just think about what your basic feelings are today. Are you feeling light and cheery, highly organized, dreamy, overwhelmed, walked on, loved and cherished, cuddly, sleepy or foggy? Understand clearly what your feelings are in this moment and write them down in your journal.

Now I want you to wander around the house. Look at everything, even touch it. Think about what it is. For instance, a cozy lounge chair is comfortable, cuddly, and supportive, while a wooden straight-backed chair without a cushion is very practical, straightforward, and simple. A large oak dining room table might represent strength, service, a strong center, or a love of entertaining. A desk might represent organization and compartmentalizing, while a fireplace might represent warmth, passion, and determination. A vase could model your feeling like an accessory in life, holding beauty, or feeling decorative but not too significant, or it could seem to you to be the piece that creates the freshness, the drama, the joy. Which is it? Is that you today?

Spend some time wandering from room to room. Look and touch many different items and decide what represents you. Trust your interpretations of anything you choose to label. It's like interpreting your dreams. No one else can tell you what a particular sofa says to you. Only you know. Begin to notice how this work is strengthening your interpretive skills and your willingness to trust your choices and your own feelings. It's very important work for your life as well as your design!

Sooner or later, you will come upon something that represents the feelings you recorded as to who you are today, or at least at this moment. When that happens, you have found an outside representation of your feelings. Simple! Now write down the object you chose in your journal.

Finding this representation is the reason for the exercise. I want you to understand the connection of inner and outer being. It's fun, and it begins the process of finding your home design personality. You might even decide to do the exercise for a couple of days until you feel comfortable with it and confident in your findings.

As you begin to recognize what you feel and what represents your feelings, you'll begin to make choices that support those feelings. It's truly inner work to get more in touch with your feelings and to trust them, and then to make your choices accordingly. This is called *being in your truth.* Neale Donald Walsch says in his book *Meditations from Conversations with God* that our highest truth and our deepest feelings are actually the same. You see that we're not just playing here! This is powerful stuff.

"Oh," you say, "but I feel different every day. This isn't going to work."

It's true that every day brings differences in the nuance of feelings, but remember, we're only working on a small scale right now. We're creeping up on this concept.

You *do* have feelings that are big and that represent you most of the time, and we want to get in touch with those and really use them for your design, to make your home perfect for you. But not yet. We're exercising the muscle and perfecting the posture so they can teach us how and what's best. We're taking one day's feelings at a time.

Now continue the exercise by writing down everything you can think of about the object that identifies who you are right now. Is it still the object that represents you after all? If not, you might want to start again tomorrow, and again the next day, until you feel comfortable with an object that you feel most connects and represents how you feel.

How to Interpret Your Choice

Example: "I feel like a chair. This chair is large and cushy and is covered in velvet." You could interpret this as: You feel like curling up and being cozy. If this is a feeling you have all the time, you will want to concentrate your design on providing lots of comfort. If it's just your feeling in the moment, then just know that you're learning the process well.

If you felt like a desk, you're probably in an efficient mood and feeling like putting everything in its compartment or place. If you felt like a rug, you might be feeling walked on. Hopefully, you'll get past that one tomorrow, but if you don't, it may mean you need better boundaries or more help with your identity. Both can be done through the decoration and design of your home. Read on!

So again, the purpose of this particular exercise is to illustrate how an internal feeling can relate to an external object. It shows that certain feelings (temporary or permanent) can be taken care of or supported by something in the environment of your home (for instance, the need for comfort might lead to the creation of soft, cushy surfaces and spaces).

If You're Working in a Group

If you're working with others, have each person tell everyone what their object is, then immediately interpret it, with everybody giving their two cents. The more input the better. Talk about the concept. Talk about your feelings and how you've neglected them in the past or honored them. Talk about how each person's opinion is theirs to cherish—as are their choices, their interpretations, their feelings. Talk about whether (and how) this has affected the way you've designed your home in the past.

Even if you're not doing the process with a group, these topics would be well worth journaling for your own reference and contemplation.

Results

Each exercise in the book ends up with a representation of who you are as well as your feelings, needs, wants, and loves. I have you select a household object as the first exercise just to illustrate how internal feelings can be represented and supported in the external world. The more you accomplish this, the more your feelings are supported by your home environment.

I made this exercise and example simple for the sake of clarity. Some of your interpretations in the future are going to be subtler. If you understand the whole process of this exercise, it will help you as you get into making more complicated choices.

I hope you journaled a lot throughout this exercise just to get into the practice of interpreting.

exercise 2
Define the Lifestyle You Want Now

What you'll need: magazines, your small spiral notebook and large spiral sketchbook, and your favorite pen or pencil. If you're doing it in a group, you might do the entire exercise together.

In Exercise 1, you started by getting in touch with your feelings. In this exercise, you are going to trust your feelings to guide you. You're going to allow them to rise up and sink back down as we put external visuals in front of you.

Your feelings are always present, but you don't always honor or listen to them. In this exercise, you will practice listening to them and choosing according to what you respond to most strongly, what makes you feel good, what attracts you. This will create a very clear dialogue between your mind and your heart.

This exercise begins to focus on a *broad* perspective of who you are and the lifestyle you want *now*. The results can be quite a surprise. I've talked about how you can follow a routine for years and lose touch with feelings or yearnings that are emerging and want to be expressed. Work, family, and responsibilities can keep you from changing the way you do things or adding newness to your life. If you do this exercise very spontaneously and with a lot of pictures, you will get a very precise overview of who you are now.

What to Do
Do this exercise quickly; it should take only 15 to 20 minutes. Choose 20 to 30 pictures.

• Put on some favorite music and let yourself have fun. It will help support your mood and your search.

• Wander through the pages of some of your magazines and randomly pull pictures that feel really good. They might be pictures of social gatherings, travel, race cars, high fashion, quiet secluded spots, animals, nature, history, family, or fantasy. They can be ads, sayings, illustrations, or pictures of rooms. Whatever you choose reflects you and the lifestyle you are drawn to.

• When you are finished, spread all the pictures in front of you.

• Notice curving lines as opposed to straight lines, color versus lack of it. Notice shadows, busyness, an abundance of nature, light, etc. Notice if there are lots of people or none at all.

• Look at the photos and write down a list of words that you feel represent the overall selection. The list could include adjectives such as *colorful, highly social, quiet and meditative, sunny and cheerful, reverent and sacred, romantic and sexy,* and so on. Trust that the words you choose are very connected to who you are.

How to Interpret Your Choices

Now, evaluate how you laid the pictures out. Were you very methodical? This might mean you love organization and neatness. Did you put them in cat-

*a*NOTHER WAY to find clues about yourself is to go to a museum or gallery. Just wandering around and listening to your feelings will give you tons of information about what's going on with you right now. I went into a gallery in Taos, New Mexico, at the time of my divorce. I wandered around observing all the gorgeous crafts, art, and jewelry.

I was literally dumbstruck by a wooden sculpture of a woman's head on top of a wave. It had huge motion, incredible strength. It rivaled everything else in the gallery.

Later, I looked at its title: "Woman Emerging." How powerful that my favorite piece was mirroring me in the moment. I began to test this exercise with museums, stores, and books—and it worked every time!

egories? If so, it might mean you like areas to have just one purpose. Did you cluster, tear, cut, or fan them?

If you went way beyond 30 pictures, you probably love abundance and want more space filled up rather than less. I find that people who desire abundance are very sensuous. They love softness, spontaneity, lots of bowls of fruit, fresh flowers, and cushy fabrics. But don't take my word for it. Check it out for yourself.

Some people find that their pictures show a few or no people and give off a feeling of needing time alone. This could be a surprise if you've been very social. It is truly awesome how what you choose can talk to you. The reflection has tremendous integrity.

If You're Working in a Group

If you are doing this in a group, each person should place their pictures separately somewhere on the floor so that everyone can look at them. As a group, look at each selection, commenting on what you see and interpreting. Then journal everything you can think of that deserves recording.

Results

All of the words you record are data that represent you, colors you're drawn to now, themes, ways of being. Your environment needs to represent these words. Say your pictures are filled with groups of people and you've considered yourself a loner. Perhaps it's time to look at that. If you are yearning for society, you need to figure out how to bring that into your life. Do you feel like entertaining? Or instead, will you want to be with groups outside of the home? Each option would ask for different needs from your home environment.

If you want to entertain more, you will need to adjust the space in your home accordingly. You'll need to address how you want to entertain (casual or formal) and decide what kind of entertaining you want to do.

If you want more social life outside of the home, the environment can be set up accordingly. Once you have decided your direction, you can design your support system. If it's travel, where will the suitcases be stored for easy access? Sports? Where will the equipment be stored?

exercise 3
Visualize How You Feel

What you'll need: a tape player or a person to read the visualization script to you, plus your small spiral notebook and favorite pen or pencil.

This is a meditation for you to do. It is going to go deep into your subconscious mind and bring up visuals that will speak to you. It needs to be done when you're peaceful, with no distractions or tension standing in your way.

Have someone read it to you, or you can record it yourself. Do the visualization as you're lying on the floor (cushions make it softer!) or sitting in a comfortable chair with your eyes closed. Allow images to come freely into your mind. As thoughts and forms come to you, don't reject them or try to change them because you don't like what they are or you think you can do better. Your first thoughts are always the "right" thoughts for you. There are no wrong thoughts or images.

When you are finished, journal everything that you remember. You will find that the mind holds almost all the details, so recalling your images will not be difficult.

If You're Working in a Group

If you're doing this in a group, definitely record the whole piece and have everyone lie down and listen together. Then do your journaling and move on to sharing and interpreting each visualization separately, just as you did in Exercise 1.

The Visualization

Here's what you should record to play back to yourself when you're lying down. Or have someone read it aloud to you.

Close your eyes . . . feel every part of your body . . . relax completely into all those parts . . . notice your breath as it moves in and out . . . follow the breath in a very relaxed way . . . let go of all your challenges, errands, activities of the day . . . move into total awareness of all the sounds and feelings in the room . . . begin with your feet, relaxing the toes and then the soles . . . relax your ankles . . . let go all through your calves . . . relax around your knees . . . up your thighs, front and back . . . let your pelvic bone hang loosely on the end of your spine . . . relax the small of your back . . . relax around each vertebra, staying with each until there is no tension . . . relax around the shoulder blades . . . relax the shoulders, allowing them to lower and rest on the floor . . . relax your fingers . . . the palms of your hands . . . your wrists . . . let go in the lower arm . . . all around the elbow . . . relax the upper arm . . . rest all the muscles in your neck, allowing them to hold no tension . . . relax in the base of the skull . . . around the ears . . . across the forehead . . . down the nose . . . behind the eyes . . . in the cheeks . . . around the mouth . . . relax your heart . . . totally let go. . . . Now see yourself lying in a sunny, soft, and grassy field . . . soak in the sun . . .

enjoy its warmth. . . . Now allow a second image of you to lift out of the first and slowly walk down the field . . . notice a path . . . follow this path for a while . . . are there any trees? . . . notice a pond . . . take it all in . . . come to a bridge that crosses a stream at the end of the pond . . . notice what the bridge looks like . . . follow the path on the other side until you see a hedge . . . follow the hedge until you find an opening . . . go through the opening . . . there in front of you will be a house . . . go up to the front door . . . notice the doorknob or handle . . . notice the type of door . . . open the door slowly and go inside. . . . You are in a room just beyond the front door . . . notice all its details . . . then move to the next room . . . what room are you in? . . . notice all the details . . . what does the ceiling look like? . . . the windows? . . . the walls? . . . the views beyond the windows? . . . the woodwork? . . . the furnishings, if there are any? . . . the art, if there is any? . . . Go on to the next room . . . notice a bookshelf there, with lots of books . . . go over and choose three of your favorites . . . what are they? . . . Now notice a desk in the room . . . on top of the desk is a portfolio with your name engraved on it . . . what do the letters look like? . . . also on the front is a word that describes you . . . what is it? . . . open the portfolio and see what's in-side. . . . Now notice a figure coming toward you . . . the figure has a gift for you . . . re-ceive the gift . . . what is it? . . . Move away and turn to leave the house . . . close the door behind you . . . follow along the hedge and notice if it has changed . . . find the opening and come out onto the path. . . . As you cross the bridge, notice if the pond has changed in any way . . . continue on along the path . . . what are you wearing? . . . Return to the relaxed first figure of your-self . . . join it . . . slowly return to the room, counting from five to one . . . open your eyes.

When you've finished listening to the visualization, journal all the de-tails that you can remember. Note down sounds, colors, feelings, words, facts, objects, essences, and names of books.

How to Interpret the Visualization

This exercise is telling you a lot about how you like to feel in a space and the essence of what you like to see. *This is the information we're looking for!* The interpretation is a little tricky, because your vision might not be showing you your style of visual pref-erence but instead the way you like space to feel. I need to tell you this, and then you need to go on reading for more understanding.

If your spaces came up with lots of places for you to sit and read and cuddle and daydream, you are prob-ably a nester. If you had wide-open doors, windows, and lots of bright open space, you probably love freedom and spontaneity and are in and out all the time. The first type of space would suggest focusing on coziness and the other on organiza-tion. These two environments repre-sent two different perspectives and would be set up quite differently. Maybe you are a combination of the two. If so, you need to have nests *and* be highly organized. Think about your images and interpret them so you know what you need in your surroundings.

Even what you were wearing had a definite message. Often, women see themselves in flowing chiffon, which speaks of wanting romance and softness. Some see themselves in blue jeans. See the difference in style and message? Sometimes, men see themselves dressed very elegantly, which may mean they love sophistication or may mean they're romantic. You have to decide what it means for you.

You may have found yourself in a kitchen in the visualization, and perhaps you never left it. This usually speaks of loving warmth, being nourished, being near the hearth. This would suggest someone having a large kitchen that is social, or lots of different places to have meals in the home, or more than one fireplace (or *at least* one fireplace). The way the kitchen looked might not suggest the style you want, but it might suggest a love of history if it is old with a walk-in fireplace, or it might suggest coziness. Be as interpretive as you can.

In one case, a woman's visualization had her walking into a house where the foyer was like a prison cell. The next room was magnificent, with flowers, colors, and great abundance.

We finally got to understand and interpret that she was going through a very difficult time and that by passing through that space in her life, she would end up in a beautiful place. The way she used this information was to slow down on her designing and deal with a pressing issue in her life.

If you had gardens or shrubs that were very precise and trimmed, you probably love order and neatness. If they were bushy and scattered, you probably prefer less structure, more abundance, and more of a casual, relaxed look. Not being able to find the opening in the shrubs could mean you're frustrated or blocked in some way.

As you interpret the data, you can decide whether it represents freedom, formality, brightness, highly social times, isolation, gaiety, simplicity, warmth, or whatever. Then you can create your home to complement those dynamics, so that your life is powerfully connected to *you*. Be as precise in your interpretation as you can.

Some Questions to Help

To clarify your visualization and your interpretation, ask yourself these questions. The questions ask about what you saw; my thoughts are in parentheses after each one.

1. Was the hedge bushy or neatly trimmed? (Casual and easy versus trim and orderly.)

2. Was the pond surrounded with lots of foliage and people, or was it sparse and secluded? (Abundance of objects versus simplicity.)

3. What was the season? (Is it your favorite, or does it represent your feelings?)

4. What was the style of the house? (Does it represent your feelings or your preferences?)

5. What was the doorknob like? (Crystal doorknobs often speak of psychic ability or purpose.)

6. What was the door like? (Easy to open? Large and grand? Painted red, the color of passion?)

7. What clothes were you wearing? (Loose or tight, formal or informal, colorful or drab?)

8. What did your bridge look like? (Elegant, old and creaky, mysterious, mystical, easy to cross?)

9. What did your portfolio say? (Often, it shows where your heart is right now—on a project, in love, ready to take a life-changing step, afraid, etc.)

10. What were your three books? (They really pinpoint your focus, your main priorities and values.)

Results

Big, open windows usually mean a love of the outdoors; lots of doors speak of ease and freedom; and on and on and on. Be a good detective. I feel that there are some people who have actually gone into a past life during this visualization. Do you think you did?

your ACTION PLAN

Now that you've finished this chapter, you have started to open up and understand the inner you, the one you want to take care of. Your visualization gives you lots of data on your current feelings, what your subconscious has to tell you about your present preferences, and what lifestyle you want. Make sure you journal all this information, either in your spiral notebook or in the back of your sketchbook.

When you look over your journal entries from these three exercises, it's very likely that you'll start to see a pattern. If so, write it down. It could change, but noting any pattern makes you more observant. Save the pictures and journaling and use them anytime you plan on tackling any decorating or remodeling job.

You should be getting a general sense of your home design personality and of how it's going to help you create your dream home.

4

YOUR OBJECTS SPEAK
to YOU (*and* ONE REALLY MAKES *Your* HEART SING!)

All of you own hundreds of objects. A percentage of them
are new, some are old; some you keep polished, some are dusty
and hidden away. You bought most of them for yourselves,
but some were gifts. Often, they were gifts from very special
people. Your gifters may still be around you, or they may
have gone away, and now those objects may be
even more special because of their absence.

Your feelings differ from object to object. Some you couldn't care less about. Some you are always wearing or never let far from your sight. Some are very special, but they lie in boxes you abandoned a long time ago. Many of your objects would never be missed if they disappeared, and others would make holes in your heart if you lost them.

I could go on and on, but I'm sure you get the idea: You have in your lives these scattered objects that all hold different

The TIE CLASP'S TALE

i CLAIM THAT I can design a whole house from a person's most beloved object. I'll give you an example.

My friend Marcia wrote to me about her choice of cherished item after she read this chapter. It was her father's Pi Kappa Phi pin, which she said had been converted into a tie clasp. Marcia said she didn't even know where this item was at the moment, but there was no doubt in her mind that this pin/tie clasp would be her choice.

So I'll tell you what I know about Marcia from her object. This object is very connected to Marcia's feelings and mirrors how important relationship is for her, simply because the object came from an important relationship. She can trust that information as being a part of who she is, and she can take it as a given that for her, relationships are a priority. It can help Marcia when she designs elements of her home, for it reminds her of this important truth about herself.

Marcia will be happiest if she sets up her seating arrangements to enhance conversation or touch. If she enjoys relating over tea or meals with friends, she'll want to enhance the space where she eats to make it conducive to cozy conversations. In fact, she'll be smart to have many areas for tea. Her father's pin can also remind her to allow time for relating when she organizes her life and when she chooses what activities she wants to pursue. It also speaks to Marcia's love of family, and especially of her father. She needs to have pictures of her father and pictures of herself with her father around her.

degrees of value. They are attached to your feelings—and the deeper the feelings, the more precious the objects.

Some of you love a particular type of object so much that you begin accumulating as many of its kind as you can house or afford. These collections grow as your families learn of your loves. You buy shelves, cabinets, and even large, appropriate pieces of furniture to house the numbers as they grow. And when you're sharing these collections with a friend,

The symbolism of the fraternity pin is about the intellect and excellence, and it reflects Marcia's love of literature, words, and writing. She will most likely be drawn to anything that relates to these parts of life. That is a great message about her, her life, and her design. She needs to set up spaces for reading, writing, discovering. These spaces need to have good light and a supportive environment for enjoying the intellectual side of life.

The pin is also sending Marcia messages about her visual preferences. The pin has a hard surface, so I would suspect she would prefer hardwood floors, leather furniture with brass nails, wooden desks, and brass lamps. They also lend themselves to a library feel. Fabrics that have small patterns and are filled with detail would remind her of the inside covers of old books and would be perfect choices. Oriental rugs would be another choice, as would anything to do with history or culture. I know she'd want shelves and shelves of books, probably open, and if she's lucky, bound in leather.

I checked all this out with Marcia, and she said I was right on! I knew I was, because this object was connected to her heart, and remember, it was her *most* beloved object. So I just began to think of Marcia's space relative to the world of a Pi Kappa Phi pin. This is not difficult, and it is profound.

There's one more subtlety worth looking into. Remember that the pin is now a tie clasp. It has been converted. This probably suggests that Marcia also loves alternatives, ingenuity, and creativity. She could support this by using furniture in unusual ways, lamps made out of vases, and documents as framed art. She also might enjoy creating spaces that convert from one activity to another.

you usually point out each one that has become a favorite, either because of the story behind it, the person who gifted you, or some other notable reason. It could, of course, be its color, style, ornamentation, or rarity that designates it as better than the rest.

I find that of all the treasures that have accumulated in someone's life, one or two own a very sacred space in that life for very important reasons, and it's because they cause good feelings. These feelings and the reasons that an object is cherished are the parts you're after. It's the intimate part that is a direct mirror of your values, your priorities, your focus in life. And the way a beloved object looks gives you very powerful messages about the visuals you prefer. Each dynamic has important messages for you.

WHAT OBJECTS SAY about US

The beloved object is an intimate statement of what lives deeply and profoundly in your soul. It is what you are about, even if the object is lost in the attic or lost from your life.

This exercise is the closest I can get to you. Often, its story is your favorite story, or it tells me what lives profoundly in your heart. Peter, a successful businessman, showed me the black, white, and red ceramic mug that belonged to his Armenian grandmother. It was his choice as his object. It's the mug he uses now for his coffee. This mug represents a relationship, and it tells him that relationship is a priority for him, as is sentiment.

Another successful corporate executive showed me his small Asian tea bowl. I knew for sure that he has two very separate lives: a corporate life and a life of spirit and ritual. He assured me I was correct. I knew these things because it was his most cherished object. I know it, and so can you.

Here's another example. Follow along with me and see if you can "read" the object's meaning: When I was working with one couple, the husband shared his unique choice, a small spiral note-

Whether your favorite object is a wooden spoon, a Tiffany diamond, or—in this case—a Japanese tea bowl, the thing that matters is that it's meaningful to you.

book that fit in the palm of his hand. It was a birthday gift to him from his wife. She had written her feelings and words of love on all the pages of this small missal.

I could tell her for sure that this man is living totally in the now. His current life is more beloved for him than any other time of his life. Words of intimacy on all levels, spoken or written to him, will always nurture him and the relationship. It is what he cherishes most. Very clear expressions of her love will be more profound than any object. Size is not important to him. Depth that he can hold in the palm of his hand is everything. I also suspect that accessibility and ease of use are important for him in his life. Spaces set up with ease of accessibility will please him immensely, as will sentimental objects as accessories.

What if I did this with your objects— objects like a gold necklace, a sterling silver teapot, or a china vase? I have been dumbstruck in the past by the depth of these objects' messages. I literally could design a home from your choice. This has become one of my favorite exercises. I uncover a piece of the inner self, and in some cases, the object can stand alone to give me powerful, succinct, colorful, and psychological input. I now call it the beloved object exercise and see it as a powerful design and communication tool.

In this process, you're only allowed one choice. One beloved object. From that choice I know you, and so do you.

RELATING the INNER to the OUTER WORLD

I hope you are beginning to see how your inner world and your outer world are best when they're in harmony, even in your home. Your inner world is made up of all your special events and memories. It contains the faces and spirits of your most beloved family and friends. Your spirit holds the words, the looks, the gifts that have formed great feelings of love and safety. They have created your values, your world. If your outer world, your home space, holds the characteristics of your inner world, then you are living more in your truth. You have surrounded yourself with support and caring, which will assist you as you live day to day. It also makes creating a home more relevant to who you are.

Now, I'm not saying you have to surround yourself with your history. My beloved object is not from my history. It is a sculpture I purchased as a young adult as soon as I could save the money. I saw it in the window of an accessory shop in New Hope, Pennsylvania. I had to have it. It is five lean dancing figures sculpted out of metal. They are all connected.

The piece is titled "Celebration." It reflects my love of dance, community, and celebration; my love of touch; and my belief that we are all connected. It has very few details, is made of rough metal, and stands on a simple wooden block. My favorite visuals are more abstract, often in metal or stone, simple and light. I purchased this long before the concept of a beloved object came to me. You can imagine my surprise when I did the exercise on myself!

Something that is very significant about my object is that I purchased it myself when I was alone. It was not given to me or passed down through my family. This speaks of my independence and love of contemplation: History is not as important to me. I own things that date back 100-plus years in my family, and I love them, but my beloved object is not one of them. It is something I bought. And the information that has for me is that I place more value on my independence than on sentiment; that I love time alone to think and wonder. My outer world needs to reflect that back to me. My time and my house need to provide the space. If, instead, I am holding on to things I don't love just to preserve relationship, my surroundings will neither nurture me nor hold my identity. This is important!

Finding Your Truth

Your object can hold discovery, laughter, and delight because it says so much about you. Often, it clarifies your thinking, crystallizes choices you've made, and embodies parts of yourself that you've forgotten. There is never anything right or wrong about an object. Its beauty is its truth about you.

Objects as Tools

One of my students, Carolyn, presented a wooden spoon as her first choice. It was an ordinary spoon that you might have in your utensil drawer. The spoon had been her grandmother's from years past, which tells us that Carolyn is sentimental and does love history. Small and practically nondescript, the spoon also shows her love of simplicity, the basics, and primitive forms. It shows that she cherishes things that have a purpose. The wood of her spoon was old and dry, with little color left. This says that she appreciates practicality, function, and history more than the visual—for her, something old and used is beautiful.

A spoon is a profound object. It is held in the hand and helps prepare food. It stirs things up and is easy to handle. It is a tool. A tool is something that is an extension of you that you use to make something better, to build or blend. A good representation of this in Carolyn's home is the blend of the old furniture with new, soft colors and fabrics. She is constantly working with tools, of which the spoon is one. She sews her window treatments, builds things of wood, and upholsters old chairs and sofas.

One of Carolyn's special innovations is an antique chest converted into a vanity and holding a beautiful sink. Carolyn made this long before chests as vanities became a trend. This gives us (and Carolyn) some great clues as to what she appreciates and why she would cherish a tool as her beloved object. The spoon also tells us that Carolyn likes to say it like it is, with no fluff! She is realistic, straightforward, and down-to-earth. She likes things that last.

Objects and Couples

One couple showed me new ways to use this information to assist in a relationship. The husband came to me with his beloved object, which he had to describe. It was his computer nest. He had created a space that housed all his technology. He had arranged everything so it all was within his reach. He absolutely loved being there. He was in bliss. The characteristics of his object are complexity with a lot of ease, accessibility, and the ability to do more than one task at the same time. Yes, freedom.

His wife's object was a teddy bear that she had given to a special friend as a gift long ago when he was ill. He passed on, and his mother gave the teddy bear back as a memento. Her characteristics as a result of her selection were sensuousness

SANTA'S PLATE

*a*T ONE of my seminars, when I asked students to choose a beloved object, one of them chose a plate. But not just any plate. Sandy's beloved object was the plate that her childhood family had used to hold Santa's cookies and milk on Christmas Eve. Sandy heard the assignment and immediately knew that this would be her object, but she had to tear the attic apart to find it. We know lots about Sandy from her choice. We know that she is a communicator (a plate with cookies to say thank you!). We also know that Sandy loves Christmas, is very sentimental, enjoys security from the past, and is a giver and a nurturer. She sees cooking as gifting, loves the details of ritual, is grateful, and is a lover of home. Such a bevy of information!

This information helps Sandy focus on what's important for her, what she can emphasize as she creates her home. She'll want to be sure she uses items that honor her nostalgia or have meaning or history. She also has a love of whimsy, as she connects with the character of Santa. As she designs, she will probably always have a tendency to set up areas where she can communicate. Her object speaks about ways to nurture (soft fur), affection (she loved her friend and liked to express it), sentiment (she had given the bear as a gift to him), a need for lots of cuddling (the cuddly textured fur), and lots of meaning (he had passed on and the gift was returned to her). She needs to have soft furniture, cuddly spaces, lots of bowls of fruit and pictures of relationship, and framed snapshots of meaningful times.

This couple are opposites in their objects, but the combination of characteristics can definitely go into the same space. The environment can be both sensuous and accessible, organized and meaningful.

Other gifts that these objects offer this couple are ways to deepen their relationship. She will help him by offering him lots of freedom with time, schedule, spontaneity, and ease of living. She needs to be sure things are accessible for him.

He needs to offer her meaningful, well-thought-out excursions, lots of affection, herself, her family, and her friends, coming up with touches that add warmth to times of sharing. Do you see how we use the object as a metaphor for the person, their style, and finally, their home?

The visual of Sandy's plate is fun. The plate was not that special to the rest of us. It was ceramic with dull colors. Even Sandy didn't think it was pretty. But as Sandy went on with this process, collecting visuals, the class began to pick up on how many times the plate's center motif—a spray of flowers with lattice behind it—showed up in her choices of paintings, fabrics, and accessories. It was really amusing. All of the bouquets in the pictures were the same shape. This tells us that Sandy's emotions are connected to her visuals. It also says that she puts more importance on meaning and nurturing than on beauty. Aesthetics take a backseat. It doesn't mean that Sandy doesn't love beautiful things—it just means they aren't as important. She's going to choose message over beauty, or better said, her beautiful things need to have meaning.

and gifts that connect to what's happening in their life. Do you see the wisdom this object can bring to your life and relationships?

Objects as Echoes

There have been many funny moments doing this exercise with students. One time, I was holding a student's sterling silver teapot etched with wreaths and lines of leaves, I said that wreaths were important to her, as were borders of leaves. Everyone began laughing as they pointed to a huge 8-foot wreath painted on the wall behind me, along with the line of hand-painted leaves surrounding the entire room just above the chair rail. It was all there on the teapot, her most beloved object, and unknowingly, she had used it in her décor. She was fascinated that it would be reflected back in her most beloved object.

The funniest incident may have been when a young woman stood in front of me, totally unaware that the vase she was holding was an exact mirror of her outfit. It was aqua, and so was her dress. The beading around the neck of the vase totally repeated the design of the beads in her necklace. Her hair was exactly the color of the beautiful horse painted on the surface of the vase. It was priceless, and I assure you, she could hardly believe it.

So, choosing your most beloved object and finding the reason it is dear is the part we're after in this process. It will assist us in choosing shapes, textures, colors, details, styles, materials, focus, and types of patterns. These objects will also remind us of what we value in life. Beloved objects have far more to say than we are aware!

Now it's time for you to do this exercise for yourself!

exercise 4
Choose Your Beloved Object

What you'll need: your small spiral notebook and your favorite pen or pencil.

In this exercise, you must select your most beloved object. The hardest part may be limiting yourself to one choice. Perhaps it will help if I tell you that when it comes down to it, two choices may give you exactly the same characteristics. But making one choice really focuses you.

Your choice has only two limitations. First, I ask that it not be a snapshot or picture of someone. You already know how much you love your family and friends. Second, do *not* choose your wallet. I know that's close to your heart, but it won't give you the information we're looking for—or maybe it will!

What to Do
Take some time choosing your favorite object. It's worth it. Choose something you really cherish. When you look at it, you remember something so important about yourself. Or you remember someone who was one of the most important people in your life. Perhaps it's the appearance that just warms your heart more than anything else you could choose. Or maybe it's something that you always have with you in your pocket or your purse. I don't want to say it's something you can't live without. I think that's misleading, and it doesn't give us the appropriate information. Instead, think of what makes your heart sing.

Once you have chosen, find a time

when you can relax and contemplate your object without distractions. Begin to write down everything you can say about this object. Describe its visual details, size, texture, and color, unless you're working in a group.

If You're Working in a Group

If you're doing this exercise with other people, choose your objects individually, but wait to do the analysis until your group gets together. Have each person take a turn placing their choice in front of the group. Select one person to be the facilitator, who'll ask the questions that follow. Everyone will get the chance to hear the answers together, which will stimulate thinking and result in lots of input. See how much more you'll know about each other and yourself in just a few hours. This is my favorite exercise.

How to Interpret Your Choices

Once you've chosen your object, it may be obvious what it says about you. Then again, it may not. And even if you think you know all there is to know about it, you might be surprised. Don't give up on it too soon.

Some Questions to Help

Ask yourself these questions as you look at your object. Write down the answers and see what you find out!

1. What is your object?
2. Was it a gift or did you purchase it, or maybe find it?
3. Did someone own it before you?
4. What adjectives would you use to describe it?
5. Is it handmade?
6. Did someone make it specifically for another person or for a reason?
7. Who was involved when you received or purchased it?
8. Is that significant information?
9. What does it represent to you?
10. How long have you had it?
11. Do you consider it a symbol? If so, of what?
12. What do you love about it?
13. How do you use it?

14. How does it make you feel?

15. What part of your life is it from?

16. Is it something that has a history?

17. What material is it made of?

18. What condition is it in now? (For instance, if it is a baby spoon that has tooth marks, it's going to say something different than one that is in perfect condition.)

Results

All of your answers typify who you are. Figuring out the metaphor, as you did in Exercise 1, "Select a Household Object That Represents You," helps give you the same kind of valuable information. For instance, goblets and teapots are very social, which means you are social, while mirrors are reflective.

Boxes represent gathering and privacy, organizing and containment. You probably are the gatherer of lots of information. Locked boxes aren't easy to open and are mysterious. That might mean you like secret places in your environment, the feeling of mystery.

Glass is transparent, open, smooth, and, depending on the design, perhaps fragile, formal, or stately. If that's descriptive of your object, it is also descriptive of you. Please assume that these are traits of yours. You might not like them, but they are your traits—I promise. And these are the characteristics that need to be represented in your environment.

Next, consider your object's origin, where you got it. If you bought it, you probably prefer choosing for yourself. If it was a gift, you are very sentimental and might use things that are nostalgic for you so that you support that part of yourself. If it came from an important person in your life, then relationship surpasses the visual for you. (Although, as I've stated before, if an object has great importance for you, that may cement your love of its visual characteristics.) If, on the other hand, the way something looks is its primary pull for you, then visual beauty is your main focus, and you need to honor that.

Trust the object you've chosen. It's now part of your direction. It contains tremendous information within its characteristics—information about you personally, socially, visually, and tactilely. It tells us what you consider important, what media you prefer. It is connected to your happiness, to what you love, and to what you need. This *external* object is profoundly connected to your *internal* being, to who you are.

a DESIGN REVELATION

*J*OANN BROUGHT a large wooden box to her seminar. When I say large, I mean it was about 5 inches high, 8 inches wide, and 14 inches long. The wood was rich, deep, dark rosewood with no detail, very simple. It had no lock and an easily opened lid.

Joann and her family had built their home long before I met her. Upon moving in, she was put to bed in her fifth month of pregnancy. A designer came in to assist them while Joann was confined to bed. This designer installed light-colored woodwork, soft beige and lavender wallpaper in the kitchen, and light gray carpeting in the family room, with textured beige wallpaper. This design was not strong. It had little energy or statement. It didn't reflect Joann or her family.

Joann is a very high-energy person who got my concepts as quickly as I said them. She had done a visualization earlier in the workshop that took her to a big old house with rich brown walls, deep green plants, strong paintings, cushy furniture. After her experience with her beloved object, she was out the door before even completing her style journal. She had gotten it. Two months later, one of her family room walls was paneled in beautiful, rich, dark wood. Other walls were painted khaki. She purchased large, plush upholstered pieces done in dark paisleys. She used heavy, strong accessories. The wooden box looked right at home on the coffee table. It looked like Joann!

your ACTION PLAN

In this chapter, you chose your beloved object and got tons of information about yourself, what you love, and what's important to you. It helped you clarify what you value most, which is part of who you are. Your design personality is becoming more defined and now holds your object's information along with some current feelings, information from your subconscious, and the lifestyle you want now. I hope you did some careful journaling about the beloved object. It's some of your most pertinent information.

In the next chapter, I'm going to show you how to use brainstorming—usually a technique reserved for the office or for other people's problems—to work for you and what you want. To make it happen, you first have to dream it!

5

DREAM *for* REALITIES
(*a* FANTASTIC ADVENTURE)

Brainstorming is something you most likely have done with a group at work or with a friend. It's that process where you go all out—beyond all limits—and think of things larger and more fantastic than you've ever imagined. In this process, you open your mind to all ideas, even if they seem ridiculous, insane, or impossible. You don't judge. You accept it all. Passing no judgments when brainstorming allows flow to really happen. It gives permission to your imagination to be crazy, creative, bizarre, and absurd. What you will find in the process is a way to discover new possibilities. The flow expands you.

Brainstorming is a lot like dreaming, because it has a great element of fantasy built into it. As the dreaming evolves, it often shows hopes, desires, and longings. It helps you discover new ways, programs, and goals that will expand and inspire new horizons for all concerned.

The technique of brainstorming also works in design. If you open all the valves of what could be, you'll come up with new ideas, projects, systems, and visuals that take you way beyond the scope that your first thoughts involved. Lively concepts, colors, and structures take flight when you eliminate boundaries. You know you will always eventually come back to reality, and with that return might come the seed of a new design or idea. Then you can get real and figure out how to build it, connect it, or make it work.

I know I keep pushing your limits in this search for *you*. I'm looking for ways to bring you all the possibilities, so you'll see your present desire for life and your present perspective clearly—data that will inspire your design and your spirit. Brainstorming is another way, and in this chapter's exercise,

you're going to do it with a fun twist. It will reveal interesting data as it works with your imagination as well as your feelings.

HOW to BRAINSTORM your DREAM DAY

I'm about to get you started on this chapter's creative exercise. When you begin, I want you to create an imaginary 24 hours for yourself. In other words, if you were given this gift, what would you choose to have happen?

Do this exercise now. If you wait, you will have too much information, and it will inhibit your writing and dreaming. Try not to be sensational. For instance, creating a trip to Europe, visiting 16 countries, and meeting the queen may sound very worldly and wild, but it may have nothing to do with where you are right now or what would really feel good if someone did hand you the opportunity. Create 24 hours that fit into the perfection of *you* right now, and what you would do, if only you could. . . .

exercise 5, part 1
Create Your Own Fantasy Day

What you'll need: your small spiral notebook, a pen, and at least an hour of time.

In this exercise, I want you to picture your perfect 24 hours. Wrestle with it first in your mind. Brainstorm lots of possibilities and come to a place or possibility that really feels powerful and delicious to you. Then I want you to write it down in detail. Tell a story about your fantasy.

Once you've gotten your direction decided, begin the tale at sunrise and end it the next morning. And remember, you can change that if you wish. This fantasy doesn't have to be linear!

Write down all the events with as much detail as you wish: things you would love to do, places you long to go, people you would enjoy being with. The exercise will serve you only if you create a story or vision that is truly what you would choose, that really feels perfect. Shape the day totally to your liking. You can also choose to be alone. There is no right or wrong. Do not consider budget, particular relationships, physical limitations, or "shoulds." Be free! The challenge is to go inside yourself and choose your day as if it were really going to happen. Be as simple or as complex as you want. And most important, follow your heart.

What to Do
Write your story of a dream 24 hours. Think about it before you begin. Go

anywhere, with anyone, and do anything. Be unlimited, free, and very creative. Explore the visions in your mind. Let your imagination take you exactly where you'd choose to be if you could right now (and that might be right in your own backyard). Begin writing. Write with clarity, detail, and intent. When you finish, don't interpret yet, but instead continue reading the rest of this chapter. It will help with your own interpretation.

If You're Working in a Group

If you're doing this exercise with others, first write your fantasy day at home alone and finish reading the chapter. Then, in part 2 (see page 76), do the same thing you did with the beloved object: Have everyone bring their story to the gathering. Deal with each story separately, having the person who created the fantasy read it aloud and everyone else share their comments.

INTERPRETING your DREAM DAY

I'm confident that you'll find this exercise extremely rewarding. It will tell you so much about yourself—who you are, what you need, even how to start making it all happen. To see how this works, let's look at some of my students' stories.

A Perfect Day at Home

It's interesting that writing a fantasy day is a forward way to take a backward glance at what is missing from your life. I'll try to explain that with an example. Barbara wrote a very detailed description of her day, and it was totally spent at home. She described waking in the morning with sun streaming into her room. She decided to stay in bed a bit longer, but instead of sleeping, she chose to read. Her breakfast was delivered to her bed, extending this joyful way of starting her day.

When Barbara decided to leave the bedroom, she stepped into a swimsuit because she really hated clothes; she con-

sidered them a nuisance and very uncomfortable. She moved to a poolside chaise to read some more. She napped and then continued reading. Then she went to her basement to work on her knitting machine. On and on her story went, as she moved from place to place in the house to snack or nap or read.

Analyzing Barbara's story, I found a keyword, and that was *comfort*. She never changed out of her bathing suit, and she later admitted that she was really being polite by wearing a bathing suit at all. She would rather have been nude.

You might think this is a dull example of what someone would choose for this unlimited 24 hours. But it isn't when you hear Barbara's story and know that she lives every 24 hours of every day in a home that is uncomfortable to her. She also lives with a family that is very judgmental of what she does, wears, and says. She does not have a lot of freedom to create her own preferences. If this is true of you, your fantasy might also be a day at home doing exactly what you would prefer, how and when you preferred to do it, without anyone's judgment—and it would give you a vast amount of information.

There are parts of this fantasy that invite Barbara to move into her own power. And there is information that addresses her home environment. Barbara and her husband have inherited furniture, accessories, and art from both sides of the family. She feels obligated to use it, live with it, and take care of it, even though she forgoes her personal comfort to do so. The furniture is Victorian, with small, delicate chairs and sofas as well as cabinets, tables, and chests. It's all gorgeous. Any antique dealer would drool over the prospect of buying it. Barbara loves the furniture, but she is denying herself comfort by holding on to it. The truth is that comfort must preclude everything for Barbara, because she is *yearning* for it. She's betraying herself by not changing her reality.

I suggested that a reasonable solution might be to keep all the antiques that were storage pieces or tables and replace the chairs and sofas. She could get some very plush sofas and chairs and still use the exquisite Victorian tables, sideboards, and dressers.

Hearing Barbara's choices shows you how the fantasy day works to bring your design direction to the surface. Her day came from some very significant yearnings, and so will yours. If you read your day carefully, it will give you some significant direction. But first, keep reading.

A Little Private Time

Virginia blew me away with her fantasy. It was one line. "I would walk all day on the beach with my husband."

"Wow," I said, "what's going on in your life? That's an easy one to create. You live 2 hours from the shore. Why isn't that part of your reality? Why isn't that a reality instead of a fantasy?"

She explained that her father lived with them. As a result, she never got time alone—especially with her husband.

This is a primary life issue. There must never be a time in your life that you cannot have some time alone or with your significant other. But you must create its possibility. There won't be that special time unless you're in control of your life and have arranged it to hold what you want.

It turned out that Virginia's home was small and housed her husband, herself, her son, and her father. Her side of the family was small, but she did have a sister who owned her own home. I asked why her sister did not carry some of the responsibility of caring for their father. The answer was that her sister and her father were not speaking!

"My goodness," I said, "she worked that out well. Why does that keep her from any responsibility with your father? And does your father know you yearn for some time alone with your husband?"

"No," she said. "I don't want to make him feel bad."

"So you just take on the responsibility for being the one to feel bad?"

These are boundary issues. Setting up imaginary borders that protect privacy is so important. We all need boundaries. And we've *got* to get better at figuring out how to deal with them personally and in our homes. Every home needs privacy spaces and gathering spaces. It takes

communicating to figure out who gets what and when and then set the house up accordingly. We will go into this issue later, but I want you to see how you get the messages from your fantasy day and start to work with them.

Thankfully, Virginia was able to solve her privacy problem. She went to her sister and shared her frustration. Then she asked her to share the responsibility of taking care of their father. Her sister agreed, and Virginia got a lot of her life back.

A Mysterious Companion

Richard's fantasy had him off in the Orient with a friend whom he couldn't identify. They were at a tea farm buying exotic teas. He wrote in great detail about the experience. He then found himself traveling up a mountain on a circular path. His companion was still with him. They had long, introspective conversations about life and its meaning. They would stop along the way in comfortable settings and continue their dialogue. They did rituals at some of these places.

The companion was extremely supportive and affectionate, comforting Richard and encouraging him in his thoughts and dreams.

My interpretation of Richard's story is that he wants more time for ritual, dialogue, contemplation, and certainly a change in his work. He seems to be searching for answers and more meaning.

As you might guess, Richard loves tea. His hobby is collecting wonderful teas, brewing them in his collection of diverse teapots, and serving a cup to his friends as well as enjoying a cup himself. He makes quite a ritual of it. In his fantasy day, he expanded on something that he already has in his life—which says that he wants more of it. The companion on his journey might have been his Higher Self, for he had no particular identity and showed so much support and introspection in the sharing. I could see the visit to the farm and then the journey upward as symbolic of where Richard yearns to go. The rituals also showed his desire to make everything sacred.

So, Richard wants more time alone, more meaning and ritual in his life. He is a very busy man. Designing his home and his life in such a way that these dynamics can take place is a challenge. But his story suggests that they will take him to a more peaceful and fulfilled self. Any way that he can create ritual around everyday living will serve him. Creating spaces for particular daily rituals will be excellent. Even paying bills in a relaxed manner and designated space, perhaps with a candle burning and music on, would make life seem less hurried and more meaningful.

Making Time and Space for Play

Gayle, on the other hand, had a fantasy day partly at home and mostly away from home that was filled with sports, parties, reading, lawn games, people, and much more. It became clear that she yearns for more time to be very active and social. She needs freedom and spontaneity to do it. Her reality was working long hours, then going home to eat and sleep in a small apartment.

At the time, she and her new husband were searching for a house to buy. I suggested that they choose one that was low maintenance and had lots of storage for sports equipment, lots of doors to the outside, and lots of windows that were easily opened—all suggesting free flow and freedom, with everything highly accessible and transportable so life can be as full as she desires. I suggested that even her clothing needed to be this way: low maintenance, spontaneous, visibly and efficiently stored, and easily accessed. I also wondered whether she didn't need to examine her job and the way it consumed her life.

THINKING about your DREAM DAY

Some of you may discover that you wanted to spend this magical day by yourselves. It most likely means that you do not have enough time alone. Having no time to yourself can put you way out of balance. If this describes your situation,

I'd suggest that you create private space: a room where you can do exactly what you want. By contrast, if your fantasy story involves a huge social party or stream of social events, I would guess that you are yearning for more connection. Making sure your home and your life support social interactions would serve you.

Perhaps you'll just see that you're in a rut, and change is what you need. This exercise promises to reveal the ruts, the stuckness, purely by your creating the reverse. Please remember this element as you push at your fantasy day to give you answers.

It is a significant challenge to convert your fantasy day into an evaluation of what you're yearning for in life. The challenge continues as you figure out how your home can help you take care of the needs that you're now aware of. It's quite an achievement to really discover the part of yourself that desires care, or expansion, or freedom, and to create the home and the life that support it.

By now you're probably itching to get back to your stories, so let's continue.

exercise 5, part 2
What Your Dream Day Says about You

What you'll need: your small spiral notebook, your description of your fantasy day, and your pen or pencil.

How to Interpret Your Dream Day

Now, reread your story. What have you asked for without realizing it? What is your longing? Break it down as much as you can. I've given you only the main themes that can come through. There could be more. It's great information to work with, and there are ways to know what you need so you can know the type of environment to create. If your home begins to help you get what you need, you're on your way to happiness.

Some Questions to Help

Following is a list of questions to help you understand what your heart was telling you. Yes, believe me, that was your heart talking to you. Your answers to these questions signify what your heart is yearning for. I'll give examples to assist you. The interpretation takes effort. Do it, and you will know so much more about where you are right now in terms of your soul's desire.

1. Where did you spend your day? (Consider the place either a symbol of a type of experience or an actual desire. You'll know which it is if you're really willing to hear yourself. Barbara's choosing her home

throughout her exercise showed a real need to get in touch with herself. She was probably giving herself away to social and family needs constantly. Her soul was yearning for alone time.)

2. Who (if anyone) was with you? (If you were alone, you're probably wishing for some extra time to be in a space connecting to yourself. If you were with others or a specific person, that is what you're wanting.)

3. Was it a very full day or a simple day? (A simple day often indicates that you're caught in an overwhelming life right now, while a full day could signal that you want to create more interesting activities because your life feels dull or you're lonely.)

4. Did you go to a far-off land? (This is usually a desire for adventure and expanding boundaries.)

5. Have you seen the person in your fantasy recently? (Often, the person is someone who is missed a great deal or who is not easily part of your normal life.)

6. Were your activities of a different nature than usual? (This may mean a new interest is surfacing.)

7. Were you at ease in your story? (This could mean that you're very pleased with your present life or, interestingly enough, that you're not, or that you have a pretty clear understanding of what you want.)

8. Did you have fun? (Again, this means that you want fun. Also, it could mean you're good at imagining what you like. Congratulations!)

9. What was the essence? (This can be so helpful. If your time was very organized and structured, you may presently be living in chaos that you yearn to sort out. If it was very laid back and free, the opposite could be true—too much structure!)

Results

Whatever your answers, you can supply what is missing from your life with some form of change in your home and/or work environment. You can change routine, or you can free up your schedule with maintenance help or better organization. You can create more comfort, better boundaries, new sacred spaces for uplifting the spirit, or new places to enhance your relationships. You can add new books that expand your horizons, different cable channels, new intentions for entertaining, more ways to bring nature indoors, new music, or candlelight at dinner.

The key is how you bring the essence of your learned experience into your life. Where was the joy in your day? How do you capture that joy in reality? Go for it. It is very sacred work.

If You're Working in a Group

If you're doing this exercise with others, choose a facilitator to ask the questions that appear on pages 76 and 77. Now's the time to have each person read their fantasy aloud, then answer the facilitator's questions. Next, let the group tell each person in turn what they hear in the story. The group may gain wonderful insights, and they often catch the most important details more clearly than the person whose story was told. I've been astounded at some of the input people have given. It's good stuff.

If You're Working as a Couple

If you're a couple doing this exercise together, it's fabulous. You are getting an opportunity to visit the intimate yearnings each of you has. A word of caution: Don't take each other's story personally. If you're missing from your partner's story, it has nothing to do with your place in his or her life. Remember, the part that surfaces is the part that is *missing*—not the part that is present! Virginia's day was a great example of that. The only thing she wanted was to walk on the beach all day with her husband. Time with him was *missing* from her life. Whatever the case may be for you, I hope you did not betray the authenticity of your story by making sure your spouse's or partner's name appeared in some part. Instead, trust each other.

your ACTION PLAN

You should finish this chapter and its exercise with important information about what is missing from your life. The data you've collected is part of your design personality. You want this information now, before you create the home that will lift your spirit and fill your needs. This is information for your design.

Planning the spaces in a home and how they'll be used allows it to be whole and alive. Your response to your design needs—and life needs— will depend on what you realize about yourself and how creative you are at creating a better reality. Please journal carefully.

You now have lots of words, observations, and interpretations. Keep them safely gathered in one place, for in chapter 14, they will assist you in assessing your design personality and incorporating it into your very important journey toward home.

But first, let's talk about designing for happiness. I'll tell you how in chapter 6.

6

DESIGN HAPPINESS
into Your HOME

We rarely take stock of what makes us happy. Perhaps it's a result of the treadmill we're on. We come across the living of great moments by accident, and we fail to record them or notice what created them. What a waste! If only we would stop and evaluate, it would offer us the opportunity to re-create them. And what could be better than that?

That's what this chapter is about.

Our personal happiness—in our homes and in our lives—is our own responsibility. We can't count on anyone else to make us happy. Of course, it's easier to think otherwise, but it would be a big order for someone else to figure out what our expectations are and then have the energy to fulfill them. If we want to be happy, we need to make it happen. So, getting better at taking stock and then making happiness possible is important.

As we all discover, happiness is elusive. The Dalai Lama writes books about finding it, and Thich Nhat Hanh says that happiness is possible only in the present moment. In this process, you've been discovering that it has a lot to do with being connected to your true self and to what joy is for you. It also has to do with intention. If you let go of worry over burdens (which accomplishes nothing, anyway) and deliberately choose to do only what brings you joy, you are getting closer to living your own truth. You can be very intentional about creating happiness and creating a home that supports it. In this chapter, you'll find out that your home

environment will support almost anything that makes you happy if you set it up to do that. And in doing so, your home will help secure your happiness.

As parents, it's empowering to create an environment that generates family happiness. I also admire parents who provide their children a wonderful example in their own ability to create a happy life. This seems like a lifetime gift to the child, and the home is a tool in this effort.

Also, when you're living with your spouse, partner, or family, you'll find that it's delightful to create happy, effective spaces that lend themselves to sharing and relationship. Daniel G. Amen, M.D., in his book *Healing the Hardware of the Soul,* points out that positive environments enhance both the emotions and the intellect.

A positive environment holds the possibilities that you most desire. To get there, you need to know how you, your mate, partner, family, friends, or groups of friends relate best and are happiest. I'm not just talking about places to sit or ways to serve food. I'm asking you to be aware of what you do together and what kind of environment you need for that. The answer could be a carpet, candles, and big pillows, or it could be four tables for bridge with a buffet for serving. You get my drift. This process helps you be a master at creating nests in which to play, share, and grow. And you need to do the same thing with spaces where you can be alone.

PICKING and CHOOSING

The first step toward designing for happiness is to become aware of your sources of happiness. What moments and activities really bring you bliss? Wandering through your memory bank to times when you experienced joy will educate you. You might remember special moments or experiences on a vacation, during a holiday, or with a particular person. Noticing the patterns of these moments or their essence will help you know what you want to see happening more in your everyday life. It's fortunate when a lot of your happiness is generated in simple ways. Then you have more opportunity to assure its recurrence.

Once you've identified your sources of joy, you can begin to envision spaces that you can appropriate for its re-creation. It's really kind of like romancing yourself. You first discover what you love doing, finding, and discovering. This guarantees your joy becoming a constant reality. The concept helps you move out of habitual living—a life of getting up, getting dressed, going to work, eating, sleeping, and then doing it all again.

A Room for Living

The story of Liz and Doug and their two children, Lori and Bobby, illustrates what I'm talking about. They were very disconnected from each other. Liz and Doug had created a life and home for their toddlers years ago, and then suddenly the kids were adolescents. Their home was stuck back in a style that worked for the family during the children's first 10 years, but it wasn't working now.

Life at home was old and tired. Liz and Doug wondered whether they should buy a new home. They began looking, but they couldn't agree on anything: style of house, size of house, type of neighborhood, even how many floors. They knew they needed a change in their lifestyle and home style, but they didn't know what that would look like. They'd lost all sense of who they were today—they knew only who they'd been.

Up to now, the family had been able to agree on almost everything, so they'd created a home that really worked at the time. Their family room was where they watched TV, and it was also the playroom. They basically lived in the kitchen, the family room, and the bedrooms. As in most houses, their living and dining rooms sat empty most of the time. No matter how attractive the house was, the *living* aspect wasn't working anymore.

Activities that brought Liz, Doug, and their kids happiness were art, music, and being together as a family. They loved hanging out in proximity to each other, but they weren't happy about using such a minimal amount of the space in such a large house. Also, the children were

bigger and needed more space and some privacy! Again, our challenge was to match the home environment with the family's current life and loves. Hopefully, that would resolve their feelings of chaos and disconnection.

What We Did

We first created space in the basement for an art room for the kids, moving it from a too-small space off the kitchen. We set up a picnic-style table, some shelves for paints, and good storage for paper. There was good light, and lots of wall space for hanging the results. The kids' art could expand in creative ways, and their friends and Mom and Dad could participate, too.

Doug needed home-office space, so we created that at the back of the family room. We kept the TV in place for family viewing, and Doug was not way off in a different wing of the house as he did some evening deskwork. We then set up each bedroom for private time. The kids updated their decor and their homework stations. Liz was going back to school, so we made a space for her studies in the large master bedroom. And we were able to make all these changes without having to make any additions to the house.

New Life for Old Space

Liz mentioned that her daughter, Lori, wanted to take piano lessons. I perked up. She knew of a baby grand that was available. Bobby said he wanted to take lessons on the saxophone. Doug remembered that his clarinet was packed away in the attic. He hadn't played it for years, but he thought it might be fun to get it out and dust it off. Perhaps they could get good enough to all play together, so they decided to explore music as a new dynamic in their lives.

Well, their lovely but unlived-in living room became the new music room. We moved in the piano and purchased chairs that swiveled. They were great in the conversation area, and they could turn toward the piano when everybody wanted to be musical together. We selected end tables and chests that could store music. And we gathered African and folk rhythm instruments to use as accessories and accompaniment.

This family turned toward music as if it were a mandate. Consequently and miraculously, their life changed, their friends changed, and their parties became musical evenings with everyone participating. The family grew both musically and socially. They began to experience great happiness. And they didn't need or want another house.

Room to Grow In

Like Liz and Doug's, *your* home environment can support growth, living, and happiness. If you can get in touch with what makes you happy and then create the space for it to happen, it's probably going to work. As you create a new lifestyle and then experience what you've created, your life changes and expands. It reminds me of Winston Churchill's statement that we shape our buildings and then they shape us.

Once, a woman in an audience to which I was speaking raised her hand and said, "I love to dance, but there is no place in my home where I can. Even

Some of our happiest memories are of childhood playthings. I had a special "bottle drawer" that was like a treasure chest. It can be fun to re-create these memories for yourself or for your own kids or grandkids.

if I did have a place, my kids would laugh at me."

It's so amazing to me that we let things like this stand in the way of our joy. This woman loves to dance, but she allows the children and environment to hold her back. Doing what she loves freely in her home would be such a gift to her children. They would see her commitment to herself, and they'd !earn what makes her happy. This would then encourage them to be less inhibited themselves and to take responsibility for their own happiness.

It's CHILD'S PLAY

*W*HEN I ASKED my client Marilyn what brought her happiness, she said playing with her grandchildren. But as we talked, she admitted she had no space set up where she could do that with ease. She didn't even have any toys. She had the formal living room for entertaining and a delightful space where she could have tea with friends. But there was no place where some of the children's toys, their books, and some favorite music were waiting for them when they visited her.

We decided to put a chest of drawers near a closet in the family room. This allowed for great hidden storage. We put a stereo on top of the chest and moved things to make some open floor space. The TV was nearby, so we stored some of the grandchildren's videos in one drawer. Now she could play with them easily. It was perfect. I tell you, an activity that brings great happiness needs to be supported with space, planning, and intention!

MOVING toward *your* HAPPINESS

To make your home a place where happiness happens, I'm advising you to set up your home with specific activities in mind—activities that are special to you. You know how to take care of the basics: the place you eat, the place you sleep, the place you bathe. But do you know how to set them up in a way that makes you happy?

I find in most homes that there's always a place to watch TV. All the chairs face the TV, and the remote sits there waiting. I think it's why we watch so much: We make it so easy. But I'm not convinced that watching lots of TV brings happiness. The awareness of what does make you happy will help you diversify and set up more islands for joy.

Happiness in the Mail

In a seminar, one woman, Dolores, listed that one of the things that brought her happiness was receiving mail from friends. You all know how rare personal

I remember how my Aunt Madge had a special drawer in her kitchen. It was in a cabinet off to the side, and it was filled with very small, old, beautiful glass bottles. We were allowed to play with them for hours while the adults chattered preparing dinner. I loved this little space so much! I can still see the green painted wood of the drawer in my mind, and the half-moon metal drawer pulls. I remember the feeling of being down on the linoleum floor and lining up the blue, green, and brown glass bottles in a row. It was so special to me then that its image still brings back feelings of happiness. I knew I was loved when I was in that space. And I'm still very drawn to the color green and to glass bottles.

Daniel G. Amen, M.D., in his book *Healing the Hardware of the Soul,* says that our identity, our sense of connection to others—our very character—is formed from our memories and experiences. My "green-drawer experience" supports that.

mail is these days, especially personal snail mail. But if we enjoy getting letters, we can help create the experience by writing letters ourselves.

"Would a special place for writing help you write more letters yourself and then get more mail?" I asked Dolores.

She said perhaps it would help. I asked her where in the house that might happen—at the kitchen table, on her lap in bed, or maybe on the porch swing? She thought about it, and she decided that she'd really like her own desk in the bedroom near a window that looks out on a stream.

We purchased the perfect desk. We bought a small, comfortable bamboo chair, some new stationery, a fountain pen, and even some sealing wax. She was ecstatic. She already had a beautiful leather address book bearing her monogram. All of this assists her happiness. As you saw with Liz and Doug, this causes life to change and makes it more cozy, diverse, full, and, yeah, happy. Happiness is a choice!

Support for Almost Anything!

Another time in a seminar, I was challenged that I wouldn't be able to find a way for the home environment to support one participant's particular source of happiness. "I love to jog in the morning," Michele said. "It's the best part of my day, and it brings me great happiness."

I asked Michele if her husband was still sleeping when she got up. "Yes," she answered. I asked if she often disturbed him as she dressed to jog. "Yes," again. I asked if he minded that. "He'd probably prefer I didn't," she replied, laughing.

I suggested that Michele explore a new place in the house to dress for her run. She did so, and she found available space near the laundry room. We got Michele a metal locker (just like the one she had in high school!) where she could store her gear, including a portable tape player. She even put male pinups inside the door! "It's great," she said. "The laundry is right there, so my jogging clothes are easy to maintain, and I never waken Bill. My jogging is even better. I'm so happy."

It's such a great practice to think of all the things you love to do and how you like all of it to happen, and then figure out creatively what that means you need to do to make it work. It's really so simple. A cup of coffee first thing in the morning? Then make it happen with ease in a special "morning coffee spot." You can explore and find your favorite coffee flavor, set the timer on your coffeemaker, have a favorite china cup or mug out and ready, and always be sure you have half-and-half or whatever it is that makes it the best.

Do shiny shoes give you joy? Then make it easy to maintain them. Do you love talking to your friends on the phone? Perhaps you could install an extension near your chaise in the bedroom.

a CHAIR in the RIGHT SPOT

Some of the activities or ways of being that bring us happiness are obvious, but some are very subtle. My student Sandy was

a DESIGNER FRIEND, Barbara Jones, had been working with an elderly woman who was selling her home and moving into a retirement center. The space in her new home was limited, and Barbara was having great difficulty setting up an area for her favorite activity, bridge.

Finally, the client said, "Oh, let it go. I'll work it out."

Barbara and I talked about this topic in depth. She went back to the project determined to find a way. It was clear to Barbara that if she didn't provide space for her client's favorite activity, she was not doing her job. So, of course, she worked it out. It proved to be surprisingly simple—just a folding card table and chairs that could easily be assembled or stored near a multipurpose area. The real challenge turned out to be simply focusing on the importance of making that space—making the client's interests a design priority. Once Barbara shifted her focus, it was easy to create a solution. And it will be for you, too!

happiest when she was feeling tons of communication with her family. (Remember "Santa's Plate" in chapter 4? If you've forgotten Sandy's story, you can find it on page 58.) I found out how she made space for family communication when I walked into her home and found an old, comfortable rocker sitting on an oval braided rug right in the middle of the kitchen. Now, you'll agree that this was not a typical sight! "I have to hear the story about this chair," I said.

Sandy's kitchen was large, but it had no spot to sit down. When the kids came in from school, she always seemed to be in the kitchen. They hardly stopped on the way through. Sandy thought that sneaking a rocker into their path might encourage them to visit. This idea came to Sandy because she knew that she wanted a very intimate connection with her children. It became a great source of happiness. But it didn't exist the way the kitchen was originally set up. She figured out a couple of changes that might make it happen easily and naturally. And it worked!

To this day, Sandy celebrates the open communication and the closeness she has with her whole family. The kids head for the chair when they come in from school, and Dad likes to sit in it when he gets home, too. After a while, the kids go off to the TV, bedrooms, and the telephone. Adding the chair simply created their first stop. They grew to know Mom's tennis scores, and she knew their grades in math. This story warmed my heart. She did it without me, and so can you!

The Hunt for Happiness

Getting in touch with the things that are going to make us happy and elevate our lives takes some time and thought. So, I'm asking you to dig deep to find out what it is you want in life—what you yearn to have waiting for you that will give you a feeling of joy. What types of events would bring your present life to a higher level of pleasure, and how can you make sure that they'll occur spontaneously in your home environment?

To find out, look to Exercise 6 and begin your dig!

exercise 6
Make a Happiness List

What you'll need: your small spiral notebook and your pen. Make sure you do this exercise where it feels good! Put on some music.

In this exercise, I want you to make a list of at least 40 things that bring you a high quality of happiness and well-being. I promise you that your list will be revealing to you. As you write your list, concentrate on things that make you happy. Do not list all the activities of your life; we'll do that in a later chapter. Concentrate instead on just those things that make your heart sing.

What to Do

On a fresh page of your small notebook, write down 40 things that make you happy. Let the list form a column on the left of your page, as shown on page 92. When you've finished the list, go back and brainstorm ways that your home environment can support them. Think of as many ways as possible, just as I did in the stories in this chapter.

If You're Working in a Group

If you're doing this exercise with a group of people, do your happiness lists as homework on your own. Then, when you come together, read each other's lists and ideas. Be clever as you think out each person's style, along with innovative ways that they can create a home environment that supports their happiness. (You ought to be

What Brings You Happiness	*How Your Environment Can Support It*
Reading a mystery novel	*a cozy reading spot, good light, comfy chair, place for a cup of tea, book and glasses, fire in fireplace*

Create a list of 40 things that make you happy, then note how you can change or rearrange your home space to encourage you to pursue them.

getting really good at this by now!) Let the input flow!

Results

You'll find that this process will make designing easier. It's hard to keep coming up with creative ideas for all the different corners of your home. But when you come from "living possibilities" (function), it makes it much easier.

This list will provide volumes of information about you. Next time you face an empty space with no idea how to fill it, go back to your happiness list and ask yourself what is still missing from your life. Maybe that space is a place for a new part of you!

your ACTION PLAN

All of your work to this point has relied on your imagination and your ability to recollect. I hope that your reflections are revealing a powerful new awareness of what you want and that they're bringing you a healthy list of things that can generate design ideas, support your current lifestyle, and keep you connected to your heart, your joy, and what's missing from your life.

This awareness alone could be responsible for a revamping of your space, and make your home a far more special and supportive place. You now possess a world of data to help you know your direction and focus. But you're not finished yet. I hope your magazines are on hand and ready to be attacked, because it's that time! Let's turn to chapter 7 and get started.

7

Your PICTURE JOURNAL

The single most important step in your home design process is building a personal journal: collecting hundreds of pictures from magazines, pasting them in a book, and analyzing each one. Choose your collection of pictures because each one is exciting and beautiful to your eye. Once you've completed your collection, you'll pull together an interpretation of all these images. This time, the interpretation will be extremely practical—you can apply it immediately to your home.

You've all looked at hundreds of magazines filled with photos, room designs, people, and advertisements. This time, you're going to create your own. Basically, it's similar to a scrapbook, but you're not gathering mementos. You're gathering your story through pictures that attract you. You'll want them to be good examples of what's especially beautiful to you, what makes you feel good. They might be pictures of full rooms, tabletops, gardens, or mountains, or ads, fashion layouts, or vignettes. They'll all work.

Initially, as you choose, you must not consider whether you want to live with the look in the pictures. Don't do the picture journal with a specific design project in mind. Instead, do it as a study of what you're drawn to, how you feel about certain looks, and what gives you a charge.

Wandering through a book on photography or art is usually a great pleasure. You enjoy a collection of someone else's images, colors, and ingenuity. In these books, though, there will always be some pictures you don't like, and your favorites will be different from anyone else's. When creating a picture journal, you are putting together page after page of only things *you* really like. The book finally becomes a collage of *you*, of what you enjoy and are attracted to. When your journal is done carefully, it becomes a primary and rich representation of so much that resonates in you. You will love *all* of the pictures.

So yes, this journal becomes a metaphor of you. It is filled with the mystery of you. With it, you can get in touch with your visual/feeling side. You'll find out whether you like space open or closed, simple or complicated, bright or subdued, soft or hard, accessible or mysterious, neat and tidy or all mussed up. You'll find out if you like whimsy, shadows, circles, pastels. All of your selections make up an important part of your home design personality: the visual part.

When you have become familiar with your loves and needs and implement them into your design, your home will become a significant place of power for you, a place of strength, refuge, and total personal comfort. You'll learn your pleasures as you fill your journal. Consequently, you'll train yourself to choose design elements easily and well. You'll embrace your individual preferences on many levels and raise your confidence appreciably.

HOW your PICTURE JOURNAL WORKS

To build your journal, first tear pictures out of interior design magazines, travel magazines, fashion magazines, and so on. Then paste them in your large spiral sketchbook and analyze them. I'll show you ways to understand the meaning of all of your revelations as the chapter proceeds, but first I want to talk about the journal and how it has played out in some people's lives.

I'm sure that it's rare for you to take the time to do an overview of yourself, especially your visual self. You might end up with your personality profile after some time in therapy or after taking a Myers-Briggs personality test. But this is usually relative to your work, or solving your problems, or finding the right job—not looking at what brings you joy or helps you design your life. Remember, these visual images that you love come from within because they're constructed from your history. They subtly state your preferences, what relaxes you, what identifies you, what motivates you. They fulfill your yearnings and are therefore helpful, so you want to examine them with great care.

After doing the picture journal, some students have sold their houses and moved; others have chosen to simplify their spaces or their lives. One woman scrapped her architectural drawings. Most of my clients and students have become much more discriminating about what they choose to make their own.

You may have already worked with a designer who has had you cut out pic-

Ann's journal
was sending her
a message to
slow down.

tures for part of the initial process. But when you collect lots of pictures, as you're going to do now, and take the time to analyze them carefully, you get deeper information. At first, you may collect pictures that seem opposed. Some will seem trendy and some won't. That's your mind sorting things out and learning to give up familiarity. But as you go on cutting and pasting, the pictures will take a turn to-

ward some looks and loves you either left behind long ago or didn't know you admired. You'll see more similarities as you go along.

Actually, sometimes the opposite happens, where everything is similar because you're concentrating on what you want to create, and then suddenly the *real* you pops up. (See "A Journal of Empty Chairs" for a real-life example.) In these cases, it's the accumulation that tells the tale. The repetition of particular images or characteristics finally leaves you with the impression of your style. The resulting treasure will be a designed interior with no mistakes. And you need to cut out a lot of pictures to get there!

a JOURNAL of EMPTY CHAIRS

ANN'S JOURNAL had page after page showing pictures of chairs. Some were outside, some inside, some in alcoves—even on verandas and in gardens. At the time, she was living a very busy and somewhat fragmented life. Sitting in a chair was a never-happens event. It made her laugh that she'd put her issue in front of herself without knowing it, and she vowed in front of all of us to open up her schedule for more sitting! This is a great example of how your pictures talk to you in the same way as your beloved object and your fantasy story.

STEPS and STORIES: MAKING the PERFECT PICTURE JOURNAL

There are three steps to building your picture journal: choosing your pictures, cutting and pasting them into your journal, and asking yourself what drew you to each one. These are covered in Exercise 7 on page 106. There's also an exercise (Exercise 8 on page 109) that helps you understand what you've created. But before you get to the exercises, I want to share some stories with you of what clients, students, and even professional designers discovered about themselves and their home design personalities and preferences when they created their picture journals.

Incidentally, a favorite point in my seminars is when we're evaluating these personal journals. Everybody has labored for weeks collecting and pasting their pictures. There's a lot of built-up excitement when it's time to hear the messages the pictures bring, and there's so much surprise and delight as the revelations un-fold. "I never knew I liked stripes so much," or "My gosh, I've got the color coral in every picture!" are typical comments. Some students find pieces of furniture they already own hidden in six or seven pictures, which shows that these are real favorites.

A Designer Tries Her Hand

I presented this process to professional interior designers at the National Conference of the American Society of Interior Designers. They voraciously pulled tons of pictures and were fascinated with their self-discoveries. One designer had the human form represented in some way in every picture, whether in a sculpture, a painting, a totem pole, or a doll. This detail was obvious through a multitude of examples. We were all blown away, and so was she. Your journal will be equally revealing and fascinating for you.

Mary Ann's Life-Changing Journal

I have many favorite stories to tell because this is all so dynamic, but the story of my colleague Mary Ann is a great place to begin. Mary Ann is an interior designer who graduated from my alma mater, Drexel University. She was well trained in the classic methods used to design spaces. Deciding to do additional studies, she signed up for one of my makeover classes. Mary Ann and I became fast friends. She began to see the piece that was missing from her designing process. She had known that design needed to be personal and based on living, but she had not taken the time to explore this to its conclusion.

And that's not the whole story. When the style class evaluated their picture journals, we met at Mary Ann's home. Her journal was filled to capacity. She had worked hard. We leafed slowly through her pages so we'd see it all. There were crushed velvets; large, old, wooden candlesticks; strong oil paintings; picture frames in gold leaf. There were purples, red, golds, and deep apricots—all strong colors.

I laid down her journal and looked around. The contrast between the condo's look and Mary Ann's journal was extreme. The condo was very attractive. It had white walls and beautiful charcoal wall-to-wall carpeting. Her

a FOCUS *on* WHAT *was* UP

ONE STUDENT'S picture journal was full of photos that went through—or rather, to—the roof. Most of Joann's pictures showed moving lines overhead, such as a scalloped valance, a hanging light fixture, stenciling along a crown molding, or a picture that showed a setting under the limbs of a tree. This gave Joann a strong indication that she is drawn to an overhead focus. Who knows where it came from? Perhaps she slept for years in a canopy bed in a very nurturing family setting, or maybe she often had wonderful picnics under the branches of a mulberry tree. It doesn't matter where Joann's overhead focus came from, although that's a fun detail. It matters more that she knows she likes the feeling it gives and that she can create these overhead effects as she designs her home. It's a winning detail that gives her comfort and joy.

modular sofa had no wood and was up-holstered in black textured wool. The decor had modern simplicity: minimal accessories, black wrought iron with glass, and a beautiful glass bowl with clear water and red roses. It was stun-ning—a great design accomplishment. But it had nothing to do with Mary Ann and what she loved.

Mary Ann was very open to her results, so we had fun laughing at the contrasts between her condo and her journal. There was no similarity—and she got that! Her openness and trust of what had happened was real and clear. She sold her condo and found an old brownstone in Center City Philadelphia. She filled it with large Victorian pieces; wonderful art she had done in college; vibrant colors; big, strong accessories; Oriental carpets; and old hatboxes. She began living ac-cording to who she was.

Mary Ann had let her condo be the showplace of her professional ability. But the sacrifice of living in another style in-stead of living according to her own was taking its toll. After creating a home in a style that was true to her own tastes, Mary Ann's life became rich, and she felt much more in touch with herself. The process also put her in touch with the ways she wanted to work with her clients. She has become a very sought-after de-signer in Philadelphia.

Students' Journal Stories

Here are more real-life stories to intrigue you, this time from four of my students. I hope you find their discoveries as in-spiring as I do!

It Wasn't All Black and White

One student, Gloria, was in her forties when she signed up for my seminar. She lamented, "My family's house has always looked like we just moved in, no matter where we lived. We left the white walls and added no color anywhere. This time, I really want to move in and design an environment to suit our family."

Gloria's pictures showed a tremen-dous love of color. There were apricots, celery greens, and cobalt blues, together with lots of light-colored wood. As I looked through Gloria's picture journal,

I discovered a black-and-white motif among all the colors. It was subtle at first. A few pictures would not have revealed it, but she had gone far in her exploration. I began to see black-and-white tiles here, black-and-white checks there, black-and-white accessories every so often, and a black-and-white area rug. All of it was against this background of warm apricots, vibrant greens, and blues.

From a design perspective, the black-and-white was acting as a neutralizer of all the color. But there are many ways to neutralize color, so this was an important discovery for Gloria, one that would not have been easy to pick up if she'd just had a limited number of pictures. She had never been aware of this. It individualized her style and served her well in creating interesting rooms.

If at First You Don't Succeed . . .

Sharon, another student, had worked with a designer before she signed up for the style seminar. They created a dining room in soft lavenders, light blues, and off-whites. Not long after its completion, Sharon found herself bored with the room. She and her husband then decided to work with an architect to renovate their kitchen. They chose many of the visual elements themselves. They used a strong fruit motif in borders and fabrics, with a combination of pickled woods in the cabinetry and strong, dark woods in the bar stools, table, and chairs. When it was finished, Sharon saw the huge difference between the two rooms. Now she was really confused.

In her confusion, she decided to use another designer to do the family room. That designer chose to pick up on the dining room look, and as I'm sure you suspect, that didn't work. Because this couple didn't know what they liked, they were continually disappointed in their design ventures.

Many people are in Sharon's predicament. Even if you're working with a professional, it's extremely important that you know what you like. The designer doesn't have the ability to show you this personal side of yourself and can't possibly know your intimate history with color and line. But when you know what you like, a designer can create that look for you at its highest potential. That's really what design is about!

What Was "In" Was Soon Out

A third student, Ivana, had the same kind of story. Her journal was full of soft colors, tiny cottage prints, and delicate lines. The window treatments were ruffled tiebacks; full, quaint valances; and fluffy balloons. But prior to the class, a designer had shown her what was "in," so Ivana's living room sported drapes done in a fabric with dark greens as the background and large cranberry- and rose-colored bouquets. The treatment was beautiful, but in two short years, Ivana had come to hate the fabric and the pleated drapes. She still had the rest of the house to tackle, and she was understandably scared. Her picture journal showed that she liked small cottage prints, and that was the new direction she needed to go.

Please understand that I am not speaking against designers. I am one! But I am aware that we as designers need to use some process to trace the preferences of our clients so that our designs nourish their lives. It's very important to the success of the design and the satisfaction of our clients. I am also speaking directly to clients and encouraging a greater self-awareness so that they are responsible partners in getting what they want.

Making Home Heaven

Susan completed her picture journal and carried it everywhere in the back of her van. She wanted to take her discoveries along with her. She and her husband, Jeff, were building a home, and she began to see everything differently once she'd done the picture journal process.

One example is when Susan and Jeff were deliberating about the architect's suggestions for the exterior of the house (stucco and mountain stone). Susan drove around taking pictures of houses that used the combination. She wanted to see a variety of applications so they could come to a good decision.

When Susan shared the snapshots with me, I quickly directed her back to her stylebook. I showed her that mountain stone was nowhere in her book. Not a single example! Why would she choose it for the exterior of their home?

my DESIGN DISCOVERIES

*I*N ORDER to develop this process, I had to use all the steps myself as they came to me. As I did, of course I began to discover my own themes, my own design personality. One of my most pronounced motifs was sculpture—mostly of the full human form. These forms were usually in black, as if they were silhouettes. They were often active, dancing or jumping.

I was fascinated by how often I had pictures that showed huge contrasts in size, such as a very small accessory next to something very large, or pictures of a small village at the base of a huge mountain. My pictures also showed contrasts in materials, such as a silk couch against a concrete wall or a brilliant painting in the midst of a monochromatic and somewhat colorless room.

There was a lack of pattern in my pictures. Fabrics were usually in powerful colors, which created patterns against each other. The rare patterns I did have were usually geometric.

I saw my own styles more clearly, and it showed me how the process could work. Now that I knew these things about myself, I was making choices for my home much faster. You will, too, whether you're creating your home with a designer or working by yourself or with a friend.

Susan gulped. "Oh, my gosh, you're right," she said. After close scrutiny and exploring, Susan, Jeff, and their architect altered the design and went with butter-yellow stucco, black shutters, and white trim. It was beautiful—and, more important, they loved it. Their home is a great reflection of Susan's picture journal process.

I was thrilled when Susan called me one Saturday night after the house was finished. "We don't want to go out anymore," she laughed. "Our home is our heaven!"

Using Your Journal

This personal picture journal will become your companion, so compile it with great intention. You'll use it to make choices and to reinforce those choices. You'll love what it will teach you about yourself and how it will reflect your favorite feelings back to you.

Many students have told me that their picture journals are important tools for helping them know themselves, but some say they also turn to their journals when they are feeling out of balance or depressed. They tell me they put on music and leaf through their collections of pictures. Doing this helps bring them gracefully back to themselves.

This is a virtue I hadn't considered. It makes sense, though. If you're feeling scattered and uncentered, and you sit down quietly to take a look at your own accumulation of inspiration, it has to bring you back to yourself and your feelings of pleasure. This dynamic speaks to the authenticity of the journal and the depth of its reflections.

While sifting through the magazines to find your clippings, it's best to work on the journal for short periods of time. I took mine on vacation and did it sitting on a cottage porch overlooking a lake. Great environmental support!

If you're doing the picture journal process with a spouse, partner, or house-mate(s), refer to the next chapter before doing this exercise. It will help you find the common ground between you before you begin.

When you're ready, let's get started!

exercise 7
Create Your Picture Journal

What you'll need: your magazines, your large spiral sketchbook, glue or tape, scissors, and a pen or pencil.

Step 1

The first step is pulling pictures. Try to do this very spontaneously. Keep reminding yourself to just let yourself go. Begin paging through your magazines one at a time and tearing (yes, tearing!) out the pages or parts of pages that appeal to you. Put out of your mind any thought of needing to find your style or of needing to remember a particular room you know you're going to design. Then you can be in the moment and enjoy yourself.

Don't study the pictures yet. Just tear them out and let them stack up. Remember, this step is to *find* the pictures. You'll paste them in your book later.

Never pull a picture because it's something you *should* like. There is no such thing! Staying committed to choosing only what you like will keep the journal authentic and helpful. Remain very focused as you proceed. You are truly creating a companion for your design work.

Step 2
Sit down with your scissors and glue (or transparent tape). Now you can trim your pictures. Make them

look respectable enough to go into your book!

Next, paste them on your pages, leaving some space between pictures for writing. Some people like to separate their pictures into categories. You can do this if you want. I prefer the hodgepodge approach, since we're trying not to be specific now.

Step 3

When you've finished, carefully go back through all your pages and ask yourself these questions about each picture you've chosen. You can write the answers right on the pages.

1. What do I like about this picture?
2. What don't I like about this picture?
3. How would I change what I don't like in the picture to make it more to my liking?
4. What drew me to the picture?

Pulling the pictures is a very right-brained exercise. You are gathering. You're totally in your feelings, and that's where you need to come from at first. But this step, answering the questions, is analytical. We're moving you into your left brain and learning why you felt the way you did and why you made these choices. This step helps you be very confident because of the logic involved. Believe me, what this will do for you is very deep and expansive.

There is absolutely no right or wrong way to do the process. No picture can be more right than another, and no reason for liking it can be wrong. This is important. You need to see your choices with great clarity and understanding. That's why it's necessary for you to answer the questions about each photo. It takes you into your left brain.

As you answer the third question, about what you would change, it helps you improve your ability to visualize, because you won't see the change except in your mind. It is also great practice in designing when you take the time to analyze and change a look with a detail that works better for you. You get the chance to experiment with alternatives. You'll understand more about the value of analyzing as you do it.

If You're Working in a Group

If you're working with a group of people, the sequence is similar to the one you used in the exercises in earlier chapters. Each person should work on their personal journal at home, where they can be alone, quiet, and focused, without distracting conversations. Choose your pictures and put them into your sketchbook. Then write your personal responses to your questions. The group comes into play after you've finished the basic exercise—made your journal, asked yourself the questions on page 107, and compiled a summary (we'll get to that part on page 112).

Results

After you've collected all your pictures, pasted them in your book, and answered the four questions for each one, your journal is complete. All you have to do now is see what it says about you. That's a bit more complex. You'll need to be more objective now. When I analyze someone's journal, I can really rock some students with what I see. It comes from being very objective. Use the question-and-answer format in Exercise 8 to create your own analysis.

exercise 8
Analyze Your Picture Journal

What you'll need: your finished picture journal, your small spiral notebook, and your pen.

Remember Gloria, who had so many pictures that were colorful—full of golds, greens, blues, and apricots—and how we also discovered black and white? You want to make discoveries like that. You also want to find out what you've been enjoying without even knowing it.

The best way is to first page through your journal, just making a list of words that represent things that you see, such as lace, sculpture, books, maps, plants, or arches. Write this list in your small spiral notebook. Perhaps you list maps only once. That will tell you that maps are not a part of your template or design personality. Then again, you may be floored at how many times you write the word *maps*. If so, then you have found out something about yourself. And if you didn't know it, what a discovery!

So, create your list and come up with all the looks, objects, colors,

shapes, and feelings that occur over and over again. Let your list of "seeing" be long. Then place this list in the back of your picture journal. I would suggest that, in lieu of the small spiral notebook, you do the entire analysis there.

What to Do

Now it's time to ask very specific questions of your pictures. These questions will help you walk through the journal, missing no details. They make sure you get all the information you need. I suggest that you read through the list of questions, then page through the entire journal again before writing down your answers.

Some Questions to Help

I've included a *lot* of questions because I've found in my experience with clients and students that understanding the picture journal is the real key to getting a wonderful, satisfying, true-to-life home design. It's worth spending some time answering questions now to get the home of your dreams later!

1. Notice how space is filled in your pictures, even in the ads and pictures of paintings.

- Is it overfilled?
- Are chairs and sofas close together, tables filled, and the walls covered with art and/or objects, or is the space very open and flowing?
- Is there lots of bare space?
- Are windows large or small?
- Are there different styles of complex design within the whole?

2. See if you can find one shape, or even two, that is repeated often.

3. Are there lots of lines? Are there crossing lines or wavy and curving lines?

4. What strong themes do you see?

- Do you find repeating elements such as gardens, library features, rustic looks, seashores, birds, cottage styles?
- Is there an abundance of natural touches or Indian, English, romantic, or sporty features?
- Are there lots of conversation areas, bedrooms, workshop spaces, decks, relaxation spots?
- Do you see lots of unorthodox touches, or are they more conventional?

5. What media show up most often: wood, brick, stone, marble, stucco, tile, fabric, glass, wrought iron?

- Is there a large variety of media or only one or two choices?
- Do you see a lot of wallpaper, plants, flowers?
- Would you say there is a lot of texture? A lot of shine?

6. Do your pictures contain lots of patterns, or are there more solid colors?

- Whichever you have, where do they occur? On the floor, the walls, the furniture, the windows?

7. What colors of wood occur most often?

8. What is the predominant style—formal or informal?

9. What are the predominant moods? Are they sunny and bright, dark and sophisticated, tidy and organized, formal and sedate, whimsical, romantic, masculine, feminine, playful, worldly, cute, country, pretty, sensuous, tailored, soft?

If you have some fashion (clothing) pictures, they'll give you some great indicators as you label them with the adjectives I've suggested or your own. Pictures of models wearing very detailed, organized, or structured (tailored) outfits or with very neat, precisely combed hair will turn up in journals of people who love home environments that feel very organized, neat, and tidy. Very dramatic or exotic fashions will reflect a love of more dramatic feelings in decor also. A model who's wearing a cuddly shawl will represent a love of the sensuous, the casual, and/or the romantic. Very ingenious fashions will reflect a love of creativity or ingenuity, and so on. You can evaluate ads in the same manner.

10. Do you have an abundance of art?
• Is it large, small, traditional, abstract, cartoonlike?
• What is the predominant subject matter?

• Are there a lot of photographs, maps, documents, and so on?
• How is the art displayed? Are the frames ornate, simple, heavy, metallic, gilded, or wooden? Do they coordinate with each other, or are they matched to the art they frame?

11. Is there a high level of drama (strong statements of style)?

12. What are the predominant colors?
• Do you see strong contrasts, pastels, lots of different colors? Do you have a lot of one color and a splash of another?

13. What do the fabrics look like?
• Are they highly detailed, abstract, soft, geometric, flowery, with small patterns, with large patterns?
• Are there lots of different patterns together?
• Is there a lot of one pattern used on walls, furniture, windows?

14. Do floor treatments have a tendency to be dark or light?
• Are the photos consistent in showing one type of treatment?

15. Do walls have a tendency to be dark or light?

16. Do your pictures show primarily painted walls, wallpapered walls, wood walls, brick walls, or another treatment?

17. How are windows treated?
• Are there a lot of window treatments, or are windows left bare?
• Is there a typical window treatment?

18. Are there lots of pairs of lamps, chairs, vases, and so forth?

19. Would you say from your pictures that you prefer *symmetry,* where everything is identically balanced on each side of a center, or would you say you like *asymmetry,* with things pushed off to one side and balanced with something different on the other side?

20. Would you label the style in your pictures as precise, neat, tidy, and clean, or is everything draped, soft and cushy, scattered, or piled, looking like it's ready for you to jump into (or as if you already have)?

21. Is there a lot of light, or are your pictures shaded, shadowy, or a combination?
• If there are both, what look is more common?

22. What types of accessories show up a lot? Are there flowers, vases, sculpture, crafts, china, books, and so on?

23. Now make a list of adjectives that you feel embody your pictures. What crops up most often? *Cozy, sweet, fragile,*

pretty, handsome, artistic, creamy, silky, luxurious? The possibilities are endless. See what your choices tell you.

24. Are there any striking characteristics? For example, perhaps nothing hangs on the walls, all the floors are wood, there is no color above eye level, or everything has a border.

Results

All of these answers make up your style. Some answers will have more importance for you than others. You'll have a feel for which ones really matter. Now, write a summary of your discoveries, noting what seems especially important to hold on to as your style. What are the loud messages?

A Sample Summary

I found that I liked lots of open space, high ceilings, big windows, lots of light, lots of big art, and plants. My art was abstract and brilliant in color. My walls were often white with an accent wall in a brilliant color. There were many circles in windows, fabrics, and styles of furniture. Sculpture was important, and so were strong geometric designs and the color red. Most of the texture

My Summary

Architectural Features:	High ceilings, big windows,
Wall Treatments:	White walls; occasional accent walls in brilliant colors; large abstract paintings, often not framed
Shapes:	Lots of round circles in windows, fabric patterns, accessories and furniture styles.
Effects:	Open, with lots of space, large sculptures (usually of the human form), strong geometric patterns, red, textures from plants, brick walls, area rugs and fountains. Woods reddish or painted black. Some metal. Natural media like stone, driftwood, marble and glass. Surprise elements like kites, cartoon characters, puppets.
Lighting:	Indirect, with very few lamps

seemed to come through plants, brick walls, area rugs, and fountains. Furniture was minimal, and it was simple and sculptural. Photos rarely showed upholstery in patterned fabric unless the fabric was geometric. Woods were reddish or painted black. Tables were often stone. In fact, natural stone, marble, and driftwood were often featured. Glass, too. There were also elements of surprise: large, colorful puppets, kites, and comic characters.

You could also do this summary in a list form, as in the diagram above.

Using Your Summary

You'll always want to refer back to your journal, but it can be helpful to carry your handwritten or typed summary with you. When you're shopping, it can help you make the best decisions. You'll pull out your description (a template of your home design personality) and let it tell you whether what you're looking at is a whim or really expresses your style. Of course, you can take your picture journal as well.

What I want to impress on you again is that all of your answers are your own unique combination and represent who you are. They are authentically *you*. The more you honor them, the more you'll become true to yourself, and the happier and more comfortable you will be.

I have some students who continue to fill the first journal. Some end up making two journals. It's best if you revisit your journal every five years to see if it reflects who you are *now*. Review the pictures, go through the questions, create a new summary. If your summary changes, add new photos to your journal that represent what you like now, and then celebrate your changes by putting them into your life and home.

If You're Working in a Group

If you're working with a group of people, now's the time to get together and go over each other's journals, questions, and summaries. One at a time, in front of the group, each of you should page through your picture journal, making comments as you show everyone what you've created. I suggest that no other comments be made at this point, as the group carefully focuses on the presenter's journal. (Remember, you've already worked on your own journal, so you're getting the questions and how to evaluate your style ingrained in your head.) At the end of each presentation, the group should add their observations and any details they see.

You will get powerful input as each person brings their perspective on your journal to the group. Trust these observations and discuss them. Try to see how each journal is different. And enjoy the intimacy that is growing in your group with all this personal sharing.

your ACTION PLAN

Now you have a picture journal. If you've been a good detective, you have great information about your preferences—perhaps more than you could have imagined. You probably know yourself better than ever before as far as visual preferences and feelings are concerned. Since we've been dealing so much with your heart up to this point in the book, you probably have some new feelings about yourself, too.

As you'll see in upcoming chapters—and in real life—the information you have now will have remarkable benefits for you every time you wish to address some part of your home or make some life choice. But what if you're not the only one who has a say in your home's design? In the next chapter, I'll tell you how to work successfully as a couple, as a family, or with roommates or housemates.

8

COUPLES, FAMILIES, *and* HOUSEMATES

Now it's time to talk about the design and compatibility issues
that can arise with two or more people living under
the same roof, or when one person's picture journal has to
take others into account. How do you find common ground?
How do you discover how extreme your differences are?
This chapter will help you bring harmony out of
potential design (and interpersonal) chaos.

When it's personal space you're talking about, there is a lot of ownership on the part of every individual living in the home. Each person's comfort index, favorite way of being, and idea of the way things "should" be are at stake. Old attachments, like "Mom did it this way," "I've always liked my slippers here," and "I've always dreamt of having this kind of home," all come on the scene and clamor for respect and attention. Tempers flare, boundaries are violated, and anyone who cares gets irritated as a result.

Often, all of the people choosing to live together—husbands and wives, families, partners, friends, or housemates—are not on the same page. They want different looks or various types of space, or they have different standards of order. We see this problem reflected in the world today. Control issues, boundary issues, customs, and cultural differences all seem to get in the way of our living together everywhere. Perhaps it's happening under your roof, too. Working it out may foster healthy coexistence and in turn contribute something to peace

on the planet. Wouldn't that be awesome!

The first step is to get everyone on the same page, and that can be easier said than done. You must choose a process to get through it all. I feel that three dynamics help: pictures, dialogue, and experimentation. It's important to try to seek agreement, so put on your hats of compassion, cooperation, and openness. They're great tools for helping you get there!

GETTING to the SAME PAGE

Pete and Peg are a great example of this issue. I got a call from Peg saying that she and Pete wanted to talk renovation with me. The truth was that Pete was not interested in renovation. He was just going along with Peg, hoping it would all just go away. They'd been in their house for a long time. Pete didn't want to move, and he didn't want to renovate. He felt their house at the beach was more important, and the house in Philadelphia was just fine as it was. That was the beginning of the problem.

Our first meeting was not an easy one. Peg and Pete have been married for a long time. Their opposite perspectives were therefore emotionally charged. Often, when this situation arises, the one who wants the change has thought out every angle to persuade, and the one who doesn't is hardly listening. My first time through the discussion may be at least the seventeenth time for them, and I end up being the neutral party brought in to hear the opposing viewpoints and help the couple resolve the situation. Peg hoped I'd show Pete the wisdom of her position. Pete hoped I'd put an end to all discussion.

Peg showed me a plan that an architect had drawn up for them. It raised the floor of one room and knocked out some walls to create larger spaces. It represented big bucks. It was a good solution for Peg but unattractive to Pete's wallet and love of the ocean house. His answer was clearly, "No way!"

The plan as the architect had drawn it gave Peg what she wanted: more open space and more light. She also wanted more space for herself. In their present home, there was no spot for her to do her work, and this frustration, as much as any other, drove her to seek change.

When there is this much emotional charge, the gap seems enormous, and it blocks a couple from seeking alternatives or spending time in dialogue and introspection. I suggested that they gather some pictures to show each other what they wanted. Pete was not interested in doing this, but Peg was, and she proceeded to do so. This was helpful for both Pete and me, because we got to actually see what Peg was yearning for. There was great simplicity in her pictures, a feeling of open space, and lots of light.

I went back to my office to design a less extravagant plan that might give Peg what she needed and maybe satisfy Pete. When I presented my solutions, Peg loved them. They seemed to supply her wants without being so involved or expensive. There was only one wall that had to be shortened, no change in floor levels, and the addition of a gas fireplace. I'd planned a window seat for the dining area that just delighted her, and I'd rearranged the furniture to include a desk area for her. We were getting there.

Back to the Drawing Board

I didn't hear from Peg for quite a few weeks. Finally, a phone call let me know we were back to the drawing board. When I got there, Peg said that after talking long and hard, she and Pete came to realize that she was looking for things this house couldn't give her. They decided that in two years, they would buy a new house, and in the meantime, they asked if I could work with Peg to make the current house more to her liking.

Well, for 2 hours, we worked to seek an alternative, using the present space and the present furnishings. We moved furniture around like cars in an amusement park ride. I kept thinking of what her pictures showed me: the need for simplicity, more light, change, open space. When we were finished, Peg was shocked. She loved it! We eliminated some pieces,

moved all the art, angled the dining room table, moved one piece out of the dining room to the Florida room, changed accessories, and positioned a desk for her in a spot with a great view of the outside.

When we started rearranging, the dining room furniture began to look new and interesting to Peg. We decided to replace the dining room light fixture, put a new frame on a large, important painting, and add some simple window treatments. They were the only changes! The costs had been reduced from thousands to hundreds by using pictures, dialogue, and experimentation.

As I left, I laughed. "Tell Pete he owes me!" I said, for it was clear that Peg was happy. And now Pete didn't have to move a single wall. He only had to accept the movement of furniture, some small expenses, and, of course, a move in two years. Getting clearer on each other's objectives and finding common ground was the goal, and it had been accomplished.

This page can't hold Pete's endorsements. He was in love. I've been hired for the beach house, too! In fact, I'll be

Pete's designer for the rest of his days of living on this Earth (so says Peg). And it all works, because Peg is also ecstatic. Seeing what the couple's needs were, experimenting, and communicating brought everyone together.

PILING UP a PEACEABLE SOLUTION

There are many cases where there is agreement on the *need* for change, but that's as far as it goes. If all involved are willing to pull photos and discuss possibilities, you have a great process with a pretty good guarantee of success on the other end.

Here's how it works: Everyone collects their own pile of pictures, then they exchange piles. Each person goes through all the other piles, selecting favorites. All favorites go on the common pile, to be considered for interpretation later. Then you use the questions in chapter 7 to summarize the common pile so you can put together a group summary. This process works for husbands and wives—and all other living combinations!

If everyone is not willing to do a picture journal or even pull random pictures, the ones who *are* willing complete that process, and then the others go through and mark the ones they like with colored pens. (Everyone gets their own color, so it's easy to see who likes what.) If neither of these techniques works, it's time for the others to bow to the desires of the person willing to do the work. We've got to have compromise somewhere!

the GENDER GAP

I have found that members of the same family are rarely very far apart, but they often think they are. Even agreeing to pull some pictures will help family members feel closer. It will also help them identify their differences. More often than not, those differences are based on masculine and feminine characteristics that can be easily addressed. Men tend to go for straighter lines, while women prefer curves and spirals. A combination of both, rather than an exclusive focus on one or the other, can fill the comfort bill.

Homes are usually zoned with a combination of "public" areas where everyone gathers and private areas for individual space. Favoring a more general style in the common areas and personal preferences in the others can help resolve style disputes. In fact, it often lessens the tension to deliberately create public and private zones in the house, if everyone agrees. Then each person can choose the look for their own personal areas.

Nevertheless, I still think that there needs to be some deep dialogue on standards of order and the overall design look. It's important for everyone to be comfortable in the home, period. So work hard at the process, using all the tools available, and then resolve your design differences in ways that create harmony.

Designer or Divorce?

One example of a couple in crisis involved emergency design intervention. Sally

"*but* WE'RE *so* DIFFERENT!"

ONE COUPLE, Margaret and Alan, were truly at odds about their home's interior design. They felt there was no compatibility in what they each wanted. Again, I got both of them to gather pictures. When they were ready, we switched their "piles." She went through his pile choosing what she liked, and he went through hers doing the same. It was amazing how many of each other's pictures they liked. The common pile was large. It was apparent that their styles were very close.

The biggest difference was that Margaret loved small-patterned wallpapers, and Alan loved the look of wood. I suggested using Margaret's preference, a small-patterned wallpaper, in the kitchen area, but brought in a larger pattern in the dining room. Alan's love of wood was enhanced with dark cranberry walls in the living room that set off the woodwork and wood furniture to perfection. We used an abundance of good woodwork throughout the house. As it turned out, wood and wallpaper were very easy to balance. Once again, common ground was established.

called me out of the blue. She was very concerned about her marriage, her home, the freedom to be herself, and the adversity she and her husband, Sam, were experiencing. It seemed they had huge differences of opinion about goals for areas in their home. She knew of my work and wondered if my process would assist them in resolving their relationship and design differences. I said we might as well try. I'm cheaper than an attorney!

Their problems had surfaced when Sam's father died and willed them a grand piano. It was very large, and it swallowed up space in the not-too-big living room. No one played the piano, and Sally was distraught over the entire issue. She hated the way the piece looked in the room. Sam was emotionally attached to it. In an attempt to resolve their impasse, they struggled to find an alternative. They wondered if a new house with a larger living room would be the solution, so they began looking.

Sally and Sam were in agreement on the move but on nothing else. Style of house, geographic location, needs, and wants were lining up differently for each

of them. Both felt totally alone and abandoned—not to mention frustrated! Their "couple glue" was coming undone.

I felt the first thing to address was the problem that seeded the issue: the piano. This is where a designer can be of tremendous assistance in experimenting with arrangement. It can sometimes be the cure (as in the case of Peg and Pete). A piano, especially a grand piano, is *big*. It also has a strong presence in its design and a lid that lifts, a side that curves, and a bench, and it's an instrument to be played, to boot. Pianos demand careful consideration.

A way I have often found to deal with a piano if the room is small is to nose it into a corner, allowing the keyboard to face the center of the room. It doesn't always work, because the sound can hit the wall nearby, killing the beauty of the music. But nosing into the corner was a perfect solution for Sam and Sally. They were ecstatic. The tension was released.

Then I suggested that each concentrate on building a personal journal to bring out their individual needs and loves. When they accomplished this goal, they

Sometimes, changing a look is as simple as moving the furniture. If you need more space, move room-eating pieces like grand pianos back into a corner.

were surprised and pleased at how much of the other's style they could appreciate and even call their own. They both had a lot of the same soft colors and the same feelings. They were both traditional in their style outlook and loved art, so there was no conflict there.

The differences seemed to be gender

based: Sally chose more curvy lines and circles (feminine), and Sam chose more straight lines, squares, and rectangles (masculine). When they saw this and heard my explanation, they actually laughed. They were liking the way the living room arrangement looked and were ready to consider even more changes. In Sam's journal, he had many very organized spaces. Sally's journal showed a more casual look. We worked it out so that each got more of their personal preference in the spaces that were uniquely theirs.

So, Sally and Sam didn't move. Instead, they moved into finding out what was important to them in their present life as far as activities, needs, and happiness were concerned. There was a feeling of excitement as we designated spaces for Sally's and Sam's new interests. They considered their similar styles, made some compromises, and appreciated their wonderful openness and creativity. They had an awareness now of their current lifestyle and moved into new directions. Their idea of separating became a non-topic. Environmental changes set up new soli-

darity and new outlooks. That's how profound this work can be—I promise!

The Power of Pictures

It's interesting how couples can use the picture process to diffuse emotions. Prior to that step, each gets really wound up about what they think would work best, and it pushes them to a feeling of great rigidity and opposition. With photos, they can see that the differences aren't that great, which seems to provide comfortable proof of solidarity and creates a sense of relief. Then, dialogue and experimentation lead to consensus.

Even if your spouse, partner, housemates, or family won't participate, don't abandon the process because you're the only one doing it at your home. Just be aware that you'll have some extra work to do in exploring the differences and similarities that will inevitably show up when you show your pictures to the rest of your household.

A Cautionary Tale

One couple recently presented me with a situation I'd like to share with you.

Melody and John were marrying in their late sixties, after leading single lives for some time. Their tastes were opposite.

John had a fabulous art collection that he and his first wife had gathered over many years. He was very attached to it. Melody was not. She felt the art was un-interesting, dark, and cold. John also had many antiques in amazing woods. To Melody, they were just old. She had no feeling for antiques.

I had them gather pictures and do the evaluation to find their common ground. They breathed a sigh of relief as I saw some similarities. With the couple's similarities and differences in hand, we got to work on the practical "making it all happen."

In her pictures, Melody showed a love of clean lines; clear, warm colors; open space; and round, contemporary sofas and chairs. John chose much more traditional styles with grayer colors, and he selected photos that showed rooms full of furni-ture and art.

How could I bring the two together? I could see that using John's antiques as sculptured accessories surrounded with lots of space might work. I could also

NO SOLUTION *here*?

*t*HERE ARE SOME COUPLES whose differences are extreme. This can actu-ally be a wonderful design challenge if you persist. You might need a professional to get you through, but you can achieve a fabulous design. For example, Natalie and Bob had tremendous success balancing their extreme differences.

Bob loved contemporary styles, wide-open spaces, white walls, simple lines, and sculpture. Natalie loved antiques, Oriental rugs, wallpapers, plants, and lace. As you can imagine, one look is streamlined while the other is busy and abundant. Well, we took her love of antiques, Oriental rugs, and antique fabrics, and his love of sparse-ness, white walls, and beautiful, shiny wood floors, and combined them.

We ended up with rooms that were not "full up" but instead were sparse. We used an-tiques as sculptures against the white walls. Then we upholstered in strong solid colors.

imagine the paintings hung sparsely so they "lightened up" in feeling. I thought it would be especially important to use the paintings Melody preferred, so I had her prioritize the ones she liked.

We agreed to make the upholstered pieces such as the sofa and chairs contemporary and use John's antiques for the wood pieces, bookcases, and cabinets. We first arranged the furniture, which, as you'll see in chapter 14, is an important prelude to hanging pictures. We left lots of space, so each piece looked like a beautiful piece of art. We arranged chairs in a semicircle in front of the fireplace to make use of this space until we could have a sofa custom made for it. Then we hung John's precious paintings to Melody's liking. The couple appreciated the whole look and agreed that it worked for them.

The big reason for sharing this story is the process that came about after the search for common ground. Color was going to be an issue, so I sent them out to look for two 5- by 7-foot area rugs that both liked. This way, I could see the colors they chose together and go on from there. I left them to make their selections.

We made the hardwood floors shiny and used smaller Oriental rugs to show them off. Sometimes we clustered plants, and at other times we used one large plant like a sculpture. We used old paintings, including some oils, and tapestries on the walls.

In places where Natalie was creating a space for herself, we clustered the furniture more, but we did it against the white walls, using more antique fabrics on the furniture. That way, the house didn't look dissected. Bob made his home office his fantasy space, spare and clean, but still brought in Oriental rugs to tie it into the rest of the house.

When we were finished, the house had a contemporary look, but it had some antique wallpapers on accent walls to tie into the overall mix of antiques and contemporary furnishings and arrangements. The place was stunning, and Bob and Natalie both loved it.

Days later, I got a call from Melody. John was hanging more of his pictures and crowding the space around the ones we had hung. She was very annoyed, and I didn't blame her. John had violated their agreement. He did it while she was at work. She had no input. The balance was gone: Each of them was no longer getting what they needed. The common ground had been violated.

I share this story so you can see how this process needs to work. Both parties must feel heard. They must feel ownership and identity with what they love. They must be able to trust each other. It's a warning you need to hear!

Seeing the Big Picture

Compromise can take many forms, as I discovered in a workshop I did called "Creating Healing Spaces," sponsored by the American Cancer Society. I had everyone pull pictures. Then I went around observing. One couple's differences were extreme. Her pictures were of rooms of huge abundance. Every space was filled with lots of patterns, textures, and objects. Sofas had pillows, scarves, and trays. In contrast, his pictures were extremely open, simple, and functional. For a while I was stumped. I couldn't imagine this couple successfully living together.

Then I got it. Where her pictures were of entire rooms filled to overflowing, beautiful and dramatic, his pictures were focused images. He did not have a single picture of a complete room. No matter how much she filled up a room, he was focused on singular images, appreciating their form and statement. He in no way connected each image to the whole. Hence, she can decorate to her heart's content. It will never bother him, because he's focused on some small part that she may not even see.

This process of using pictures, dialogue, and experimenting has worked over and over again for couples. Solving design dilemmas this way creates a win-win situation. It's a good model for how couples can work on other differences in their relationships. Perhaps her focus is on how art is hung, and his is on maps as art. So hang *his* maps to *her* liking!

exercise 9
Find Your Common Ground

What you need: pictures, your small spiral notebook, and a pen.

Now it's your turn to do it. There are many ways to approach this, depending on the willingness of each of you. Both of you—*all* of you—can create a personal journal. That's one way. If one of you is resistant, don't fight it. Let that person go through your finished journal and choose what they like. Or they can tear some pictures that are to their liking and put them in a pile for you to go through. You all need to discuss the process as well as your different styles. The goal is a beautiful, practical home, with all styles represented so that all needs are met.

What to Do

Your next step is to go through each other's pictures or journals, choosing what you like. These choices from each other's piles, once you've put them together, are your common ground. They will lead you to create a design that represents you both (or all).

Next, go back to the questions on page 107 and answer them together, using your collective pile of pictures as your "journal." Be careful and caring, as if you were examining each other's opinion, life purpose, or medicine cabinet. Your job is to see each other, see what's similar, and compromise. Good luck!

If You're Working in a Group

This is primarily a chapter and exercise for two people who are sorting their tastes. If your group is made up of couples, do your own work at home and then, as couples, share what you discovered.

If there's only one person from each couple in your group, I want you to take the following precaution when you go through this exercise: Be sure that you observe any of the absent person's pictures without judgment. As part of the group, your job is to offer input, not criticism. It will not be helpful to put down someone's style. It will be extremely positive for you to see even more common ground for the couple. As I've said before, this can be one of the most difficult parts of decorating for two people.

your ACTION PLAN

You now know from this chapter that there are positive ways to help sort through differences in style. Your tools are pictures, clear dialogue, and experimenting with all possibilities. With the pictures, you can actually *see* your differences and your common ground. With dialogue, you get to hear each other's intimate feelings. With rearrangement, you experiment with what you currently own to see if what you already have can fill your needs when it's moved around or into different rooms. It's all about good working relationships between people and objects.

In the next chapter, I'll talk about one of the most common design elements in your house—and one of the most overlooked. It's fabric, and once you start looking around, you'll see that it's everywhere. It can create or destroy a design look, and because there's so much of it, it's easy to misuse. But a few designer techniques will help you pull together a look you'll love, as you're about to find out.

9

KNOWING *Your* FABRIC PREFERENCES

Choices, choices. Choices forever! Better yet, *confident* choices forever! That's what we're after. In the preceding chapters, you chose general pictures that called to you. In this chapter, you're going to move to a microcosm of the design plan: fabric. You'll get to see reflections of your picture journal choices and actually touch the object (fabric) and bring together more of the sensuality of your choices. You'll really test being in the "marketplace" and exercising who you are.

When you're cruising through show-rooms and retail stores, there are so many choices to seduce you. As you become very clear about your home design personality and who you are, you will no longer be seduced or overwhelmed by all of the possible selections.

Make sense? I hope so! This chapter is a fun exercise. Let it help stabilize this identity that you're growing so carefully.

When we're talking fabric, we're talking about many parts of the design plan, such as window treatments, upholstery, rugs, table skirts, tablecloths, and even bed linens. We're talking about how much fabric, what kind, and where you like to put it. We're talking about the fact that fabric adds softness to a room and exploring whether or not you need or want its softening effect. We're talking about pattern, too, and whether you like it best on the walls, the floors, the furniture, or all of the above.

Touch can add a lot of input to the choice of a fabric. Many times, I spot a material for a client across the show-room. I charge ahead to get its number and then a sample. When I touch the fabric, though, it can stop me cold, even if the colors and the pattern are "right." This is especially true if I'm shopping for fabric to be used as bed linens, as opposed to something that will be uphol-stered to a cornice board for a window treatment.

You see, using fabric in a design scheme addresses your preferences in color, texture, and pattern—and you *will* have preferences on all three levels. I want to make you aware of each level, so you can see your preferences clearly. It's easy to forget your favorite choices in color, ignore how you like fabric to be used, and be unaware that you have very definite ideas of pattern. I first want to address how you like fabric in general. Then I'll have you look at how you like fabric designed into your living areas.

a LOVE AFFAIR with FABRIC

I love fabric. As I write this, I think of a moment when I was sitting in my car at a traffic light on a breezy day. I looked up through my windshield, and directly above me was a huge American flag furling and unfurling wildly in the wind. Fabric! It captivated me. I was inspired about my country, fascinated by wind causing motion, and entertained by the drama of the moment. Fabric and its use were reflecting a lot to me about life and about myself. It was making me feel good!

Thinking about that particular experience with fabric reminds me of other images, too. There was the time when I sat at the window of a Philadelphia restaurant and watched a slim woman in a flared crepe skirt walk down the street. The fabric's movement was magical as it swung back and forth from her hips. It was the right design and the right fabric on the right body. All good choices!

Then there was the time I was amazed in the Zellerbach Theater, watching a dancer being bounced up and down as if she were swimming in a huge sea of pink chiffon that stretched from one end of the stage to the other: a rich and ingenious use of fabric and a great choice of color and type. And that makes me think of the aerial dancers in Cirque du Soleil who suspend themselves and twirl from ribbons of silk chiffon. The costumes and the chiffon are usually the same color, and they all become one, a drama of movement.

I love it all. I love the visual effect of lace curtains blowing with the breeze from an open window in the summertime. I even love the feeling of fabric moving on my body, whether it's a silk jersey skirt or the 300-thread-count sheets on my bed.

I find a carefully dressed round table is magic, and the perfect combination of fabric and fringe on a window can dress the whole room. As you can see, I love fabric that moves, that sculpts, that hangs in soft folds.

But I *don't* use a lot of fabric when I design for myself. When I do use it, my application is very sculptural. (Surprise!) I prefer tailored looks and down pillows as opposed to ruffles and yards and yards of drapery. I dislike the stiffness of organdy and linen that wrinkles easily.

In contrast, my daughter-in-law, Tricia, loves the look of linen—even when it wrinkles—and has it on most of her upholstered pieces. If her furniture were mine, I would go around straightening the lines and smoothing out the wrinkles all the time.

I hope you can see the value of knowing what you like and where and when you want to use it. I have a great list of questions I ask myself when I'm purchasing fabrics. The answers are different for clothes than for household design. Just having the answers stops all the mistakes from happening. You'll learn to ask yourself these questions over and over.

WORKING with FABRIC

I've gloried in selections that I've seen—or created—that have been triumphs in the use of fabric. (You will, too!) Here are some of my favorite success stories.

Linda used a splashy, pink-flowered chintz fabric on a small Louis IV chaise. It was drop-dead. Somehow, the density of the fabric was perfect for the down cushions, and the brilliance of the colors enhanced the shape and style.

Pat dressed her guest bed in different patterns of red—the quilt, the pillows, the throws. It's breathtaking.

Susan took plain white sheer drapes and let them knot through each other to form soft sculptural swirls at her dining room windows. Fabulous!

Each look worked for the woman who designed it, but it might horrify you. You need to know *your* preferences. Pat's different patterns could make you crazy, and you might pull the knots out of Susan's design so fast we'd figure you installed them only to vacuum. I learned this lesson when I got creative on a TV show I was doing. I took an Oriental silk scarf and furled it across a coffee table. A friend who saw the segment reported that the idea made her crazy. She knew she'd be straightening it all the time. That's great self-awareness.

I've seen people buy handsome leather sofas and hate them because they forgot that they don't like the feeling of sitting on leather. I've seen others buy fabulous old Oriental rugs and not be happy with so much pattern, especially on the floor, or fall in love with the colors and design of a French Aubusson rug, only to end up hating its lack of body on the floor. I've seen windows dressed with heavy fabric treatments, then watched their owner discover that soft sheers that flow when drawn are their heart's delight.

Some people like rooms filled with fabric. Others like just a whisper—a very tailored whisper, to boot. If you're very tactile, the surface feel of fabric will be very important to you, too, and the pattern printed or woven into the surface will open up a wide field of choices. You'll prefer some over others, and you'll want to be well aware of those preferences.

I could go on and on, but I'm sure you're getting the gist. We're still talking preference, we're still stalking awareness, and we're still begging for individual discrimination. The "shoulds" are still out. Finding who you are and what turns you on continues to be our goal. Your picture journal gave you many clues about what you prefer, and going through the questions probably helped you get closer to some of your answers.

AVOIDING FABRIC MISTAKES

More mistakes are made with fabric than with any other element of design. Therefore, fabric deserves a bit more attention than other design elements. The next exercise should help you eliminate all future problems in selection. (And since fabric—especially upholstery fabric, carpets, and drapes—can be quite costly, avoiding mistakes is an excellent plan!)

Choosing Fabric

When selecting fabrics, even choosing what you like, there are three criteria to consider.

1. Surface. Do you like the surface effect? Is it shiny, dull, soft to the touch, dressy? Does it have a nap (a soft, furry texture)?

2. Color. Are the colors of the fabric in the same family as your discoveries in your picture journal?

3. Pattern. Does the pattern fall into the types you're discovering are part of your home design personality?

Often, fabrics are chosen without thoroughly considering surface, color, and pattern. Beware of making this mistake! Think about all three aspects before you commit to any fabric.

A Note about Pattern

Pattern is an important aspect of fabric. The patterns you choose are *very* personal. Your journal answers hold some of the keys to your pattern style, but I would like to have you do an exercise that will significantly sensitize you to your precise personal choices.

You most likely already know whether you prefer geometrics, stripes, florals, or some other type of pattern. This next exercise will take you even deeper. In addition to thinking about texture and color, you'll discover whether you are drawn to great detail, such as outlining or realism; whether you prefer abstracts; or whether you tend to choose dark backgrounds.

Fabric can be a wonderful dressing for an older piece, really bringing it to life.

You may find that there's always a subtle design behind the main motif, almost as if it is a sketch or a suggestion of another dimension. You'll notice whether you like flat images or very three-dimensional, lifelike bunches of flowers. You'll test whether you're drawn to whimsy, a repetitive pattern, or a particular subject matter. You'll see whether you prefer the background field open or the design to be very intense and full. My list could get longer, but I think you're ready for the exercise!

exercise 10
Choose Fabrics You Like

What you'll need: your pen, your small spiral notebook, your picture journal, and some paper clips. You'll also need to find out where there's a great fabric store or a store with a fabulous fabric department, and how to get there.

What to Do

I'd first like for you to think of moments, as I did on page 135, when fabric—its essence—struck you. Think about the situations and the characteristics of the fabric. Think about how you feel wearing particular fabrics: wools, silks, cottons, chiffons. Journal these thoughts in your small spiral notebook.

Then ask yourself whether these ideas work when you're designing. Really take some time to relate to times in the past, your picture journal, and your reactions in others' homes. Again, journal these thoughts.

Next, I want you to go to a nice big fabric store or fabric department for the completion of this exercise. Try to find one where the bolts are standing on end and there is good lighting so you can see the fabrics easily.

Take your time wandering around, feeling and looking. Go up one aisle and down the other. Do not choose fabrics for a specific project now. It's very important that you just look for fabrics you like. When you're working on a particular design project, the emotional pressure to choose "what's right"—and the resulting tension—is huge. We don't need or want that pressure and tension now. We're discovering *you*, so we want freedom from tension.

As you wander spontaneously through the fabrics, choose at least 20 that you like. Write down their positions in the rows or put a paper clip on the edge to remind you of your choices. Then go back to each choice and write down the characteristics that you see, such as colors, type of pattern, texture, and anything else we've talked about that occurs to you. Answer the following questions to further your observations.

Some Questions to Help

Use these questions to really focus in on the fabrics you've chosen.

Texture

1. What are the majority of textures that you selected: shiny, soft, napped surfaces, flat, hard, nubby, ridged, silky, furry?

2. Do you tend toward very shiny fabrics such as silk, brocade, or chintz?

3. Are your choices full of soft, napped surfaces (not just flat) like corduroy, velvet, chenille, fur?

4. Are the threads in your choices loosely woven, with an almost see-through effect?

5. Are most of your fabrics "hard," flat surfaces that are tightly woven, such as cotton (especially chintz), matelassé, raw silk, and cotton damask?

Color

1. What colors seem to predominate in your selections?

2. Are there warm colors (reds, yellows, oranges, golds)?

3. Are your tendencies toward cooler colors (aquas, lavenders, purples, blues, greens)?

4. Do you choose pastels (ice-cream shades of pink, green, raspberry, yellow, blue)?

5. Are you in love with intense primary or jewel tones (emerald green, ruby or fire engine red, sunny yellow, indigo blue)?

6. Are they the same colors that appeared in the photos in your picture journal?

Pattern

1. What are the types of patterns you've chosen: small cottage prints, large abstracts, plaids, stripes, floral bouquets, historical prints, old-world looks, or whimsical prints?

2. What is the scale of the pattern: small, medium, or large?

3. Are there some woven patterns, or are they all printed?

4. Is there lots of open space in the

background of the patterns, or are they pretty much an overall design?

5. What are some of the predominant shapes?

6. Is there is a variety of flowers or just one type? (If your answer is one type, it could mean that the shape is what you love and gravitate toward.)

7. Are there fruits?

8. Are there birds or people in your designs?

9. Are the patterns stylized or very realistic?

10. Is the pattern three-dimensional or flat (two-dimensional)?

11. If there are plaids or stripes, describe them. Are they large, open, random, multicolored, and so on?

12. Are the backgrounds dark or light?

Results

Whatever your answers, this is what you prefer. Trust this step. It guarantees that if you buy according to this new list of preferences, you will not grow tired of your choices, and you will enjoy the look the fabrics provide. I hope you did this honestly and carefully, and that you chose a store that had an abundance of styles. The information is golden—and money-saving in the long run.

I suggest that you write out this summary and add it to your journal summary. Then, when you're fabric shopping or out looking for art or accessories, you can easily access your information in your wallet or purse.

If You're Working in a Group

If you're doing this exercise as a group, go to the fabric store together. (It's just too much fun!) Each of you should work separately at first as you choose your fabrics. Then, one by one, parade the group around to see your choices. Tell them what you learned, and then let them tell you what they found out about you.

If You're Working as a Couple

If you are doing this exercise with your spouse or partner, do it the same way you exchanged pictures in chapter 8. First, you should each make your individual choices. Then share your choices with each other and choose the ones you both like.

your ACTION PLAN

In this chapter, you have considered all the possibilities of fabric and zeroed in on your favorites. In doing so, you've also become very discriminating about fabric designs. This will safeguard you from making mistakes, but more important, it expands your awareness of pattern and of your fabric tastes.

Now it's time to move on to the last stage of self-examination. We've looked at who you are; we've explored your tastes; we've examined what you want out of life and out of your home. In the next chapter, we're going to look at what you *do*—your daily activities, how you move around your home. And once you've figured that out, you'll be ready to dig into the actual designing!

10

DISCOVERING *How* YOU WANT *to* LIVE NOW

This is the last chapter in which I'll take you through the process of getting to know yourself and your home design personality. (You'll put this knowledge into practice in part 4.) All the information and self-awareness you've accumulated so far will help you now as you consider how you like to be and act—whether you like to sit or stand while you're working or puttering around;

whether you're a closet artist, a frustrated cook, or an impossible romantic. Do you like a separate room for each of your activities, or do you like it all happening in one big space?

You'll be making some important decisions as you design, so stay very centered as you read this. It's time to come to terms with what makes you feel ecstatic as you move around your home on this beautiful planet. You're in the chapter that bridges the inner and outer work. I'm really challenging you now to embrace who you are and change your life to match it!

Your task now is to examine your current realities, what is missing from your life, and what would make your life better (all the material that you've brought to the surface in this process, plus more). You're going to witness yourself, as if you were floating just above your own head and pondering, "Hmm, is this what I want to be doing? Is this where I want to be doing it? Is this the way I'm comfortable doing this in this moment?" When you've answered those important questions, you will contemplate how to create all of your life accordingly. You're going to observe your movements, your feelings, your way of working, and your way of relaxing as you think about every day of your life and see what you could possibly change to bring yourself happiness. The Buddhists call this *witnessing*. You do it by being mindful—aware of yourself, your thoughts, and your surroundings—and by living with intent.

We all can set up our basic lives pretty easily. It's harder to move beyond basic setups to surroundings that make for a full life that is going to feel good and help you grow. I can easily create a delightful meditation corner for you, but I'll do it differently if I know that you meditate more deeply when you're on the floor in front of the fire!

SUCCESS STORIES

Scott Bedbury, a former marketing executive for Starbucks, wrote a book entitled *The New Brand World*. In it, he speaks of

Starbucks and how they created such a huge success around a simple cup of coffee. They didn't invent the cup of coffee; we've all been drinking quarts for years. Bedbury says they did it by creating a *new experience* around a cup of coffee. Their process was to find out how their customers might enjoy a cup of coffee and then create the opportunity for them. He's talking about the Starbucks success like we're talking about home design.

I'm not even sure their coffee is that delicious. Sometimes it's a bit strong for me. But Starbucks discovered that we want ease and speed in purchasing a cup of coffee, that we like a huge selection of flavors, and that we enjoy the option of spices and/or whipped cream. Along with that, they discovered our desire to sit down in public at a table—alone or with friends, inside or out—even if we're only having coffee. They found out that we'd bring along our newspaper or our book and stay a while. In some branches, they even found out that we'd relish fireplaces and soft sofas and chairs.

You see, they did the work you're going to do. They uncovered people's enjoyment of relaxing out in public, feeling part of the community, and being comfortable in attractive surroundings having a cup of coffee. I think we've all been looking for this kind of experience without even knowing it. And Starbucks figured it out!

Likewise, we've always had homes. Once, they were caves; now they're as diverse as those coffee flavors. And we're all looking for the best possible experience of home and life according to what we personally like. How do we figure out our best experiences? How do we add the dynamic of *us* to our lives? We do it by observing ourselves and experimenting with our feelings and what we like. This will lead us there. I hope you will be as successful as Starbucks has been profitable!

An Apartment Makeover

Here's how the process can work. About 12 years ago, one of my clients was my bachelor son, Carl. He asked me to help him set up his apartment near the city. Carl is a happy, busy guy who loves life, and he's very clear about what he wants. At that particular time, he knew exactly how he wanted to experience his living space: "Give me a space completely set up so that when I come in the door with my Chinese food in one hand and my briefcase in the other, I can go directly to the sofa. I want to sit there and be like a jet pilot, with the ability to put my hands on everything—my remote, my book, my guitar and music, my pillow—and eat my Chinese food pleasantly. And by the way, Mom, I love to see the sunset." This is the way Carl wanted to move (or *not* move) once he arrived home.

I suspect that, as you read his desires, you can conjure up an image of the space. That's what I did, and I successfully made his apartment over so it met his needs. It was easy because of his self-awareness. He was so in touch with his style of order, I knew I just had to listen carefully and then create it for him. (Nice when your mother's a designer!)

I created a nest that included a sofa, love seat, and chair. I put a shelf on the wall behind the sofa for lamps, remotes,

and books. I placed a coffee table in the middle of the room. It had a drawer for some paper napkins, silverware, and guitar picks. (The guitar was at one end of the sofa.) The TV was across the room, and the sun was setting in the window opposite the chair. Voilà!

Together, we worked on what Carl needed for a kitchen. When he talked about walking in with his bag of Chinese, it didn't strike me that Carl was moving toward being a gourmet. And his kitchen was small, so the space needed careful thought. He mentioned a morning bowl of cereal, vitamins, and a cup of coffee. He was also sure he'd want a midnight snack. Having the storage for those items was imperative. Storing china for eight or luxury pots and pans didn't make sense.

The apartment was also small, so there were even questions concerning where his briefcase could go. Carl loved sports, but he wanted all his equipment out of sight. We decided to stash it all in the front closet, where he could organize it and get to it easily.

Now Carl is married, with a beautiful

daughter, so his home environment needs to be quite different. But in those years, Carl liked his apartment near the city. Some of us prefer a wide-open house in the country. Some of us want to be on the first floor and some up where we can see forever. Some of us like having the neatest, tidiest home possible, and some of us feel best when our spaces look like we're still sitting there doing our work.

Our diversity is delicious, but the sad news is that some of us are living in homes that were set up to accommodate what we wanted at one time in our lives, and we never changed them when *we* changed. If this is true of you, it means there is no correlation between your life and your home, and your spirit is displaced. If that's the case, I suspect that your life has probably lost its juiciness and comfort.

What, Where, and How

It's time to get this kind of information into your self-assessment. In the exercises starting on page 161, you'll examine your current life and make some decisions.

Like Carl, you're going to get in touch with what you want *now* and how you like to work and live *now*. If this sounds dry, let me reassure you that this is some of the liveliest part of the work. This is where you really get going! You're going to focus on exactly how you want to set up your home. You will begin to plan its orientation in the way that works best for you. The whole process will give you an ideal space to entertain, meditate, or pursue your hobbies just the way you want. Living and loving will become your heart's delight.

MOVING through your LIFE

This chapter is all about your style of moving; your style of sitting, viewing, communing; your style of working (at any hobby, chore, or task); your style of order. Notice, though, that I have *not* used the words *neat and tidy*. It's definitely not about being neat and tidy or how to be neat and tidy. That could be your goal later, if it's your choice!

Our goal now is placement of the things or activities in your house according to how you like to move, how you want to live, and what you want to do in your space. It's about where you would like to write, think, relax, and doodle, and how you want to do all this. The goal is to set up your spaces so you glide through your life, and your spaces are ready to meet all your desires and needs. You'll be able to move easily and logically around your kitchen, office, and bathroom, do what you want to do with pleasure, and leave without hassle. It's a dance plan, and you decide the style of your dance.

This process stresses your needs as an individual. In home design, it's a radical approach. That's because of our mass-market mentality. Today's kitchens, for example, are often put together in a stereotypical style, designed by one person for millions of others. This just cannot work, not in any part of the house. We are all different.

Let's say you're going to look at your experience of reading. So, when you decide to read, do you want it to happen spontaneously in the best way possible? It will if you are in touch with your favorite experience of reading. You know what I mean: just like Starbucks. I bet you like to pick up your book in a delightful place that has the kind of light, softness, warmth, and support you desire when reading. And where is that? Do you like everything around you to enhance your reading experience (a cup of coffee, a pen for underlining, a clock for keeping you aware of your time, an attractive bookmark, a pencil and eraser for crossword puzzles)? I'll put money on it! So you spell out the things you need and then put them into the space.

In your mind, designate this oasis as "your reading place." If you create it well, it will always be ready for you. Your planning will guarantee your enjoyment. Other stuff will not be there, unless that one space has two purposes. You'll have thought about that in your planning, too, so you won't have to think about sorting as your reading is about to happen. Some people like to read where they have a view, others like to stare into a fire between chapters, and still others like to just roll over and go to sleep when they're ready. It's the vanilla-chocolate thing: Which flavor is your favorite? Be sure you've made it available.

Really Dive In!

This personal planning will help your home support every activity in your life, whether it's painting, cooking, sleeping, or relating. Anything. Let's talk about relating for a minute. Let's say that relationships are very important to you. This process will help you create places where people love to gather. First, you'll decide where you like to interact: inside, outside, on the floor, on cozy chairs, in a hammock, on a window seat, in the living room, in the bedroom, on the patio. Then you'll choose those spaces in your home and set up all different dynamics of interaction and what you need to make it meaningful. One of my clients has a wingback chair in the kitchen. His wife loves to cook. He reads the paper there and they share their day. It's another kind of relationship space.

When you're setting up spaces, it helps

if you know some of the dynamics of each experience you're trying to create. For example, where relationship is concerned, knowing that skin changes texture, eyes tear, and voices change when people are really moved can actually help you when you design your home. You probably don't want to miss that kind of intimacy when you're with others, so you'll want to be sure the furniture isn't strung around the edge of the room so it's hardly connected. Instead, you'll arrange it so you sit close enough to experience it all. This is another way you heighten all design—by contemplating what makes each part of life wonderfully deep.

HOW (and WHY) SPACES WORK

Before you start in on the exercises, I'd like to talk about one more thing: using space. When you live in your house, you want to enter it, unload everything, move into the next segment of the day, find everything you need, change easily, romanticize constantly, function profoundly, relax immediately, and relate exquisitely. Whew! None of that can happen perfectly for you unless you know what you like, because there are so many ways to do each one of those things.

A simple example is that I hate to have to search for my pocketbook, especially when I'm about to leave for an appointment. I've resolved the issue by creating a special place for it, and I make a point of always putting it in that place immediately upon entering. It's a system that I established to take care of my needs and wants. I've found that if I set up a system well and use it carefully, it takes care of me forever, or until I change what I need or want.

This thinking about your life applies to work spaces, dressing rooms, entryways, closets, kitchens, laundry rooms, and mudrooms, as well as to home offices. You'll need to set them all in order so they'll keep *you* ordered.

Working Spaces

I'm fussy about where I work. I am writing this book in a conversation nest that has built-in seats around it and lots of windows. I'm doing the work here because as I try to pull all these memories out of my brain, I can't sit at a desk. It's too confining. My style is to be on the floor with all my notes, quotes, and tea around me. When I get stuck, I lie down on the floor. I roll around. It's a sight. But the writing gets done! Then I move to my computer, where I can see the oak tree or watch the squirrels and the cardinals or see the gardens I am creating.

One day, I picked up my pages and went to the dock of a nearby lake to write. (I was claustrophobic at home and couldn't seem to get any thoughts on paper.) Leaving home kept me flowing, but I knew it was important to return my finished pages to my work space. If I'm going to be spontaneous, I have to be careful to keep the book together. When I returned from the lake, I put the new work right back in sequence with the rest of the book.

My system will let me write next time in my designated space or anywhere else I choose. I need to plan everything for the writing moment—the moment when inspiration hits or time is available. But the entire book needs to be filed in the same place all of the time so none of it gets lost. I know myself well, so this is protection! I'm making sure that my book is ready and I can flow back into its process easily and quickly. Without this setup, I might lose the sequence, lose my train of thought, or start another chapter! *Eeek!*

Some people can work without these precautions. They can leave things scattered about as they work on a project. Darma Singh Khalsa, M.D., coauthor of *Brain Longevity*, writes a very humorous account of Robert Sapolsky, Ph.D., professor of biology at Stanford University in California. Dr. Singh relates that he found Dr. Sapolsky "half-buried in a rat's-nest of papers and books." Yet, when asked for a specific paper, Dr. Sapolsky—without looking around—shot a hand backward and extracted that precise paper out of a pile.

I think that story is a riot. It's a humorous and descriptive way to illustrate that everybody has their own style, and the style may be extremely unorthodox. But if it works, it's fantastic. When you're aware of what works for you, it's the best. There will be no formulas from me for the way you *should* do it. I'll provide only the guidance to get you in touch with *your* way. You've got to do the rest.

I know too many people who struggle with very basic daily activities because they're oblivious to their own activity style and haven't set up the systems to support it. If you're not like Dr. Sapolsky, but you work the way he does, you're in trouble and have lots of headaches!

Different Work Styles

So how do *you* like to work? If you're a very busy person with many projects, you have to know how to keep them separated and accessible. Some people separate by space, some by closet, some by drawer, and some by container. If you like things to look neat and tidy, you need to have doors on cabinets and closets to close away the chaos, or you need baskets and containers as attractive sorters. We'll talk about this more in part 3, as we address organizing, but you need to start thinking about it here because you're going to designate space now.

Some people never do begin the projects they're passionate about, just because they don't like the clutter they create or because they haven't designated a space where the project can live. That's why I encourage you to select a space and organize it to accommodate the way you work best *before* you begin a project. This supports your success and prevents a mess!

I know people who love to work standing up. For them, I create desks on tall legs, with bar stools and counters all around and lots of cubbies above. Some people like to work in a circle. That means they sit or stand in one place, but they want to have their work around them on all sides. These folks need different types of furniture. Some people like to put everything away. For them, I've created a large, tablelike desk that sits in front of a bank of six file cabinets, all housing a huge volume of in-

ASK, *then* ACT!

ONE OF MY FAVORITE STORIES about work space was told to me by a mother who had read an article in a magazine about creating study spaces for children. Her son Tommy's room had never been organized well, and he was studying on his bed. This article really inspired her, so she studied the suggestions carefully. Then she took her son to Ikea, where they bought everything the article recommended: the perfect desk, the perfect cubbies, pencil holders, blotter, chair, and cabinet. They were both excited.

The bedroom makeover got done easily, and Tommy moved in. Then one day, Mom passed Tommy's door and found him doing his homework on the bed. She was crushed, and she scolded him, "Tommy, we worked so hard to get you the perfect study area!"

"I study better on the bed," he said.

formation filed in a way most personal to them.

It's so important to think through or talk through how you like to work. How you want to work, to live, to be, to relate, to relax, to make love. Really take your time with this. Stretch it out. Think of the smallest parts of your life, the most mundane bits, and think how all of those times could become favorite times. Then develop systems and storage that works. That way, your house or your room really ends up being yours. And so does your life.

No Gender Preferences

Couples, listen up! Thinking about how to set up your living space applies to both men and women. I say this because, in some cases, thought is put into how the man wants to live and work in the house but not into how the woman does, or the woman plans no spaces for her own living activities because she's so busy taking care of everybody else. In other cases, the man has no input. He doesn't do the entertaining, the cooking, or the cleaning, so why should he even

After sharing a good laugh with her, I asked if she had ever had a discussion with Tommy about *how he wanted to work* before they started. She hadn't. The article had convinced her that there was only one way to set up the area. Well, she found out otherwise! The suggestions would have been right for a child who loves working at a desk, but they were definitely wrong for her son. Another amusing part of the story was that the school had no problem with where the kids ended up doing their homework. It could be on the ceiling, as long as it got done.

If she and her son had had that important discussion beforehand (or if they had done this process!), they would have avoided a lot of heartache and expense. She would have bought him a blue denim comforter and never worried about the spread getting soiled. Bookshelves would have been more useful—and more used—than the desk. For much less money, they'd have made Tommy's room perfect for *him*, not for some mythical child from a magazine.

think about it? Often, his wife or partner hopes he *doesn't* give any input, because she wants control over the choices.

Instead, if you're working on re-designing or making over your home (or setting up new living quarters), you need to get better at including everyone—in-cluding the kids! Let everyone take re-sponsibility for their own space choices. It will guarantee that each person has a more vital space. Consequently, everyone will be a lot happier in their space and in their work, and they will get more enjoy-ment from living in every moment.

So, now it should be clear: You're choosing how home is going to be. You're planning where, how, and with what, so you can create it. Believe me, you'll love being in your home, and it will become your island of ecstasy.

HOW *a* DRESSING ROOM SAVED *the* DAY

*P*AMELA HAD A RELATIONSHIP ISSUE. She was a great dresser. Her husband usually loved the way she put herself together, but often when he wit-nessed the process midway, he was critical of her choices. It was very frustrating to her, and it often ruined the beginning of a lovely evening.

Pam wanted to stop this pattern. She wanted to put an end to the criticism and enjoy the appreciation. This meant that she needed to be hidden away until she was ready, avoiding the stifling criticism. So she took a bedroom that was being used for storage and made it into a dressing room for herself. There, she could stay hidden while she dressed, then emerge radiant and ready for compliments. She resolved the problem by changing spaces. (This is a great example of how changing your home environment can resolve relationship problems.)

Because Pam was in touch with her feelings, it helped her transform a tough situa-tion in her relationship. She didn't like the way her husband's criticism made her feel, so she removed the possibility of it happening. The professional you hire cannot be counted on to know what you need. You have to be in touch with your own feelings and communicate them to your architect or designer.

EXITS and ENTRANCES

Marilyn came to me because her family didn't want to move, but their home was in chaos and they didn't know what to do about it. The biggest problem was at the back door. It was the entry everybody used upon arriving home at the end of the day. It brought them smack into a part of the kitchen where there were stools and a counter. Nobody came in the door empty-handed, either. They had whatever had gone out with them: coats, schoolbags, lunch boxes, briefcases, pulled-off neck-ties, newspapers, you name it. Yep, the counter got the books, the tie, and the newspaper, and the floor got the bags and briefcases. And you guessed it, the ladder-back stools became instant coatracks!

Marilyn had already been to an architect to discuss her situation, but she questioned whether his solution was appropriate. His answer had been a closet in the entry space. I knew, just as she knew, that a closet could never hold *all* the stuff (if the family would even have used it, which I doubt). I could see that it would have created even more of a bottleneck by reducing the space.

The question was how to change the flow or make a different suggestion for that specific space. The back door opened off a deck. If we brought everyone an extra 20 feet across the same deck, they would enter a sliding glass door into the family room. There, we had a very available wall where we could build some good-looking wooden lockers, one for each person. When they came inside, everyone could pack every-thing into their lockers, then come around the corner to the kitchen for their snacks.

It's what we did—and boy, did moods improve! An unexpected bonus was that with the lockers, the mittens, boots, and books no longer got lost. When some-thing was needed, everyone knew right where it was: in their own locker!

When I consider a situation like Mar-ilyn's, I think in terms of activity and pat-tern. In her case, the activity was arriving home. The pattern was to drop every-thing and get a snack. Our goal was to im-prove the arrival with a better entry. The question was, Could we change the

Fireplaces have come a long way. Now you don't even need a chimney! Just set up one of the new gas fireplaces, turn it on, and settle back to enjoy the cozy ambience.

family's pattern—their habit—so they'd use another door? Consensus said, "Yes." The new door was close enough, and the advantages were huge.

A Picture-Perfect Solution

Doren's problem was also about arrival. She shopped often, and she often purchased old frames for future use. When she came in the back door, she had no specific place to store them—and it was usually time to start dinner or do something entirely different. In her haste to get on to the next thing, she'd place the frames near that back door, where they joined the lacrosse sticks and schoolbags. This was dangerous for some of the beautifully carved frames. Doren also said she often left them there for a long time.

As we worked to solve her problem, we found a second coat closet in the foyer that was always empty and could be a perfect storage space for the frames. The closet was on the pathway through the house.

She had only to walk around a few more corners to get there. Now she had a system.

Same Needs, New Space

Years ago, I created an addition for Jennifer and Tom as they were in the midst of raising their family. Not long ago, Jennifer called me back. "The kids are now grown and gone," she said, "and our layout needs some new thought." They were also trying to decide whether to stay or sell. This is often the discussion as chaos begins to persist, and it usually comes up because the present house hasn't been brought up to date.

Jennifer and Tom were very frustrated. Again, one of the problems was about entry. It seemed that when Tom arrived home, he liked to spend about half an hour in his office before enjoying the evening. His office was on the lower level. This was perfect when their children were small, and he could go there for a half-hour before he got involved with the family. Now he hated going down there. It seemed dark and lonely.

Jennifer had the same kind of dilemma. She would come in from work and want to unwind before cooking dinner. But the only spot she could find to do it was in front of the TV, and she hated the fact that she always turned it on. It wasn't the kind of wind-down she wanted, but she hadn't taken the time to consider what she *did* want. She remembered how, in the past, the kids needed her immediate attention. Now she needed to attend to herself.

Both of them were faced with the same kind of problem: It didn't feel good to come home. The old way wasn't working, and they couldn't figure out how to change their flow. I felt that there were many good options but that Tom and Jennifer needed different solutions to their problems.

Jennifer said she was most comfortable with returning home to a cup of tea and light reading. Her work was very intense, and she needed a release from the intensity. The TV seemed to be the aggravator, so we found a nesting spot away from the TV, where she could sit and stare or read a periodical to clear her mind. It was near a fireplace, which we could easily convert to a gas log unit. Then she could just turn it on when she came in.

I love this new fireplace convenience. There's even one model that has a remote that will turn the gas logs on when you're within a mile of home. Silly? No! It's a product that supports comfort and ease and pleasant living. I'm for that. I love a real fireplace, but if I'm too busy to ever build a fire, the gas logs are golden.

The next step was to set Tom up in a home office on the first floor, possibly near the front door. There was the perfect room, which had been used for other activities—activities that were long gone from their lives. The room was junked up with things that were no longer vital; it had unwittingly become a storage space. Things were getting pushed into the space to get them out of the way. We transformed it into Tom's dream office. First, we cleared out the stuff. Then we painted the walls a soft color. We brought Tom's desk upstairs to the room and used a small Oriental rug they had to add deeper color. He loved it.

Doren's and Tom and Jennifer's turn-abouts were created with very little cost—just enough to make the areas pleasant and help sort out the big question of whether this house could possibly provide a new feeling of home or catch up with the owners and their current desires for life.

SORTING it all OUT

The four exercises that end this chapter will guide you toward making your everyday life easier, better, more pleasurable, and more meaningful. You, like the people in this chapter, need to figure out what you want in your life, where your problems exist, and where change needs to happen. Is it when you want to stop your day for a cup of coffee and it's too difficult? When you simply want to gather and do the laundry? When you want to leave for a spontaneous weekend? The exercises will guarantee the answers, so you'll get spaces, systems, and ideas to support your living and loving.

Because all these exercises are related, this time I'll save the results and analysis for the end, rather than including them with each exercise. If you're working in a group, do each exercise individually, then get together to review, compare, and discuss your results.

exercise 11
Explore Your Daily Itinerary

What you'll need: your small spiral notebook and your pen.

Step 1: Map Your Daily Itinerary

It's time for you to walk through your day to get an idea of what's working and not working in your home. To help you with this, I've provided Wendy and Phil's example, starting on page 170. You can describe your day in bullet points, as Phil did; in a stream-of-consciousness narrative like Wendy's; or in whatever way will give you the necessary information. The only way you could improve on Wendy and Phil's job is to be even more explicit with yourself about what is working well and what you'd like to change.

If writing your life out in this way is difficult, you might be more comfortable drawing pictures that connect and map out a vision of your ideal flow. All we're looking for is your typical movement through your day, pinpointing what is missing in the space and what's not working. Feel free to put your pen aside and pick up some crayons—or whatever assists you in achieving a clear picture of your life today.

Take your time. Have a lot of fun. You can even be dramatic in your descriptions. As you get in touch with multitudes of thoughts and feelings, you'll want to question them or interpret them for yourself.

All of this information is going toward designing your home. Desires that you didn't know you had will emerge. You'll get in touch with favorites and new ideas. Let it all come in. Let your heart tell you what serves you and the use of your energy the most. What do you really value holding onto, and what desperately needs to change? You may see negative or positive aspects of your life that you didn't see before. Welcome all honesty and clarity; they will only serve you.

Step 2: Summarize Your Itinerary

Write a paragraph that summarizes what you see as highlights, just as I did for Wendy and Phil. What must you be sure to remember, correct, and honor from all that writing?

exercise 12
Make Your Life List

What you'll need: Yep, you'll still need your pen and small spiral notebook.

Let's jump from your daily itinerary and really examine all your life priorities. We'll do them in a list format. It will be a rundown of what you want and what has to be in your life now. To help you create this list, remember your happiness list and your fantasy story. In fact, all the work you've done to this point will help you with this step. This is a continuation of a complex walk around you, finding all your idiosyncrasies and basic traits. Be patient. You will have thought through your present so clearly and be so familiar with it that you'll hardly have to refer to the lists to move ahead. You will truly understand the present *you*.

Here is my present life list as a sample. It includes my entire current life inside and outside the home, inside and outside of me. You won't necessarily find it that interesting, but you'll see the scope of the exercise. You're tapping the roots of your desires, walking through your dreams (daydreams, too), and even checking out your purpose.

Sample Life List
As of today, I want my life to hold:

- Writing my book
- Promoting my book

- Research for my book
- Social life with friends
- Work with clients
- Eating
- Sleeping
- Grooming
- Romance
- Painting
- Reading
- Cooking
- Easy financial management
- Meditation, prayer, and yoga
- Dance
- Gardening
- Speaking engagements
- Work with community church
- Lots of personal time
- Comfortable evenings watching TV
- A fireplace
- Kayaking
- Biking
- Hiking
- Friendship

- Time outside
- Computer for e-mail
- Ease in doing laundry
- Ease in packing for trips
- Warmth and beauty
- Lots of travel
- Overnight guests
- Good health
- Time with family (grandchildren)
- Deep sleep
- Dream journaling
- Personal journaling
- Comfort
- Easy maintenance of home
- Community
- Play
- Growth
- Good transportation
- A dog or cat

What to Do

Now it's your turn to make your list. Include everything in your life just as I did.

exercise 13
Make a Household Activity Inventory

What you'll need: Keep your pen and small spiral notebook with you.

Step 1: Record All Your Activities

Your task now is to create a list of the activities for which you need new or better spaces. Refer back to your daily itinerary (Exercise 11) and your list of what's in your life (Exercise 12). These exercises have prepared you, so you can be very specific. List the activity, decide how and where you're going to do it, and note all the things you want with you to make the task efficient and enjoyable. Again, I've provided an example to help you see how this step works.

Sample Activity List

This is how I might go through my list and think out what I want.

Writing my book. A space that is light and comfortable, pens, computer, candle, storage for notes, music, open floor space. (I prefer working in the daytime.) Might be in the conversation nest.

Research for my book. A space where books can be stored, file folders, file drawer, magazines and books for research, light, comfort, daytime, like to do it on the floor, pencils, paper. Think a corner in my office will work (away from the desk).

Social life with friends. Nice dining

space, like small groups of 6 to 8 people, eating at table, china for 10, music, fire in winter, candles, flowers, cozy space in living room for conversations, also comfortable seating in kitchen! Good phone list in computer, some blank invitations, blank thank-you notes. Present dining room works, but want to also create a beautiful outside dining room. Will do it on the end of the patio near the kitchen.

Meditation, prayer, and yoga. Open space in one bedroom, yoga mat, altar, meditation books and poetry books, oracles, music and recorder, water fountain, candle, incense, view outside. Will use middle bedroom. It gets the morning sun.

Speaking engagements. Space at a desk that contains promotional materials, mailing lists, pens, pencils, blank paper for thoughts, music, good light, stapler, punch, stamps. Needs a phone extension and a file cabinet. Will create space at a second desk in the office on far wall.

What to Do

Now make *your* list of activities, including where you want to do them and what you need, considering everything in the process to this point. You make the list, and then it clarifies your life. You will begin to see what is realistic, what cannot possibly happen in your present life, and whether your life and your home are mutually supportive or your present layout is fighting with your needs and lifestyle.

Your activity list will answer questions like: Is it time to sell my house? Should I get a dog or cat now, and if so, how will I create a comfortable and workable arrangement for it? It helps you address small questions, like why it takes so long to do the laundry. Look at your whole life, so your choices are relative to your present situation. You can see what you want to keep in your life and what you might consider dropping. My list was so long that I'm doing a very necessary revamping!

I used the paragraph format in the preceding sample to do this exercise. You might find it easier to use the prototype on the opposite page, which forms a chart. Or feel free to create your own system. You know the information you're looking for, so choose your own style of getting there.

Step 1

Activity	Where I Do It	What I Need to Make It the Best

Step 2: Record the Activities of All Family Members

List the specific activities of the other members of your household. Again, mention what the activity is, where it will happen (it can be more than one place), and what is needed to make it the best possible experience. You may want each member of your family to do this exercise themselves. If not, they certainly need to give you lots of input. Remember Tommy and his mom from "Ask, Then Act" on page 154! Talk to each other, and ask questions as often as possible.

Step 2

Individual's Activities	Where They Do It	What They Need

Step 3: Record All Group Activities

Finish this exercise by writing down all the activities that your family does together, other than the basics. Again, make sure you decide where they will happen and how you can make them happen well. (Create a chart if necessary.)

exercise 14
Summarize Activity Space Needs for Your Home

What you'll need: If you guessed that you'll still need your pen and small spiral notebook, you're right!

In this exercise, you'll decide if room labels in your home need to change. This is a powerful moment because you may startle yourself with some of your decisions. Ask yourself these questions: Is my home big enough to house all these activities? Does the house need to have multipurpose spaces? Does the current orientation of rooms accommodate our lives? Are there rooms that are never used? Can we convert them to help fill out our lives?

What to Do

Look at your lists in relationship to the house, then decide whether some room—such as the living room—needs to become a home office or a music room or a library. Really use your imagination here, writing it like a letter to yourself. You still need to be journaling. This is an important part of the process. In fact, journal your feelings, thoughts, frustrations, confusion, everything! It will help you sort it all out, and you might suddenly write yourself the answer.

Results

When you're finished, take an overview of what parts of the house are being overused or underused. This often creates a moment of truth, where you see that all activities are happening in small, out-of-the-way places, and the general area of the home is serving no one. This could be the time when you trash or give a new purpose to many spaces because you've discovered the need. Sometimes a living room becomes the perfect place for you to work on photo albums, do your embroidery, or have family discussions. I've seen many families become quite creative with living room space after doing these exercises—and the room also remained a beautiful space for entertaining.

Be very flexible in your thinking. Move activities around. Reinvent rooms. Put odd things in new places just to try them out. You're not actually doing anything yet, and thinking doesn't cost a cent, so experiment with all sorts of ideas in your mind. Forgo the fear that you're sacrificing beauty. Remember that inventive storage pieces as your main furniture pieces can be golden.

A wonderful outcome of all this work can be that your home becomes 100 percent inhabited. People who are working, eating, and sleeping in 25 percent of the house suddenly wake up to new ideas for their time and spread their lives out into the many wonderful spaces waiting to be used.

Trust the process! It's the best.

i WANT TO SHARE with you some very thought-filled material that was written for me by two clients who wanted to add on to their present home. They really loved their log house and didn't want to move, but they needed more space. They wanted their son to have a larger bedroom, and they wanted a larger guest bedroom and a separate dining room. They also were at different points in their relationship and in their lives, so they had new wants and needs. I needed to know how their lives played out daily, both physically and emotionally, so I could see how to create these new spaces and relate them to existing rooms.

As you'll see, their narratives were brilliantly thought out. In fact, they apologized when they gave me their lists, feeling sure they would overwhelm me in terms of design. On the contrary—the design just rolled right out of their process! It allowed me to be extremely creative, based on what they needed in order to live their lives exactly the way they wanted to, today, now, in this present situation. Read the flow of their day. I have included a summary for you at the end so you can see what I did, using all their information. This real-life example demonstrates how to pull together the information you need for the preceding exercises.

The Cast of Characters

The parties are:

• Phil: dad, head of his own health-products company

• Wendy: mom, teacher of deaf children

• Nate: 6-year-old son, student

Phil's Day and Lifestyle

Morning

• I get up and reach over to put my glasses on so I can see.

• I use the bathroom and then get some coffee, clean up the kitchen, and make Nate's lunch (Wendy is gone by now).

- I wake Nate up and go down to work out for 35 to 40 minutes while listening to NPR. Nate watches some TV.

- I go upstairs to shower, get Nate dressed, and we go to the bus. I come in, clean up, think, make some lists, and head off to work.

Afternoon

- I come home with stuff to unload and bring it in to unpack (usually, supplies for the kitchen). I hate the way I have to bring it all into the house.

Evening

- If Wendy is out, I make dinner for Nate, and he eats it in the living room in front of the TV.

- I do some paperwork or go to the basement to play with Nate.

- After Nate is in bed, Wendy and I sit on the couch and talk or read. I retire to the bedroom and watch TV for a short while until I fall asleep. Wendy sometimes complains about the loudness of the TV. This could be a continuing problem unless we plan well.

On the Weekends

- I always go to my den room in the morning so I can do all my noisy things and not wake anybody up. I could also use a sunroom for this.

- I usually get up early, before Wendy. I go to my computer in the basement (after I've made coffee and cleaned up). I do some work, modem in. I also listen to NPR. Then when Nate gets up, I get him settled, and he comes downstairs to play while I work.

- This will change eventually, but now we enjoy the parallel activity. Often, we play ball. At some point I work out, and then eventually I go up and shower. During growing season, I often work in the garden.

(continued)

• On weekend afternoons, I do a variety of things, ranging from work to computer, TV, sports, reading, and listening to music. I would really like a very comfortable chair with all remote devices right near the music.

• Wendy joins me when I'm watching TV; she does a jigsaw puzzle, reads, or plays a video game with Nate.

• In the summer, I would envision hanging out at various times on an enclosed balcony, perhaps off our bedroom.

• I might Jacuzzi at night after Nate is asleep.

Phil's Summary

As you read Phil's itinerary, could you begin to see the plan emerging? He needs private space and relationship space, but his private space has many requirements. Since his relationship with Nate is close, planning their spaces close together for now will serve their relationship but help each continue with his own interests at the same time.

Now, let's turn to Wendy's day and lifestyle. As you'll see, even her style of thinking and communicating is different from Phil's! Where he thinks sequentially in lists, Wendy thinks in paragraphs.

Wendy Sorts Her Day Differently

I love my home, but I would like for it to be larger. I love the property size. I am a homebody. I enjoy hanging out and entertaining. A favorite time is when I have the house to myself for several hours and I can just relax and enjoy it, especially if it's a sunny day and I don't have anything pressing. I'd love a cozy fireplace and private space for myself. I'd like it to have natural light. I rarely use my office, because it's on the second floor—too far from the family. Now I just dump into my office. Occasionally I file things there, wrap gifts, and do projects. It's small.

In the past, I always wanted my bedroom to be on the second floor. But I've become used to the first floor. I would spend more time in our bedroom, but it's not cozy. At night, I might use it to get away from the TV in the other room. I sit on the bed with my reading material spread around me, and occasionally I talk on the phone. If I'm in there on a sunny afternoon, I find myself on the floor, absorbing the warmth and reading or folding laundry. When I can hear the TV, I get angry. At night, I often read in bed after Phil falls asleep. It is uncomfortable if one of us reads in bed while the other is asleep. A king-size bed?

My favorite time of day is late afternoon (4 P.M. and on). This is the time I relax the most and seek time for myself in a separate room. I may be reading, writing, doing a house project, whatever. Now I only have the bedroom or office to retreat to. I can read in the living room, but I am only in there if the TV is not on. There is only one sofa in there and nowhere to put my stuff (drinking glasses, snacks, magazines, books, whatever) and let me curl up at the same time.

I tend to sit in a cross-legged position or with my feet up. I never sit with a straight back and feet on the floor—even at the kitchen table or in a restaurant. I feel cramped on the sofa, and it gets messy when Phil is also using it and his papers are spread around. Originally, he had a desk built and used it often, but lately he prefers to sit on the sofa. I like to gaze out the windows and to sit in the chair near the small window where the afternoon sun comes in. But the chair is not comfortable, nor is there a table for stuff.

I use the kitchen table to go through mail and hang out there, writing or chatting on the phone. I love looking at the deer every day as they come out of the woods and wander around. I also enjoy watching birds with binoculars.

I would like more space in the kitchen while I'm cooking. I'd love to have a small sitting area for hanging out in when I'm perusing recipes or waiting for the oven buzzer to go off. I love to entertain and have people gather in the kitchen.

(continued)

I'd love to have a fireplace. Fireplaces relax and soothe me. Going out on a cold day and gathering the wood, arranging the wood in the fireplace and setting it ablaze, tending it during the day, and having the luscious smell of burning wood in the house and outside thrills me to my toes. I like to sit close to the fire and feel its warmth on me.

I would like to have additional entertaining space added on to the living room area. I would enjoy more sitting zones, cozy areas for people to hang. I would like to be able to use the living room at the same time as Nate and Phil, yet be able to curl up in another part and do my own thing or play a game with Nate. I am a big game player and always wanted a Ping-Pong table.

I want an in-law suite. Both our families are aging, and I would like to know that I have a space for them to be in my home. This could also act as a library and guestroom, but we'd need to think of a bathroom to serve this possibility.

Wendy's Summary

Wendy reminds me of a cat. She loves to sit comfortably (preferably on the floor or the bed) and observe, contemplate, or just be cozy. She is a homebody, so it is more important for her to create lots of islands for herself instead of concentrating on the organization of spaces to get her in or out of the house. She mentions the desire for more entertaining, but her writing suggests that her main priority is her everyday way of being cozy in the house and in touch with nature and the family. Her dislike of the TV (even its noise) needs some special attention.

Nate's Day

Nate's day played out for me in Phil and Wendy's writing. Someday, it won't!

Wendy, Phil, and Nate: Making It Work

Phil's very structured time- and activity-wise. Wendy's a sensual cat who follows the sun and curls up wherever she is. They both are very sound sensitive, and they need to do more to protect that. Each might be noisier than the other appreciates. Her needs are much more unfulfilled than his. Consequently, I felt that the design of the new addition needed to create a room with a fireplace but no TV. I designed it to look into the woods so that Wendy's nature watching can happen easily.

Expanding the kitchen was difficult while staying within their budget, but I added a space for Wendy's computer in a corner. In another corner, I put a round table that was cozier than their formal table.

A big change was moving the bedroom upstairs. It is far away from the noise. I also suggested insulating inside walls to protect this auditory sensibility even more. Wendy's office went to the first floor (she needed the space, and the new office room had a door). She could be untidy or take projects out to other spaces to work, returning them to her office afterward and just closing the door on them so no one else would disturb them. Wendy needed comfortable chairs near the fireplace and a comfortable chair in the TV room, with a place to do a jigsaw puzzle.

Phil's office and workout area and Nate's playroom are side by side in the basement. The space is aesthetically dynamite, with art, a foyer that's gorgeous, and a very open look with angled walls. Everybody should be happy now! Oh, and that all-season porch Phil spoke of will probably go off the bedroom at some point. Then everybody's needs will finally be met. But this family's needs could be met *only* when they were thought out and put in a list. (You'll find that the same is true for your family and your needs.) Their new home is beautiful visually, artistically, and functionally, and it's now comfortable for all of them.

your ACTION PLAN

Moment to moment, you choose what, where, and how you're going to live your life. If you update your scheme of home spaces, activities, and systems so they are all on the same page as your feelings, you will improve your life. If you include in that scheme ways that you personally prefer moving and being, you will *enjoy* your life. If you manage to get your life in order, then romance, fun, and creativity can happen at any time. It takes planning and being aware—aware of who you are now and where and how you most want to be. It is profound.

3

CLEARING THE CLUTTER

11

CLUTTER *and* EMOTIONAL CHAOS

Well, you knew we had to get to some dirty work, didn't you?
Here it is. Take a *deep* breath! It's time to ask the big,
important question: Is your house a clean canvas?
What this question is really asking is whether your home
is ready to receive all the beauty and high function that
you've uncovered as you've discovered your home design
personality—free of chaos and clutter. Does it have good
working systems and lots of open closets, drawers, and shelves?
If it does, you're ready to begin creating. I hear some yeses,
and I hear some nos. And I definitely hear some sighs.

This is the muddy, murky chapter. We're looking at your stuff! Your clutter is made up of the old unused objects, unworn clothes, obsolete toys, dusty old books, and other pieces of life's leavings that have been sitting or hanging around for a long time. They need to go, and I promise it will feel good when they do. Here's why.

They've got you stuck. Have you ever thought of starting a new painting on an already painted canvas? Of course not. It's silly. But it's just as silly to begin designing a new space without cleaning up first. Going through your closets, your drawers, your shelves, your garage—everywhere—and getting rid of the stuff is hard to do, but it's so necessary!

All the work you've been doing has formed a very clear and powerful template of you. This template is your tool to help you make decisions with confidence. Clutter is the "stuff" that will block that action.

If your space is freed of the clutter of your past and is ready to receive the design changes that will bring you bliss, you can probably skip this chapter. (But then again, you might find some new ideas for clearing out that you can use the next time things start piling up.) That's because this chapter and its exercises are a pathway to finding your way out of the old and into a new way of being in the present moment. It's the first step to the clean canvas.

CLARIFYING CLUTTER

A friend of mine gave me a wonderful metaphor for decluttering. He said to imagine a tree that chooses not to drop its leaves in the fall and carries them through the winter. Then imagine that tree in the spring, when little green buds are trying to come out! It's a great way to see how important it is to let go of your stuff. How can new life bud and come forth if your space is clogged with the old life?

Life can get so stuck when you let it. Imagine this scenario: Tony wakes up late. In a rush, he falls over a pile of books that have accumulated by the side of the bed. He can't find his toothpaste, he finds that he has no clean shirts, and his favorite tie has a gravy spot from the last time he wore it. He can't locate the pen he keeps in his briefcase, he left the stereo on, and he can't run the dishwasher because he's out of detergent. The heaped-up trash smells foul. Not only that, but he's lost the phone number of the girl he was excited to call, and today is the day he'd arranged to do that. This is only his first hour up! It gets no better.

Tony's life could read differently if the chaos, clutter, and systems changed. Let's try it: He wakes up with his new Sting CD breaking the silence of the morning. The pleasures scheduled for his day flow through his mind as he pours his automatically brewed cup of coffee. Turning on the news, he grooms and dresses, finding everything quickly and easily, and ends up looking forward to the day ahead. He dials a special number he'd placed carefully by the bedside phone. This call, he knows, guarantees the quality of the events ahead. Toast and egg go together easily, and as he eats, he enjoys a note from a friend and the morning newspaper. All ready, he sets out for the day ahead. Nice start!

If you have clutter everywhere and a lack of systems, both the excess and the lack are in your way. Your disorganized spaces deny you effective activity, freedom, ease, and even romance! Failure to stop your life for a moment, redefine, initiate, and interact with what you want your new life to be piles one passage on top of another, and your life gets stuck. You get depressed. Or perhaps it all happens because you are depressed or ill or scared. It's a vicious cycle that spirals downward and makes matters worse. You feel awful. You now attract *awful*.

Some of us are living in houses that are too big for our present lives. Some of us are living in spaces that are much too small. A lot of us are living with our objects of the past, which are now "stuff," or we're living out of boxes. All of us who fit into any of these categories are not living the reality of who we are now. The trick is to know that this is what's happening and do something about it.

All of the work you've done to find your home design personality has been very important to this topic. You are not shifting gears in any way. Your personal journal and all the exercises have put before you your own powerful images of life at its personal best. If you did your work well, these images should pull you through the cleanup like a magnet, with the power of anticipation and possibility. If Tony had done this process, he'd be *way* in touch with himself and powerfully determined to get his life together.

How to Get Started

You need to face letting go. To do it, you will need help from friends, patience with yourself, time, and objectivity. You will also need incentive. That's why we've done most of the process in the first 10 chapters. It's given you powerful "carrots" to pull you forward. All those visions of beautiful rooms, new projects, and new relationship possibilities will keep reminding you that it's worth it to let go of all that stuff.

Decluttering is hard work because it's powerfully tied to the emotions. You can't

just say, "Oh, well, I guess I'll change." Your mind and my mind don't work that way, and you've worked hard at getting all this accumulation under one roof! So you need to help yourself see the dysfunction behind the attachment. You see, your ego is convincing you that you have to hold on. It's saying to hold onto everything you've ever owned so that it keeps you feeling safe and comfortable. It's all of who you were! The truth is it's dysfunctional, but the stuff is making you feel better for some reason, and it's assisting you in creating a stuck life. It's time to sort out all the stuff and get healthy so you can love your home and live in it serenely. It's time to make sense out of your nonsense.

I've often tried to separate this part of the process from the design personality work, but it's not that simple. Sitting in the seat of the lecturer, I see wet eyes and hear tight throats when I get to the part about moving on. I can see that many people have issues that are in the way. And everyone seems to pull me into speaking about clutter. I can see that everyone—or at least many of us—has lots of accumulated clutter that is no longer giving pleasure; it's creating misery.

I can truly say that there are many of you who are suffering from this chaotic state. Somehow, the answer isn't obvious either, and that quandary is truly causing pain. If you are facing a need to release and clean up in your space and can't seem to do it, please know that there are emotional reasons why you're stuck, and there are ways out. Determination is the key.

The trick is to find the root of your dilemma. Doing so will be both powerful and helpful. I will tell you some great stories to help you see more clearly. Just know that there is some reason you're choosing to hold on and that finding the reason will help you let go, give away, and move on.

Mountains of Everything

One woman, Amy, called me, distraught. She and her husband had begun to renovate. They'd renovated bathrooms halfway, set up sitting areas halfway, created a patio, yes, halfway—and, of course, they felt worn out and frustrated.

Amy had also taken to flea-market shopping. She kept seeing so many things that caught her fancy and then buying most of them. I guess the things began to feel like the solution. In the accumulation, she began to lose the focus of what she really liked, needed, and wanted. When she took all of her accumulation from flea markets, secondhand clothing stores, and garage sales and put it in the same house with what she already owned, Amy was in such chaos that she truly felt ill. She could not see her way out. Therapy and doctors' appointments had become necessary, and they were robbing her of available time to deal with the confusion of the home. The family was slowly falling apart.

Amy is an extreme, and that allows me to clarify the issue for you. She and her husband, Phil, had started a lot of projects, but nothing seemed to reach completion. They had lost the focus of where they were going or what they had meant to create. They were not living; they were only *surviving*, and barely.

When something like this happens, know that something emotional is going on with you. Your problems are stopping

When your home is overstuffed, it's often a sign that your emotional life is in chaos, too. Fixing one is often the beginning of fixing the other.

the project; they're blocking your creativity and sapping your energy. Your behavior is numbing something deep inside. Sorting out and/or doing some therapy makes sense. I've seen it enough to know that it's a positive step. In Amy's case, her mother had died about a year before our work together. Amy had most of her mom's possessions filling an entire room,

floor to ceiling. Sorting through them was a huge and painful project, so she kept putting it off. In her heart, she hadn't even begun to deal with her mom's passing.

No Place to Hide

Add to this story the tale of Howard and Gloria, who literally had stuff crammed behind the long stereo cabinet in their living room. Each vacated bedroom was now crammed with suitcases and racks of unused clothing. The home office could not be entered. Gloria had 100 lipsticks in her master bathroom drawer, and she had enough sheets to outfit all the beds in the neighborhood. Howard called me, desperate. He felt he and Gloria had a great relationship, but he was in a huge muddle with this state of being.

Our job now was to set up a dialogue to process what could bring their lives back to a pleasurable, realistic level. In other words, we needed to figure out the cause. Then we could resolve and change the environment to support their new choices. It was a process they could have done 25 years ago, but they just hadn't.

I loved these people. They were intelligent, fun loving, and happy. But their house wasn't working, and Howard was very frustrated. I don't mean to say he didn't have anything to do with the problem, because he did, but he was the one who was bothered by the gargantuan amount of stuff. He couldn't figure out what to do, and he couldn't do it alone.

We began our work with long conversations. Like Amy and Phil, they needed to find out what was going on within them and between them that contributed to creating all this chaos. It didn't just suddenly happen. It was created out of some particular behavior. All of it for all of us is just a mirror of what's going on inside.

The home Howard and Gloria were living in was not one that they had chosen together as a couple. It was Gloria's parents' home. They had moved in when her parents got sick and needed caretaking. After long illnesses, both parents passed away, and Howard and Gloria decided to stay.

The house was very beautiful. It didn't need a lot of structural repair at the time, either. So Howard and Gloria didn't sit down and address whether to remain there and make it home; they just stayed. Their lives were busy and money was scarce, so they were grateful that the house was sound and didn't need work. Raising a family was their biggest priority.

In that process or lack of it, they had never had the conversation about "Should we stay, or should we sell?"

They didn't move through any kind of decision making to decide that this space really answered their needs. Maybe each was afraid of what the other would decide, so they just continued. Certainly, because of their lack of communication, they had never broached other questions like, "What shall we do with the space now that it's ours?" or, "How do we want our home to be?" This was a huge disservice they did to themselves, and it set up a pattern of living without much thought to the wheres and hows.

Patterns like this are easy to fall into. We all do it from time to time. Gloria and Howard missed their chance to decide what they wanted to keep and what they wanted to let go. They never put in place an image of what they wanted their home to be. They moved into someone else's image of home and lived in that image for years and years, accumulating but not throwing away, storing everywhere there was open space. The house supported this living well enough, and their life outside was full of travel and tennis and basketball. But then, one morning in a series

of many mornings, Howard got up and made the bed in order to pull out his desk blotter, calendar, and pens. He placed them on the bed again to start his business day. His home office no longer had a passage into it, and he'd moved his work area to the bed.

In our discussions, we addressed their omission years ago of not making plans or decisions. This was very beneficial. It helped them see their past pattern of poor processing and no dialogue about how to move ahead in their lives. They could see how they never decided what to let go of and what to keep. Space was never dealt with according to how to use it. It was just filled up, and then they'd move on to the next space and fill it up.

Since the house was large, it took a long time for this problem to confront them. But once all of the space was finally filled, it became necessary and very difficult to face. They could see their priorities or lack of them. There had clearly been a great addiction to immediate gratification. They just kept putting great moments on their calendar and allowing themselves to be blind to what was happening in their home. The immediate gratification addiction helped keep them unaware. Everything seemed really great. They were happy and having fun!

Sometimes owning the responsibility is half the battle, and sometimes getting both people on the same page and in agreement is what has to happen. In this case, it seemed that choosing a project for the house that both of them would be excited about was the best solution. The kitchen was in need of remodeling, so that was where we began. Getting that part of the house in order brought up their enthusiasm about addressing the rest of the house.

I worked with Howard and Gloria for a long time. We organized the "keepables" and set up a platform in the garage as a launching pad. We canceled magazine subscriptions and newspaper subscriptions and figured how to organize the ones they still wanted to receive. We set up designated spaces for audiotapes, videotapes, and workshop notebooks. It was very meaningful work.

Other People's Stuff

Another favorite of mine is the story of Rita, who was in a "Design Away Chaos" class that I was teaching. We would go to the home of each person in the class and address their chaos problem. It was a wonderful group, and I always felt that everyone was very brave to open up their problems to each other. But the beauty of the class was that it brought resolution. Participants got input on why they were living the way they were and stressing themselves, and they got answers to help them crawl out of the abyss.

Rita's session was fascinating. She took us into her basement and pointed out her washer and dryer stuck way back in a corner. In front of these appliances was a sea of black plastic trash bags. "This," Rita said, "is completely impossible and making the laundry task unreachable and insurmountable. Consequently, my life is a mess. I am really stuck."

The class was in awe of this mass of plastic. We asked her what was in all those bags. She shared that they were filled with all the things her father had decided to get rid of. She'd put them in the basement because he had passed them on to her to go through. She was to remove anything she wanted before they were tossed.

None of these bags had been opened. I asked Rita if she intended opening any of them. She shook her head no. "It's all junk," she said. "Nothing I want!"

The big question then was, Why were they sitting in Rita's basement? Well, it turned out that she didn't want to hurt Dad's feelings by throwing every last bit of it away.

It's interesting how many of us betray ourselves for someone else's feelings. We're willing to take their stuff, inherit their furniture, and store their old china because they're giving it to us! They *want* to give it to us. This pulls on our heartstrings. We become the caretakers of someone else's stuff— even when we don't like the stuff or want the stuff—just because they asked. We really think it shows them that we love them. And we thank them!

The sad thing is that if we would stay in our integrity and admit what we want and what we don't want, our relationships would be so much more honest and intimate. But we don't want to hurt feelings. We choose to protect the other person, so we stuff our houses and our feelings, and we end up with resentments that get heavier with each new bag. We don't do this just with fathers or other relatives but also with friends, children, and business associates.

When we talked about all of this, Rita got it. She realized that there were far better ways to tell her father that she loved him than storing his trash. In fact, she shared that with him using those very words. He agreed that it was a ridiculous way to show love and said, "Get rid of that stuff pronto, Honey." I think it took a truck to get it all out, but the end result was that Rita went off to art school and became a very successful artist with a whole new life, new friends, her own studio, and wonderful self-respect.

ENDING the CHAOS

If you can see the way you need to think your problem through, you can find ways to explore your own issues. You need to ask yourself questions like:

- What would I rather be doing?
- What feelings am I giving in to?
- Do I like my life just as it is?
- What really pushes my buttons?

Honest answers will not only help you know yourself, they'll help you pinpoint the problem. And once you've done that, you can move toward a solution.

Some Root Causes of Chaos

By now, you can see that there really *is* an emotional connection to your stuff. There are hidden reasons you're holding on and not getting what you want in life. I know it's agonizing, and you aren't resolving the issue because it's all connected to deep feelings. I'm going to give you a list of possible causes. This list comes from years of discussing students' lives in my seminars. In presenting it to you, I am not attempting to be a psychologist. I'm only sharing some of the discoveries my students made when they were willing to be vulnerable. I hope they'll be as helpful to you as they've been to my students and me.

Issues of codependency. There is a caretaker alive and well in most of us! It dictates to us the importance of our service to others. It says it's the way we keep someone's love, say thank you, get approval, and stay in everyone's good graces. It means we hold onto all gifts, mementos, and objects that were given to us by someone else, so we don't hurt any feelings. It is okay if you love the things and want them around you. But if you're holding onto something to show affection or out of obligation, you are codependent, and your affections are misplaced. Melody Beattie has written some great books on codependency, which you can find at bookstores and libraries.

Fear or insecurity about yourself and your life. Yes, it could also be a fear of death. Here, you're holding onto everything because it may be needed in the future. This is because you're afraid that you don't have all you need within you already. You keep old high school notebooks, scrapbooks, and so on to create a false sense of safety and identity. Accepting yourself where you are right now and knowing that all you've learned and all your memories are vivid within will help you move on. It takes so much energy to take care of and store all this stuff. I think it finally causes a loss of identity through its demeaning nature.

my OWN CHAOS STORY

*M*Y STORY isn't about clutter, but the way I dealt with my dilemma is the same way many people deal with clutter. I'm actually pretty good at throwing things away, but writing presented me with my chaos issue. I really wanted to put all my design discoveries into a book—this book. It was a dream. But I had an emotional issue that kept me floundering.

I don't find it easy to write, and I tend, therefore, to put it off. The way I do that is to find many unrelated activities that I "need to do." (Is this starting to sound familiar?) This is called procrastination. I was ignoring my problem by seeking immediate gratification, just like Howard and Gloria. It was its own form of chaos because all the tasks I came up with succeeded in taking me away from my writing. I'd suddenly realize that I hadn't seen the eye doctor in a while, I was missing all the good movies, there were six friends I'd fallen out of touch with, and the mattresses needed turning. It began to seem very important that I tend to this list, and it freed me from having to write. I was *very* serious with my procrastination!

Immediate gratification for me is also filling up life with lots of good feelings in the moment. It's been my lifetime pattern. It was audacious for me to even take on this task of writing a book. Anyone who begins such a task knows you've moved gratification far into the future. Putting off a paragraph, let alone a chapter, would put me that much farther from the goal and make me crazy.

At the same time, I knew how much the writing of this book meant to me. When I stopped to think of the satisfaction I would get from having gone deeper into myself to

A strong attachment to the past. If you're a parent, the kids' things might remind you of good times gone by when the children were younger and not so close to leaving. Holding onto them might be creating a kind of denial that life is changing or make you feel like it hasn't changed. Perhaps instead it's a past relationship or job. Part of the solution is just seeing what it is and identifying whether

complete this manuscript, I kept on working. But I also kept working with the real issue—why I was so easily distracted by immediate gratification.

When I looked carefully at my behavior patterns, I could see myself as a child with a dysfunctional family. As that child, I had to find ways to make myself feel okay and make life feel good, safe, and happy. That wasn't true now, and I wanted life to get bigger and deeper. I needed to stop choosing only what would satisfy me immediately. I needed to start focusing and give up my impatience. I was an adult putting a very important priority (my book) on a back burner.

The only way to get past this was to go through it. I didn't need to feel constantly gratified anymore, but I had to discipline myself out of it. It was so familiar. I knew my energy was highest in the morning, so that might be the place to start. I'd devote my first hours of the day to my most important task.

I began. The morning ended up being a perfect choice. It was when new thoughts were coming in, and I had high energy to move ahead easily. The rest of the day, I felt I'd accomplished something wonderful. Thus, I had chosen a schedule that suited my style of being (you need to do this, too) and healed a longstanding issue with immediate gratification. Oh, believe me, I still sit at my computer writing, and hundreds of things go through my mind that I'd like to be doing. I just smile and let them pass through. The one thing all those thoughts do for me is to show me how much abundance there is around me and how good life is. I know I can always get to them after I write.

it is a fear of or resistance to the future. Talking to someone, feeling the grief of loss, and journaling your feelings about it are all positive ways to deal with this hard issue. Also, just *seeing* your tenacious hold on the past can help you loosen your grip and make up your mind to let go of everything. Trust the future, make plans, and move forward in whatever way or ways give you the most enthusiasm and anticipation. *Necessary Losses* by Judith Viorst is a great resource for this issue.

A feeling of obligation or guilt. The belief that you should "save things for when the kids are on their own" or "never throw anything away" is really an obstacle. In seminars, we've explored this completely. The truth is that kids don't want your old stuff—believe me. When you reach this realization, the letting go can really make you laugh. Holding onto gifts that no longer appeal to you is exhausting. It says that you don't trust the relationship, and you'll do anything to protect it.

The old self-esteem bugaboo. This is a lack of self-worth. It keeps you convinced that you don't "deserve" current clothes or new gadgets, so you hold onto everything in case you can wear or use it again. This can overlap with the preceding cause. In fact, there is an interrelationship between all the items in this list.

The issue of feeling deprived. Having a lot of things (the clutter) can give you temporary feelings of abundance—of not being deprived. Unfortunately, this feeling leaves as the accumulation grows and chaos moves in. Finally, there are no feelings of well-being left. Recognizing this source of fear and releasing it can give you incredible freedom.

An inability to see what you want or where you're going. Indecisiveness keeps you from moving ahead. You think about it, and you think about it, and then you think about it some more. You're not sure where you're going. Things begin to pile up around you because you're not sure what you'll need or won't need once you decide. This is often a fear of change or a lack of trust that you'll decide correctly. It really saps your energy.

Perpetuating the "Starving People in India" syndrome. This actually is often a leftover from the Great Depression. Coming from a place of "waste not, want not," it can be traced to fear, lack of self-worth, obligation and guilt, or all of the above. Certainly, we are a wasteful society, but I don't believe the solution to that is hanging onto everything. Suddenly there is no joy. There's got to be a balance somewhere.

A life that is just too full. This happens to those of you who cannot say no. You can't say no to requests, gifts, or affection. This is another codependency and boundary issue. Your belief is usually that if you say no, someone won't like you, or worse, they won't love you. "If I say no, you'll think I'm an awful person." Out of this belief, you jam your schedules and your houses.

Needing to prove yourself. This is usually the case when your house is too large, your job is too complicated, and/or you have too many relationships because you need things to show how important you are. You decorate in trends; create showy, dramatic looks (even if they don't suit you); and buy very expensive items because of the showy price tags, not the showy objects. This can be based on lack of self-esteem, overachievement issues, or fear, and it's overwhelming.

Lack of planning. I think this probably relates back to self-worth. You just don't take the time to think through how you want to live, which is a process of how you honor yourself. This is a great way to sabotage yourself. Planning may be learned, and it's never too late—but it takes time and peaceful consideration.

Addiction to immediate gratification and/or collecting. Shopping to feel good can be so addictive. It's filling a hole somewhere inside of you. Another way this comes up is not dealing with life's issues because someone just asked you to lunch or another activity. These are actions that make you feel good in the moment but keep you from what really matters. This one takes real awareness and persistence to get past.

Fear of death, loss, or illness. This reason is like most of the others, and it's a biggie. If you haven't dealt with these issues and are in denial, you're stuffing yourself in some way so that everything feels okay.

This is a long list, and it's many ways of saying a lot of the same thing. But we're all different, and perhaps hearing it in a way that resonates in you will help you know what you need to face and change in yourself. I hope it stimulates some thoughts or discoveries for you. It will be very helpful if you can identify anything on this list as an issue for you.

IS it HIM or HER or THEM?

In all of this discussion, we've talked as if the problem is with you. It is possible that the problem lives outside of you, in your partner. In the case of Howard and Gloria on page 184, Howard wasn't sure where the problem lived, but he was willing to explore all possibilities. It turned out to be them, both of them. With Amy and Phil (page 183), there may have been many things going on, but Amy knew a lot of the responsibility rested with her, and that's how she chose to approach it. And Rita, whose story is on page 187, knew the problem was with her.

I have talked to many clients and students who are living with someone who is a "packrat," and they haven't been able to supply the right cheese to solve the problem. I encourage you to push the issue! It is wrong for anyone's issues to destroy the freedom and serenity of the home.

Keep talking—and talking. Present your case, ask questions, examine all feelings. Discuss causes. Insist that this is important work and that no one has the right to turn their back on a life companion's pain. There may be compromises that have to be made. I've seen the opposite extreme, and I call it being anal or just being too neat and tidy—to the detriment of living! If you're living under one roof with someone else, it is powerfully sacred work to find out the page you both can live on happily. Bless you on this journey.

Okay. Take another deep breath, because it's time—whether you're living alone or living with others—for you to plunge into the source of your chaos— and your clutter. Exercise 15 awaits!

exercise 15
Uncover Your Reasons for Chaos

What you'll need: your pen or pencil and your small spiral notebook.

It's time to process your feelings and come up with your answers. I suggest the following steps to help you. If you have a mate who is contributing to the chaos, try to involve him or her in some way. Perhaps this sequence will help.

What to Do

1. Go somewhere comfortable and quiet. Take a box of tissues if you need it.

2. Put on some music that pulls on your heart. It will help you get to the truth.

3. Identify your chaos. Write it out very clearly for yourself.

4. Identify your goals. Where do you want this all to lead? Journal carefully.

5. Reread "Some Root Causes of Chaos" starting on page 189. Stop at each cause and consider its place in your life. Are you a good time planner? Are you afraid of the future? Can you say no? Do you practice misplaced affection by keeping things you don't want?

6. Choose which root cause is yours. If it isn't on the list, decide what your issue could be.

7. Try to remember many ways that you've played this out. Ask yourself all the questions about why you're stuck in this situation, and answer them as honestly as you can. Try to zero in deeply on your issue.

8. Try to remember where the issue came from.

9. Journal all about how this behavior makes you feel good and then leads to your present status of *not* feeling good. Journal why you want this chaos to end. Make promises to yourself.

10. Contemplate what it would take to change your behavior.

11. If appropriate, think of ways to connect with those who need to hear your thoughts or your new choices.

Results

If you explore these questions carefully, you may see more than one root cause, you may identify events or situations, and you may realize that therapy would be helpful. I urge you to keep journaling past these questions. Journal until you're clear. Journal even past clarity to ways you would prefer to behave in your life. Journal what it might feel like living in a chaos-free environment. Be poetic when you write, or be any way that you need to be so that you can go back and reread for clarity, coaching and sustaining yourself as you clean up.

I don't think there is anyone who doesn't have some issue of chaos. Sometimes you clean up one part of your life, only to notice (oops!) that there's something else. I love the statement that says, "Life is not a problem to be solved, but a mystery to be unfolded." Delight as much as you are able in these revelations. I've heard it called peeling the layers of the onion. So there's another layer. But remember that one layer is gone.

If You're Working in a Group

This issue is powerful to address in the group, but you know, becoming intimate with each other is part of the new paradigm. It's great for creating feelings of not being so separate.

You can do this chapter the same way my chaos class worked. If you're courageous enough to let everyone stand in front of your clutter and chaos issues, you will get support, I promise. But the feeling of support comes only after you drop your embarrassment over showing your imperfections. Each person will share their issues and their discoveries and then get input from the group. Trust the intimacy that has been developing in your group up to this point.

I would suggest that you do the exercise alone, then come together to share what you discovered. Allow input from everybody on the emotional stuff, as well as practical advice on how to let go. It would be wonderful if everybody helped each other do some of the actual shoveling away.

your ACTION PLAN

If other steps in this process haven't wrung you out, this may be the clincher. There is probably no sadder state in your home than when it is stuffed to the brim with old, "dead" objects that no longer serve your or your family's life. Or when you can't make decisions that move you along in your life. Maybe it's a life partner who is contributing to the chaos. Figuring out who and why, coming to grips with it all, journaling, talking, and then sweeping the canvas clean is work that must be done to be free. But first you must connect with your emotions, or stuff will just pile up again.

Now that you've done the hardest part—thinking through your reasons for having all that clutter—let's buckle down and get rid of it. I'll tell you how in chapter 12.

12

LETTING GO
of the CLUTTER

I knew you could do it! You've slain your dragons. Let's back up the trucks, get out the shovels, and make more lists. You're ready to act. Believe me, even your decision to move ahead is going to feel *so* good. You'll be taking excellent care of yourself, throwing away the old, figuring out how to deal with the junk, and setting up spaces that fill your needs. You are on your way to feeling safe, in control, nourished, and happy.

You know that most of our chaotic circumstances come out of our lives changing as well as *us* changing. Change happens so fast that sometimes we don't recognize it or take the time and the steps to alter our patterns, our environment, or our relationships. Our homes will accommodate change only if we address what has happened and where we're going now. I know single female executives who are working fabulous top-tier jobs, earning buckets of money, and living out of boxes. They don't take the time to hire an organizer or ask for a buddy's help. Consequently, they are so out of balance. I've heard them talk about it. They laugh about their situations and work on. This is very dangerous territory.

By this point in the book, I hope I've convinced you that you especially need your home for your days that aren't so good. At those times, you need it to ground and comfort you. The restaurant takeout menu and the boxes can't do it, especially on an ongoing basis.

But it's hard to face the necessary throwaway and reorganization because you see value in front of you: books you've loved, objects that were beloved gifts, toys that were cherished, clothes that you still love but that don't fit anymore or are out of style. It's truly a difficult task, and an important one. Getting our houses out of chaos or moving out of the spaces that are creating the chaos is timely and important work.

When it comes to decluttering, however, the job can seem insurmountable. A large part of the problem can be caused by the inaccessibility of places to take all the stuff. Where can it all go when you get rid of it? A person looks at the task and can't see the steps. Junk shops are overloaded, garage sales are hard to organize, trash haulers won't take it, and the Salvation Army's "base" is almost impossible to drive into because so many other people have been there before you and dumped their discards—or it's at the ends of the Earth. (I know, I've been there.)

WHERE *to* START?

Remember Amy and Phil from chapter 11? Let's follow along and see how their

KEEP *your* ENERGY UP *while* CUTTING CHAOS

*a*S YOU PROBABLY KNOW, it's easy to get overwhelmed when you're confronted by seemingly insurmountable chaos. Then the old excuses start pouring out: "I don't have time for this!" "I've got other things to do." "I'm tired." "*You* do it." The result is paralysis—and unhappiness. To keep out of this trap, you need to keep up your energy. Here are 16 ways to stay energized for the work at hand.

1. Use a priority list constantly.

2. Redo your priority list.

3. Do one job at a time.

4. Get a buddy to help.

5. Get the family involved.

6. Share the project you're working on.

7. Ask for help.

8. Delegate.

9. Reward yourself.

10. Break a job into parts and schedule them (with time limits and deadlines).

11. Be realistic.

12. If in doubt, throw it out.

13. Take a day off.

14. Schedule regular maintenance.

15. Be flexible—if your energy level is low, give yourself a day off.

16. Set up good systems and remember that they need to be maintained.

Add more ways as you think of them!

story ends (at least as far as we're concerned). Amy's process was to first discover her home design personality by building her picture journal, happiness list, and so on, just as you have. That helped her pull up good feelings, dreams, and memories. The exercises helped her sort, sort, sort, and she began to feel more self-esteem. Ideas of what she wanted began to crystallize, and she began to believe that she deserved all she was thinking of. She dealt with her mother's death and dialogued with her family to build a new dream, and this began to bring her the energy for the huge task ahead.

Choosing and eliminating possessions as Amy did begins to help you reach a higher level of energy and personal awareness. You've done the inner work of finding the wonderful photos of beauty and new possibilities that show you how you want to live. Now you're going to make lists upon lists of what you need to do, chunking it down into small increments so you can breathe in the process and not lose your ambition.

The Process of Making Lists

Amy and I literally journeyed through her home with a clipboard. We went to every area of the house. The lists we made represented what needed to be done in each section. They gave us an overview of what was going to pull Amy and Phil's home together. As we walked through the house space by space, we listed what had to change and what the family needed. We made no decisions about filling those needs during this tour. We resolved nothing. It would have been too frustrating. We just looked at all that was there and got tough about what needed to change.

When I saw how much there was to do, I suggested that Amy create a notebook with index tabs, where each section of the home could be addressed separately. With neat sections for rooms, specific areas, needs, and empty space available, I felt she could come back at any time and fill in the blanks with ideas and ways to do it better. She could develop notes about where she wanted to build shelves, what closets she wanted to sort through, and what areas she wanted to change in regard to how they're used. It became a work in progress that got recorded and allowed her creativity to manifest itself.

I confess that we stumbled a few times figuring out what this notebook would look like. First, it needed to be very clear and practical to use. Second, it needed to represent the entire house. Third, it needed to change with Amy's progress, so she could feel her accomplishment.

After a bit of trial and error, we designed each page with columns that had specific headings. You don't want a complex notebook to add to the complexity of the job! Our columns were

Room, Specific Area or System, Needs, and Ideas, as shown below.

We used index tabs to divide the sections of the notebook according to the person in charge. You'll be making your own notebook in Exercise 18 (page 217), and when you do, you can decide how to use your index tabs. They can divide the floors, the types of jobs, the systems, and so on.

To show you how this process works, let's use the laundry room as an example. The laundry area is well placed on the second floor, but when we got there, I saw that Amy had a mountain of clean but unironed clothes sitting in the middle of the half-renovated laundry room. Going through the pile and making choices was going to be a long day's work—if

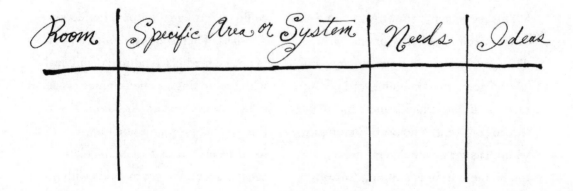

Room	Specific Area or System	Needs	Ideas

Room	Specific Area or System	Needs	Ideas
Laundry	Second Floor	Sort the pile	Figure out a new system

not more. So she filled in the columns as shown above.

Now, when Amy goes to her notebook, if she has the right amount of time or energy, she can eyeball this job fast and decide what to accomplish and when. Her fourth column of "figuring out a new system" might be addressed separately beforehand, so that she knows where all those clothes are going to go.

This particular chaos of Amy's indicates a need for a behavior change. There are lots of resolutions to any situation. Seeing this problem, sorting through different ideas, and adopting a way to resolve it is helpful. Coming up with ideas for new behavior prevents the problem from continuing. In Amy's

case, if she doesn't think of a new way, she'll get the clothes pile down—and it will come right back.

So, what *is* the problem? I would say that Amy clearly doesn't like to iron, so she puts it off. Her solution could be to buy nothing that needs ironing. This would eliminate a step in the laundry process, and things could go straight from the dryer to the closet. Another solution could be letting go of some perfection standard. Then she could put things away in an assigned place unironed and deal with the ironing when each piece is going to be worn. There are lots of pitfalls to this system, for something may never be worn again. But that's actually okay, because it's a way to get in touch with how important that item is or how the system is working into the lifestyle you want. It shows that the item or the system needs to be checked out and maybe chucked.

Using the Organizing Notebook

By recording "jobs to do" in an organized way, Amy set up a system so that when any member of the family had a little time, they could page through the notebook and find a small job to accomplish. They could also see their progress. Amy color-coded her book, making red items priorities, orange items the next most urgent, yellow the next, and so on down the list.

The notebook took time to set up, but I understand it has remained a workable system for the family to record jobs that need to be done. Phil found it a great way to keep himself organized.

How It Worked

Let's look at what happened for Amy and Phil, so you can see how this technique might work in your own case. Amy is the one who called me. She had a severe problem with holding on to possessions. Here is the sequence that she used to heal.

1. She first did the process of exercises I present in this book to discover her family's home design personalities and reconnect with who they were, what they loved, and what they wanted in their lives.

2. Then, the family tried to sort out what this was about for them emotionally.

3. Next, Amy and I set up their notebook to efficiently record everything.

4. We did the "walk-through" of the house, spotting all the problems and making a list of jobs to address.

5. Then, they identified some intentions, such as:

- Keeping only what they needed. (Example: two salad bowls were kept and four were given away.)
- Working on one room at a time.
- Not moving ahead until each job was completed.
- Working at least 1 hour every day.

6. Finally, working with the notebook item by item, they did one job at a time until they were finished.

Something I noticed early on in our process was that Amy's daughter Marcia was picking up the same trait of accumulating much too much stuff. Do you have children who are showing these symptoms? Watching her mother deal openly with this issue provided a powerful model for Marcia. I saw a lot of healing happening on many levels through our work together.

In fact, all of their relationships were healing. Life was moving out of a helpless place and into a hopeful state. Also, the home was beginning to breathe—and so was Amy.

TALKIN' to the CLUTTER

Clutter is a sign of being stuck on all levels. If we can see it, it's a great moti-

THE 6 RULES *of* HAPPINESS

i CALL THESE the 6 Rules of Happiness because when you follow them, happiness follows. And, best of all, you'll have found all the answers just by going through the exercises and self-discovery process in this book! Reflect on them often and make sure you still know the answers. Don't be afraid to change your answers as you change!

1. Know who you are and what's changed.

2. Know where you're going.

3. Know what you need.

4. Know what you want.

5. Know what and who is going with you.

6. Know what makes you happy.

vator to push us forward into a better perspective and a better space. Sometimes, the stuff we ought to get rid of is stuff we've loved but no longer use or wear.

My daughter, Robin, called me one Saturday faced with a chore she'd assigned herself: throwing away at least half of her T-shirts. She wasn't looking forward to it. She said she loved all of them. I gave her a formula that I'll give to you now. It really works! I told her to hold each T-shirt in front of her and ask two things:

1. Where am I going?

2. Are you going with me?

Robin called me back when she'd finished. She sounded so free. "It worked!" she said. "I had no struggle at all. I gave the recipe to all the girls in the office. It's wonderful."

It really is. Of course, you have to sit down for a few minutes and get the vision in your head of who you are now, what your life looks like, and how you want to look. In other words, of where you're going. As soon as you do that, the job is a snap.

If you're doing a throw-away job on objects, it's the same two questions, with a third added if the item is staying.

1. Where am I going?

2. Are you going with me?

3. Where is the best place for you to live?

Life is too precious for us to be taking care of other people's stuff or clutter of our own that no longer serves our lives. It crowds our consciousness to have too much stuff, and it crowds our time to take care of it. Our closets get overstuffed and inaccessible. Our drawers get impossible to open and close. We lose everything and can't find it when we need it. All systems break down. For our own sake, to become who we want to be and be free to do what we want to do, we have to de-clutter our lives.

Just Keep Digging!

In one of my lectures, a woman at the back of the room raised her hand near the end of an hour and expressed her annoyance that I hadn't spoken to her problem. I asked her what it was. She said that she was from a large family, and everybody willed their treasures to her when they died. She said it had become very difficult to move through her house. *All* the space was occupied. She was tearful, which I understood. She said the things were beautiful, but she didn't have any more space.

I listed the options I thought she had to heal her situation. First I suggested that she do a very careful study of what she wanted to keep and what she was willing to let go of, using the questions I just gave you. Then I asked if she could find a buddy to help search out sources that would take the furniture or help advertise that it was for sale. I suggested she also consider creating a garage sale with the help of this buddy. If those choices didn't work, I told her, "get yourself a shovel and go out in the backyard, dig a very big hole, and put it all in!"

Do you know what she said? "Thank you!"

She just needed permission. And that's something we all seem to need, permission to take back our space, to say that we're not willing to be the caretakers of stuff. It's hard to take this stand, but if you really value yourself, your time, and your space and understand their importance to you, then you will get very good at saying no when it's appropriate for you. It truly is a matter of you being in your own integrity. It's about not betraying yourself for someone else's feelings. And it's raising your own feelings!

Ready, Set, Go!

It's probably easier if you chunk down this job of sorting. You might try Amy's system, creating a list of tasks to do that's organized by urgency. You and your family can then refer to it whenever you have the energy. It's fun to cross off your accomplishments. Let your lists go closet by closet, room by room, system by system, or job by job.

As you accumulate items that you're going to give away or throw away, create a place where you can store them until it's a convenient time to deal with their disposal. I call my spot a launching pad. It's in the garage. It never gets too full because I've made a habit of taking things away periodically. And it does move everything out of the living area, so I can immediately see some results. Walking around the stuff "to go" is impossible and aggravating if it's piled right in the middle of your living space. You feel no accomplishment at all.

A Launched Item Needs a Destination

You'll need to create a list of places that will take your old treasures. Building a relationship with this source can keep this process ongoing. I did a garage sale myself, and for two months preceding it, I continually took anything that was to be sold to the garage. My daughter-in-law, Jackie, and son, David, became my partners in this project, and we took one night to ticket everything. The sale was very successful—and it amazed me what people bought. It is

for sure that one person's junk is another person's treasure!

In the Case of Clothes

I find that if my closets are too full of clothes, I don't dress easily or as attractively. It's because I can't see everything, so I end up wearing the same seven outfits over and over. Sometimes I'll discover something I forgot I had, and I'll wear it purely because I've kept it so long. With an overstuffed closet, when I'm trying to combine clothes to make an outfit, I find that my choices can't be as well thought out. At one point (before I decluttered), I found a gorgeous and expensive Eileen Fisher dress that I'd forgotten I had. It was smashed deep between old blouses. I was horrified and cleaned up my act fast.

When you pack for any kind of trip, you are quite efficient at taking just what you need, or close to it. Dressing is much simpler then, and you probably look better. Having less just seems to simplify and enhance the wardrobe. Now that I understand this, I pare way down.

*t*O ME, decluttering is very sacred work. (Here's one place where my minister's hat and my designer's hat are the same—or maybe I'm just wearing both at once!) There are no right or wrong answers. But there is a reality: that we all want freedom and ease. Another reality is that we ourselves are responsible for creating it. If you need more inspiration at this point, here's a meditation that might be helpful. You can read this meditation out loud like a story, read it silently to yourself to contemplate, or ask someone to read it to you. Some people have put this on the other side of their visualization tape (the tape you made and played for yourself in chapter 3) so they can replay it for inspiration.

Chaos Meditation

Winston Churchill said, "We build our buildings, and then they grow us."

If this is so, then our buildings need to be impeccable.

If this is so, then we need spires, carved arches, grand tall walls, and domes.

We need leaded glass, crescent moons, tints of majesty, and miles of marble and mica,

So that the richness, the grandeur, the creativity and the nobility

Can become our own, and make us feel grand.

And if the architecture is magnificent and vast, creative and significant,

It will connect us with our magnificence, our vastness, our creativity and significance.

So too our private spaces,

Our own nooks and crannies:

They too must be impeccable, for they cradle and nurture, and shelter and support us.

They too must be held sacred, beautiful and filled with color and light

So they connect us with our holiness, our sacredness, our beauty and color, and our light.

It is our responsibility, you know, our public buildings.

And it is our responsibility, our private nests.

Think of the perfection of the natural environment,

Think of the beauty of the pine and the maple,

The oak and the spruce,

Streams that bubble,

Skies that are blue,

Breezes so balmy.

Wander through the wonder feeling the sun,

Feeling the shade,

Seeing the flowers and ferns.

Sit down by the flowers in a garden,

Perhaps on a smooth stone,

And think about the perfection of nature:

How it sends its winds and rains to cleanse,

And its light to energize,

And its seasons to keep life in order.

It moves the nonessential out,

And keeps the wonder abundant.

Now I will tell you a story that may inspire.

My story is about a family, and

My story is about beauty and energy and
    feelings;

Energy moving and light pouring into this
    family's home.

But it wasn't always so for this family.

Well, it was in the beginning, but the days
    and the years of this family

Had brought them so much to remember,
    and they wanted to hold it all.

And they did!

The books they'd read, the albums of
    photographs,

The tapes of songs, the fashions of great
    design,

They loved them all!

And labeled them all, and piled them all,

So finally no one could see them.

And no one could use them.

Yes, finally they could not be shared.

Finally this family and their past were one.

Old concepts couldn't give way to new, and
    old discoveries were no longer stepping
    stones.

The books and boxes were standing where
    someone else needed to stand,

They were sitting where someone else
    needed to sit,

And they were lying where someone else
    wanted to make love.

They were littering where folks wanted
    to dine.

The now was gone, the tools of being alive.

The peaceful vessel was gone, and the
    darkness of holding blocked their lives.

The past blocked the sun, the breezes, all.

(continued)

They felt as if their cells were crowded with
lead.

They felt as if their shoulders were laden
with iron.

They couldn't dream, they couldn't cook
or sew.

They couldn't go out and fight for great
causes.

They sat with the ghosts of their long ago.

There was no space for new friendships
and new celebration.

Awareness of their darkened space finally
crept within them.

They saw that unlike a river, they could
not flow,

And unlike birds, they could not fly.

They looked around this place called home

And knew it needed grace.

It was time to turn the tide.

They carefully chose the objects most precious to them

And made sure these objects held their
loves the best.

Then sadly, but gladly, they moved all the
rest of it away.

They passed on the garments that they
wore no more.

They released the boxes of old scribed notes

And boxed the volumes of books they'd
read.

As they worked and worked and cleansed
their space,

They felt the universe turning.

Their limbs grew stronger, their minds
quicker.

Their veins felt gorged;

Their eyes began to see more clearly.

It was truly a metaphor, for they were
letting go of what they needed no
more,

And the light was filling all those dark
spaces.

Now their lives were filled with the present.

The past is long gone.

Feelings of peace and joy are good now.

Now light fills all the spaces,

And music plays its score,

Fresh flowers adorn sweet places,

And peace is evermore.

Strength and courage brought this.

Their mountain—it collapsed.

Their lives now have the spaces

For living unsurpassed.

exercise 16
From Chaos to Freedom: Focusing

What you'll need: your pen and your small spiral notebook.

Before starting out to tackle the chaos, since that can seem so overwhelming, I'd like you to take a minute to focus on what you're planning to do and why you're doing it. This exercise is fast, and it will gear you up to get all that *stuff* out of your hair—and your home.

What to Do
Note the categories below in your notebook, then jot down everything you can think of that applies to your situation under each heading. Ready? Go!

Why It Would Be Great to Eliminate Chaos
Here are just a few of the reasons that occur to me.

- To enrich your life
- To connect you to yourself and others
- To support your personal identity
- To inspire the feeling of motivation and possibility
- To give you clarity about your life
- To empower you

Now add yours.

Why We Want Simplicity and Order
Here's my list.

- More time
- Health
- Easier to get to work
- Joy
- More choices
- Serenity

- Spontaneity
- Romance
- Creativity
- More energy
- Ease
- Accessibility to everything
- Fun
- Convenience
- Freedom
- Ability to live on a higher level
- Beauty

Jot down all of mine that apply to you, then add yours.

Why We Have Clutter

Now, list all the things that tend to turn into clutter, seemingly when your back is turned. These are my top picks.

- Memorabilia
- Old letters
- Collections
- Gifts
- Recipes
- Notes from high school
- Notes from college
- Mail-order catalogs
- Something really unusual
- Old birthday cards
- Clothes you've outgrown

- Toys the kids no longer play with
- Too many clothes
- Too much of anything
- Furniture, linens, and other items you're saving for the kids' marriages
- Stuff that's still in good shape!

Now add your list.

Where All the Clutter Can Go

Aha—hope at last!

- "Launching pad"
- Extra locker space
- Flea markets
- Garage sales
- Friends
- Homeless or other shelters
- Organizations that distribute used stuff
- Antique dealers
- Consignment shops
- School libraries
- Prisons
- Homes for the elderly
- Recycling (check the Yellow Pages)
- Nonprofit organizations
- Auction houses

Add more. You can do it!

exercise 17
Create Your Clutter-Clearing Checklist

What you'll need: Yep, your pen and small spiral notebook are what you need. Have your new organizing notebook nearby.

This is a short exercise, but I think you'll find it helpful. I've given you a list of questions to summarize what brought you to this point and how you're going to approach clearing out your clutter. The questions go from abstract ideas to very concrete action items. When you've finished all 10, you'll be ready to go!

What to Do

Write each question and your answers in your notebook.

1. What is the major chaos in your home or your life? Identify it carefully. You can have more than one!

2. What is the weakness in you that causes this chaos? Cut to the quick here.

3. Make a list of possible solutions, such as: throw away, build a closet, and so on. (Refer back to Amy's list on page 204 if you need help here.)

4. Do you need a buddy to help you do this work?

5. What tools do you need? List them.

6. Do you want to set up a launching pad in your garage?

7. What discipline are you going to use? (Examples: I'm going to devote 1 hour every day, or I'm going to schedule one day a week, etc.)

8. What are your priorities?

9. When are you going to begin?

10. What's the first thing you're going to declutter?

If You're Working in a Group

I'm not going to say that this is the place where the group works best, because there are so many places. But I do know that emotional support from the group as you see your reality, and the physical support of the group when you're doing the mundane, are amazing. Yes, why not help each other shovel out the stuff? Make your notebooks together.

One of the best things you can do for each other is combine your lists of resources, thoughts on organizing, and local assistance that others may not be aware of. Really use each other. Confess your failures. Ask for alternatives. Share the reward. Yeah! Why not all go out to dinner together once all of your chaos work is done? Maybe dinner isn't enough—perhaps a weekend away is better. Live this out together, the yuk and the yippee!

exercise 18
Create an Organizing Notebook

What you'll need: Now you need to have a three-ring notebook or binder with unlined paper and index tabs. (If finding unlined paper is a problem, go for the lined. I just like the freedom of a blank sheet to work on.) You'll also need your pen.

What to Do

Here's where we bring order out of chaos. You're going to chart your strategy and set your clutter-fighting course here. Start by setting up your pages. Remember how Amy set up hers? If not, reread that section (page 202), then refer to the illustration on page 218.

Once you've set up your notebook, decide on an appropriate sequence for walking through your house. This walk is to record all instances and areas of chaos and clutter you find, along with how you're going to address each of them. Allow a good amount of time. Take this walk and discuss your options with the other members of your family, if possible. Don't get too hung up on solutions unless everybody feels especially creative. Your main goal is to identify all areas that must be decluttered. Walk through your entire property: house, basement, garage, sheds, outbuildings, playhouses—everyplace.

Room	Specific Area or System	Needs	Ideas

If You're Working in a Group

I think doing your walk-through together as a group might be more thorough, although I'll leave that to you. My thought is that someone in the group may zero in on a detail that you miss or see a solution that's perfect!

your ACTION PLAN

This is the "hard work" chapter. It's where we really take responsibility. It's where we chop wood and haul water. It's not easy, but the other side is so incredible that it makes every step worth it. You're going to feel full, free, and alive. So, you just gotta take the journey. Get yourself ready to face the hauling, the tossing, the aching back. Move into your life: "magnificent," rid of the past, the stuff, the ugliness, armored now with strength, hope, and willingness. Life doesn't get better than this.

But it does get easier and a lot more fun, as you'll discover in the next chapter. There, with our space uncluttered at last, we turn to home design. Come on—your dream home awaits!

13

STORAGE SYSTEMS
That FIT *Your* LIFE *NOW*

By now, you've got a profound awareness of what you love
visually; a significant connection to your heart; and a real
awareness of what is missing from your life, your personal
happiness, and your style of moving and working.
I hope you've managed to cut through the clutter and now
have lots of opened-up space, cleared shelves, empty
hangers, and roomy closets. If you have, congratulations!
Let's fill up those spaces with useful and usable storage!

Before we start, I want you to be aware of this: Storage is *not* about the part of life that isn't happening. We're not trying to find places for stuff you're not using. It's about the part of life that *is* happening. It's about storing all the tools you need for your current life, your life that is happening now, and it's about storing them really close to the actual place where they will be used.

You see, storage, just like all the rest of design, is about you, your lifestyle, and the things you need to live it today. It's about your family, and your family's friends, and what you all do alone and together in work and in play. You want to place everything (the CDs, the games, the candles, the equipment for building a fire) nearby so it helps create paradise whenever you need it. You want to store what you're going to use to cook, to play, to dress, to entertain.

Your newly empty closets, drawers, and containers are ready and waiting. And when you make sure the storage and the activity are living close together, it will make every corner of your home vital.

Whether you're storing your current collection of clothes that work for your present weight and lifestyle, the bedding you use now (the current favorites), or the dishes you love, their efficient organization and storage will add to the quality of your life. I'm talking about the appliances that you use currently, the toys that the kids bring out every day—all the things that serve the life that's being lived in front of the closet doors.

The fun part of this is that it makes storage an art. I've already talked about designating spaces for favorite activities. You should designate your storage spaces the same way because, when you do, it contributes to the success of the activity and the design. It's why I love cocktail tables or end tables with drawers: If you forget the napkins when you're serving drinks, you can quickly recover without a trip back to the bar or the kitchen. To make sure your storage spaces are what and where they need to be, you need to visualize the different aspects of living that are going to happen on your sofa, at your desk, in your kitchen, or anywhere in your home, and the equipment you'll need to make them all happen.

DON'T STORE what you DON'T NEED

Whenever I stay over at a client's vacation home on the Atlantic shore, I observe her genius at organizing and storing. The beach bags are in an attractive box right near the door. The candles are in their own drawer with the matches and candlesticks. Each of her designated storage spaces is right at the spot where the stuff being stored will be used.

It makes me realize that vacation houses are great models for successful storage. Usually, people take only the things they really need for "in-the-moment living" to these vacation havens. The storage spaces in these homes are usually not overcrowded, so access is easy. They really embody the first important message of storage: Don't store what you don't need. (At least, not in the vital storage spaces!)

I go to so many homes where the clothes closets are bulging with apparel (old clothing *and* new clothing still sporting price tags). The kitchen cabinets are bursting with too many plastic containers and salad bowls, and linen closets are spilling over with too many sets of sheets and towels. The medicine cabinets are booby-trapped with old, outdated medicines, the kids' rooms are crammed with obsolete toys and puzzles never to be used again—and on and on.

When are we going to get it? We started in the 1970s, got more shopping addicted in the 1980s, and in the 1990s were faced with the wounds of both decades and the insecurity that makes us hold on to all of it. Simplicity, I say. Bring it on in the new millennium!

DEEP STORAGE STORIES

Let's look at storage in depth here. Over the years, clients have presented me with interesting problems: too little storage space, poorly thought-out systems, too much stuff, and on top of that, no furniture with drawers! Solving all of this brings great satisfaction.

Sometimes I'm presented with problems that are hard to fix. If a house is small already, creating storage space is next to impossible. But houses with plenty of storage space can be just as difficult if none of it has been organized well or the closets are large but have no inner structure. However, everything can be resolved with thought. When your storage situation is under control, it puts you on the way to ease, fun, spontaneity, and just about any other positive situation. Life isn't working when what needs to happen can't happen easily!

Reclaiming Rooms

For some years, I did a TV design segment for an early-morning Philadelphia talk show called *A.M. Philadelphia*. We addressed many different design issues to meet the needs of as many viewers as possible. The audience would write in telling me their problems, and I would decide whether their stories had the ingredients and information for a good show. I'd choose one that did to be aired as a makeover sometime within the next month. Our process was to go out to the home to tape the segment. We'd discuss the process on the air and introduce the clients. It was a very intimate look into homes and lives.

One couple, Ben and Judy, wrote in about their tiny house, which had no family room. Their three-year-old daughter, Isabelle, needed space to play, and they were stumped. They wanted everything: a lovely home, a social life, and a happy daughter. And why not?

We took the cameras out to their home. The dining room had become the playspace. It was filled with plastic toys and furry animals, with no place to store them. It was unsightly all of the time, and this aggravated Judy and Ben to no end. Pleasant meals with guests were out of the question. They didn't even enjoy candlelight dinners alone.

Moving all the toys to the living room was a possibility, but they saw the same problem happening. If the living room was also going to be the playroom, storage had to be the key. We had to find where the toys could go when the party wanted to happen—without an excavation. (Conversion, yes!)

I went shopping for furniture to hold toys. I didn't know what it might look like, but I just held the function as my goal. In an antique store, I found a wonderful old armoire with carved doors. The wood of the piece was somewhat dry, but lemon oil could fix that fast. It wasn't a fine piece of furniture, believe me, but it had a lot of style, and it had shelves! I saw its great potential for holding a lot of toys. Closed, it was attractive. Open, it was perfect for Isabelle's needs.

Well, it worked. But it wasn't enough storage, so I designed a large cube with doors on both sides to use as a coffee table. We covered it in an appropriate color of Formica. It literally was a big, empty box that could be stuffed, but no one knew that until you opened the doors.

Imagine the great visuals we showed on TV: The renovated room came first, with its tasteful but durable fabrics and its stunning armoire, low light, and great colors. In the next sequence, we showed cuddly bears, cars, and blocks spilling out into bright light—and Isabelle, happy as could be. Of course, we couldn't use silk fabrics and fine furniture to do the room, but with taste, three-way lightbulbs, some plants, and ingenious storage (if I must say so myself), we solved what was a real dilemma for a young couple. Fun, huh?

The House That Almost Became a Closet

A client, Suzanne, has a great example of a home I helped declutter. Suzanne called after attending my lecture on chaos. "I really need you," she said. "I need better storage."

At our first appointment, she pulled lots of pictures from magazines for her personal journal. Her choices were beautiful: soft cranberries, greens, a Victorian feeling, peaceful yet colorful. We followed with a trip through the house, finding places she thought needed storage.

Suzanne began very reasonably in the children's rooms, then we moved to the master bedroom, and finally to the kitchen and family room. There was so much to store, and I kept coming up with terrific plans for built-ins of every variety. Suddenly, awareness struck. I blurted out, "Suzanne! We've got to stop—we're making your house into a closet! All of that beauty we looked at in the beginning will have no place to happen."

Paring down was a must. Suzanne saw it, too. We could never create the amount of storage she needed inside, and emptying the garage would change the family's life—not to mention freeing up space for actual parking. She had work to do and felt the family would help.

Suzanne did pare down, and we met again to decide how a (suddenly) much more reasonable number of possessions could be stored. Remember, I want you to store only *vital* everyday things in the vital living areas and put the "storage perennials" (such as Christmas ornaments) in the attic, garage, or basement—the out-of-the-way spaces.

Suzanne had made this mistake in her kitchen. She had used a vital kitchen closet for future Halloween costumes and every other kind of costume. She not only had enough costumes for 20 children for 20-odd years, but she had used a space to store them that was needed for vital kitchen use. She desperately needed that space. So we stored the costumes in sealed (and labeled) plastic bins in her attic and returned the kitchen closet to immediate kitchen use.

SO, HOW do WE do IT?

Our kitchens need to be organized so that the bowls for salads are stored where the salads will be made, along with the cutting board and the knives. And that's a perfect model for storage throughout the house. If there isn't storage already available in a designated space, then furniture that *offers* storage needs to be found or created. I don't think you can ever have too many shelves, cabinets, and closets, but don't just keep creating built-ins everywhere and sacrificing the beauty of the home, as I was about to do to poor Suzanne.

I feel that the designation of storage is crucial. It means you assign a particular closet, cabinet, or drawer with the "job" of storing particular items, such as cleaning agents, appliance directions, vases, or gardening supplies. Don't mix in anything else unless there's lots of space for a second category of items.

I suggest that you also select furniture with drawers or doors so you can use it for storage. Designate each drawer and shelf within that single piece of furniture for specific items and categories: a drawer for snapshots and negatives, a drawer for tablecloths and napkins, and so on.

Having less to store, being creative with the storage space, and designating storage

If you designate storage for items near where
you'll use them, you really will use them!

close to where items will be used will move you forward. Don't mix up your designated areas or pile one type of storage on top of another. If you're prone to doing that, create more shelves and cubbyholes to separate your stuff. This will help your family follow the system, too.

A Closet Is a Big Hole!

A closet is only as efficient as the number of shelves, racks, and other structures inside it. It's like a pocketbook. If it's big but has no compartments, everything falls to the bottom, and you have to dig to find anything. I see the inner structure, the shelves, as a skeleton in the closet. (Excuse the pun!) You build the bones to hold what you need. Large spaces can then be worked down into multitudes of compartments, each designated. Shelves, cubbies, racks, hooks, you name it. They all have their place.

Deep closets deserve careful design. Either use them front to back, with current storage forward and "annuals" toward the back, or create them in the round with shelves and use floor space for a few standing objects. Whichever you choose, do it. Otherwise, you will have tons of empty space within the closet and

an ATTIC ROOM

*i*OAN AND BOB'S HOME had an unusual feature: a large storage room that looked like an attic but was on the second floor. It was wide open, with no partitions, so the room had become a catchall. Everyone just opened the door and put the stuff in. We decided to build shelves around the entire space and carefully plan what would be stored where. One wall of shelves was created for Christmas decorations, one wall for suitcases, one wall for winter clothes.

With our innovations, Joan and Bob could now open the door and consciously walk in to place an item in its designated area. And they could retrieve it as easily. This simple organization was a life changer. You could walk in the room and find what you wanted at a moment's notice. That's what it's about.

end up closet-poor. I bet you could consolidate three closets into one with the proper structure.

Lots of Holding Vessels

Container storage is brilliant for work areas and small spaces. You can have holders for everything from pencils to appliance instruction booklets to pennies, buttons, towels, and scissors, all contained separately and ready for use. If the containers are out in the room, they need to be attractive, and you may feel that the same is true even behind closed doors.

I have a basket for all my manicure paraphernalia. I can carry it anywhere in one hand, with a cup of tea in the other, and have a blissful manicure. I also use a silverware tray in a drawer for my cosmetics. It's a beautiful way to hold all the small parts of grooming and fixing.

That last trick I learned from Maria, who does telephone work part-time from her home. She has a blue plastic milk crate that holds all her phone numbers, papers, writing utensils, calendars, and so on. When she is ready to work, she can quickly grab them and take them to the phone.

I do have one caveat, though—a time when containers did *not* work. That was when a client used many empty envelope boxes for storage. She labeled them, but they all looked so similar that it was truly a nuisance. Sure, they stacked nicely, but accessibility (our important word) was a nightmare. If they had been housed in separate cubbies and had been well-labeled, they might have worked.

The Biggest Challenge

The hardest storage to design, I feel, is the storage of information: magazines, newspapers, CDs, videotapes and DVDs, computer disks. I beg clients to clip their pictures, recipes, and articles out of newspapers and magazines. Then do some careful filing so you can find them when you want them.

Audio- and videotapes (and CDs and DVDs) are a challenge, because they're hard to identify. If you store them by category, it assists you in identifying the individual tapes, and the category of "current favorites" can be stored in a more obvious place where you can grab them regularly. Me, I can't remember the particular category I choose for a tape or CD. That's how visual I am. So I store mine by the last name of the artist, which works best for me. This is what I mean by identifying your style of order or how you think. Who are you? How does your mind work?

Then There's Junk Mail

Where magazines, newspapers, newsletters, catalogs—all the stuff that makes up junk mail—are concerned, we're talking major chaos. Every day, the mail comes in: piles of it. It's like a dragon. It covers tabletops, clogs drawers, frustrates all systems, and makes us spit fire. Maybe we'll design a trashcan/mailbox combination. Some people do stop at the trashcan before they enter the house with the day's

the INFORMATION CLOSET

*M*Y FRIEND GEORGE has an addiction to information that is unmatched by anyone I've ever known. Helping him was difficult, but we used some of the ideas I've given you in these pages. My greatest triumph was with his home office. Our first visit to this disaster zone revealed audiotapes, videotapes, CDs, and DVDs all mixed together, never to be seen or listened to again. Something had to give!

I designated one closet the Information Closet. In it, I placed many small containers, each for a specific topic. We put all George's tapes, videotapes, CDs, and DVDs on finance in one container. I did the same for topics such as leadership, public speaking, and travel.

I organized shelves of labeled notebooks from workshops George had attended alphabetically by content. Thus, his cascades of data were organized, labeled, and stored according to subject, and all the information on each topic was in one place.

George felt he could work well with these categories, and he was beginning to smile. Hooray!

mail. Remember that you can call the post office and request that the junk mail *stop*!

Remedies for handling the mountain of mail seem to elude everyone. But I think you'll find the best solution is creating a place where the mail can be sorted immediately upon entering the house.

You know part of the problem is that mail is not just mail. It's bills, applications, licenses, magazines, advertisements, brochures, and personal letters (once in a while, we hope), all addressed individually. Each part of the mail goes someplace else unless you've been smart and have files set up where you sort it. Have a wastebasket close by to help lighten the load immediately—and use it! This is called creating a system and then using it daily. Do it in the same designated space all the time. Use containers for each family member's mail.

The catalogs that come in the mail can be filed alphabetically or in categories in a cardboard box or other type of container, but you need to be strict. When the new catalog comes in, the old one goes out!

Women who love "shelter magazines" (the industry phrase for magazines like *House Beautiful* and *Better Homes and Gardens*) and men who love *Consumer Reports* (am I being sexist?) may need to designate a closet or part of one for storage. But I think you should get brave and cut up those magazines, filing the articles away—possibly in the same closet! Then police yourself to throw out the deadwood every once in a while. But do get it all behind closed doors in the meantime, out of sight if not out of mind.

It's when we don't have the luxury of space or designated space that the problems pile up—literally—and become a burden. I say keep only six months' issues of any periodical, and never make an exception. That keeps life manageable.

STORAGE SUMMARY

The following overview of my storage concepts might simplify your thinking process.

• When a room is small and has few closets, less needs to be stored there—probably just what will be used in the space. Choose furniture for these small spaces with drawers or doors to increase the storage possibilities. Buying plastic containers that fit under beds is great. A small kitchen needs limited equipment, good interior skeletons for cabinets, hooks on walls, containers on counters, and furniture with storage possibilities, such as a kitchen table with drawers. They're out there. I saw one yesterday!

• Large rooms with little storage require the same treatment as small rooms: furniture that stores things, containers that hold things, and/or built-in closets.

• A game area needs cards, score pads, pencils, coasters, and games, all stored as close by as possible. You could use a closet or a small chest of drawers, a drawer in the table, or even a cabinet on the wall, so once again, products or tools are stored where they are used.

• All laundry detergents, softeners, and the like need to be stored in the laundry room. No shoe polish there—unless that's where you polish your shoes!

when EFFICIENCY BACKFIRES

ONE STUDENT of mine made the mistake of having good suitcase storage, but then storing sweaters in the suitcases. She thought she was being super-efficient in her use of space, but every time she took a trip, her sweaters ended up in a pile in a corner or on the bed. Then when she came back, she had to put them away again.

This is not spontaneous enough. We want things to happen easily. I suggested that she buy some storage bags for sweaters and store the suitcases empty. Then she could be on her way for a weekend much faster and more efficiently, without the dreaded sweater-repacking chore waiting for her at the end of the trip.

If you live in an apartment, I find that it's most efficient to store a suitcase right under the bed—at least, if it's used often. Another possibility is in a guest room closet, if your apartment has a guest room.

• Candle and match storage could be in five places in the house. Those areas are all places where you would want to use candles: the dining room, the living room, the kitchen, the bedroom, and the meditation space. You could also use a space in a very large closet out of the vital area for additional candle and match storage. (Out of reach of small hands, please!)

• CDs and tapes need to be waiting by the stereo and boom box, organized in easily accessible categories. If space is limited, keep current favorites out and others stored away in a less vital but very accessible place.

• Same with magazines, books, suitcases, pots and pans, pencils and pens, and glasses.

• Be sure you update your storage systems when you change your life, habits, or home design. Everything needs to be available near the place where it is used.

REVISIT your PICTURE JOURNAL

This is a good point to look at your journal and examine your pictures, which tell you so much about your sense of order. Don't just look at them as pictures. Trust that these photos will give you lots of input toward the best way of storing for you.

Look at the pictures with an eagle eye. Notice how many containers are out, how things are displayed, even how pictures are hung. If your pictures of sitting rooms look as if someone just got up from their seat and walked away, to return at any given moment and pick up their book right where they left it, then you have a very casual style. You'll enjoy setting up spaces with hand lotion in pretty containers on coffee tables, the current book left out, the permanent coaster on the table, the throw literally thrown. If instead the picture looks as if no one was ever there, you want places to put things away. The book can go back on a shelf, in a drawer, or behind a pillow. Just remember it's there!

Then think about ways you work. Are you on the phone often? Which phone area needs what? Do you wear reading glasses? Where do you need them? Hit the nearest drugstore for a bunch that can be sitting around waiting for you. (And don't forget to take them off there.) All storage needs to be supported by a system that you maintain. Car keys on a designated nail as you come in the door, your purse always dropped in the same place, gloves always taken off and stored by the door. But this will work only if it is a style that is comfortable for you. Above all, build the system that works for you.

You arrive at the ways to resolve your storage dilemmas by getting in touch with your feelings, looking at your journal pictures, and becoming aware of how life works for you—or, at least, how you want it to work. Yeah, it takes thought, awareness, and asking questions like, "Why don't I feel good coming home?" or, "Why do I get cranky when it's time to cook?" And it means setting things up a better way. It may mean using ordinary spaces in extraordinary ways, and that's okay if it works for you.

STORAGE SAVES *the* DAY

*O*NE OF MY CLIENTS hated her apartment. We spent a lot of time scoping out why. Was it a lack of light, lots of outside noise, lack of storage, too little space, a too-small kitchen?

What we discovered was that she had a negative feeling as soon as she walked in the front door. She always came in the door with packages, and the vestibule (that's what we used to call the entrance hall) was very small. She would stop, put everything down, trip over it as she hung up her coat, and then gather it all up again to transport into the apartment or to wherever it was going.

We decided to switch where she hung her coat and where she put her car keys. We set it up so she walked all the way into the apartment (to the bedroom, actually), where she dropped everything once. We set up the storage of her seasonal coats there and stored her out-of-season coats back at the front door. She used the front closet for other kinds of storage also. That small adjustment totally changed her feelings about the apartment—and notice that it's a storage resolution.

That's why I'm writing this book. If I can get you in touch with how you want to live, the designing you need or want to do will be easier, more attractive, and far more functional. It helps you specify the kind of coffee table, end table, and shelves. It orients the arrangement. It helps you choose the lighting, the comfort factor of the seating. Isn't it amazing? And you thought selecting furniture only had to do with its style and finish in relation to the room!

Interpreting Your Journal

Let's go back to your picture journal for a few more moments. What do the gardens look like in some of your outdoor pictures? Are they carefully organized, with zinnias in one part of the garden and marigolds in another, or are they all mixed up like bouquets? Look carefully, because this is an indication of what style you like: the looks, the function, the feeling.

One student had many pictures of roads, paths, and streams in her journal, each with chaos along them. I finally determined that she moved through life that way—and liked it. We needed to have a path through her house that was very open. Her storage was carefully planned along that path. We were right. Boy, did she live in her house more easily once we figured that one out! She was always on her way. She never sat down in designated places to do things.

Use your personal journal and do your own interpreting. Make notes of what you see. Go to your happiness list and review what you want now in your life. Go to your plan. Make notes for all activity areas (even where you're going to have your coffee) that tell you what items you need where and what storage you'll need in each area. Give yourself some clear instructions.

Think about whether you are a visual person (if you can't see it, you forget that you own it) or if you're more rational. If you are visual, you need to be able to see almost everything you own, or you'll lose it. It can be behind closed but designated doors. If files are very difficult for you, using colored files, categorized file cabinets, and closets designated for cleaning supplies, calendars, and winter clothes is best. If you're better at remembering through logic, then files (even done alphabetically) work.

Storage for Living

The part of this storage concept that I love is how it helps with living. My client Donna had a huge kitchen. It was so big it wasn't working. When we listed all that could be happening in the kitchen, such as a computer center, a place for perusing cookbooks, a spot for kids to work on homework, a place to bake, one where Donna could cut up vegetables for salads, and on and on, we were able to organize her cabinets to support each task and also assist the design. It was very useful.

We put a computer center at the end of the kitchen and stored the necessary tools there. Donna used it for recipes, and the kids used it for homework. We set up a baking area, a salad-making area, and a great cleanup area with nesting plastic containers (they're my favorites). We even set up a music area, using an under-the-cabinet CD player and a drawer nearby for the CD storage.

It was easy for the kids to help with dinner (they actually wanted to) by setting up these centers and storing what they needed right there where they needed it. Cooking became a family hobby. Carefully planned and set up designs ingeniously lead you to new experiences. This kitchen sends the message to the whole family that everyone is welcome and belongs there.

ORGANIZATION, ORGANIZATION, ORGANIZATION

Remember, we're talking *organized* storage. We're talking storage according to how you think (stacks and containers or file cabinets and drawers). We're talking about storage of tools and so on in the everyday living spaces where they'll be used. We're talking about keeping only what is vital to current living (including seasonal living), and what's required or important to your history. The key words here are *vital, designated, accessible,* and *your style.* We're talking paring down—eliminating the stuff that keeps us stuck—and organizing the rest so that it is *soooo* accessible. Fulfill a dream. Is it to be able to park your car in the garage? Make it happen!

Take all your school yearbooks, diaries, and other memorabilia and carefully place them in the attic or in a guest-bedroom drawer. They are not vital storage items. They're less important, and they're perfectly safe in faraway places. It's the vital items—the stuff we use every day—that needs to occupy the center of our living spaces.

It's really the Montessori schooling concept with two additions:

1. A place for everything

2. Everything in its place

3. Everything stored near the place that it is going to be used

4. Everything else stored out of the center of living

This is my formula for successful storage! It will make life simpler, easier, downright pleasant. But if you are a collector, don't panic. Collections do need to be stored or displayed so they can be enjoyed and accessed. There is a difference. Collections are cherished groups of objects that bring you pleasure every day. Clutter is stuff that died from lack of use but wasn't buried far away from your life or given to someone who could use it. Instead, it got buried in the nearest closet or the garage and is now a dangerous tripping hazard or barrier to something more important. Don't let your closets be gravesites.

I could go on and on with stories, but I think I've said it. We all need to learn how to live better, and some of the best assistance comes from good systems and fabulous storage. Look at your life, your stuff, and your needs, and go for it. It's sublime, and so is getting there.

exercise 19
Organize Room by Room

What you'll need: your three-ring binder or, if that one is full, a new one, plus lined or unlined paper and your pen.

Doing this exercise may be tedious, but it is so worthwhile. We're going to use either the same three-ring notebook you put together in chapter 12 or create another one. We'll set up the pages as shown on the opposite page.

What to Do

• We're going to go room by room or floor by floor.

• I want you to just stand in a room. Write down the activities you do in it (or want to do), the tools you have or need, and the storage you'll need for them. This may sound like the last exercise you did, but this time, we're not looking at decluttering or eliminating chaos. We're looking at storage for activities.

• There may be a point in the process where you actually no longer need or want to write it all down because you've got it. You've established a rhythm of deciding where something is going to happen and therefore what needs to be considered with storage or how a storage space is going to be used. But let's assume you're going to do it all on paper first, with the pages set up as shown on the opposite page.

If You're Working in a Group

Do this exercise on your own, then get together and compare storage solutions. You'll probably come away with even more great ideas!

	Activity	*What is to be stored?*	*How will it be stored?*
First floor:			
Second floor:			
Third floor:			
Basement:			
Garage:			

Map your storage systems like this, and you'll have an action list for making them happen.

If your group enjoys field trips, or if one of you is having trouble coming up with a particular storage solution, you might want to travel from house to house to do a show-and-tell. It's fun to do this as a before-and-after trip, too, so everybody can admire your finished storage masterpiece.

your ACTION PLAN

Inventing good storage can be one of
the most creative parts of design. It deserves your ingenuity, your contemplation, and your time. It can be reduced
to a very simple formula of storing only
what is current to your life and storing
it always in the same place, close to
where it will be used. Store the memorabilia, the tax records, and everything
else carefully "far" away, and be sure
you know the inventory and where
you've put it. You'll never be sorry you
did this chapter well.

In the next section, we can move on to
tackling the rest of interior design. Now
that you've laid all the groundwork, discovered what you need and like, decluttered, and put the rest away, you're ready
to put the finishing touches on your
dream home!

4

USING YOUR HOME DESIGN

PERSONALITY

14

STEPPING *into* *the* DESIGN PROCESS

It's finally time to step up to the plate and design! This chapter will give you an overview of the principles you need for successful design and how to put them to work in your home. I've thrown in a liberal sprinkling of design tips from my experiences with clients, too, so you can avoid lots of frustrating and potentially costly mistakes.

Your primary challenge now is to hold on to who you are and refuse to be swayed by either trends or the suggestions of all the well-meaning people in your life. This is difficult. Everyone has strong opinions about design. Everyone considers themselves part designer. It's fun to listen to advice, but it's important to then put on the brakes and make your own choices. Sift through trends and advice using the new template of your style. Then use only what suits you.

You know what you want, but you may not know how to get it. Designing a room is harder than it looks. After considering your options, you may decide to

IF *you're* USING *a* DESIGNER

*i*F YOU ARE USING this process in order to work with a professional designer or architect, you can skip this chapter. You are well equipped to assist anyone you hire in achieving exactly what you and your family want. You know your design personality, and the person you hire should have the nuts-and-bolts design skills to see the project through. You can do it without the advice of friends or outside family. All you need is good communication skills, your picture journal, and your confidence. You must believe this. My experience has been that each person doing this work gets so clear that coaching and input are no longer needed. I really hope that's true for you.

I encourage you to totally appreciate what you have accomplished. I remember, when the manuscript of this book was in its first draft, my daughter looked it over and said, "Man, this is really a large commitment." It is. It's huge. Even more than that, it's a challenge to use it, whether you're working with a designer or on your own.

Your next step is deciding where you want to go with this material. Perhaps you have used this process as a focusing exercise that helped you know who you are now. Or instead, you are planning to forge ahead and buy a new house, arrange a room, organize, declutter, or set up space for a new relationship or project. I want to thank you for taking this journey with yourself. You have helped change the concept of home and of design. Stay connected to what you love and how you want to live, always!

hand the task over to a designer. If this is what you choose to do, know that you will be an equal partner now because you know your look and how you want to live in your home. Your designer will appreciate your clarity and decisiveness. Trust me.

If you choose to design without a professional, this chapter is devoted to some great knowledge that will assist you. I will keep it as simple as possible so that you can digest and implement it with ease. I suggest that if you are starting from scratch and doing it yourself, you do all your planning before you spend a cent.

I hope you are in love with your style. You probably noticed that this process had a powerful conditioning technique built in that ensured that you came up with a lot of the same answers over and over again. That is because your style consistently shines through, whether it's brought to the surface through an object, a picture, a fabric, or a visualization. If you did the exercises with integrity, you saw the same feelings, looks, and needs over and over. This is not a weakness! This was the strength of your home design personality coming through.

I hope you'll carry your picture journal with you in the trunk of your car or when you're out with your professional designer. When you get stale about the use of your space, pull out your happiness list or your activity list and reinvent your life. The lists may get stale, too, so redo them or add to them as needed. Rewrite a fantasy day and see if you have changed. Test your beloved object. Often, people will challenge their selection and find out that the new choice has the same message. Then again, sometimes a change does show up.

If you're a designer, I hope you did the process completely. You may never do it so completely with a client, but you now are sensitized to new ways of discovering who your client is, what they might want or need. I encourage you to use this process or invent your own, so that your designs have powerful relevance to the needs and loves of your clients. The design field needs this, and your clients need it. You'll find your work going deeper and yourself becoming a very authentic magnifying glass for someone else's design needs.

DESIGN with the HEART in MIND

I was attending a weekend seminar with a group of fellow students. Our facilitator was Peter Roche de Coppens, a well-known author and philosopher. At breakfast one morning, Peter and I were exploring my thoughts on design. His eyes sparkled as he told me of his mother and her work in design in France, where he grew up. "She would engage an architect for two weeks," he said, "and they would go off in retreat together to come up with the perfect design that would fill the human needs of the possible inhabitants. They would use great care in these designs, and then they would build the house on speculation."

I loved his understanding of the necessary consideration of the human side of living, but I said, "They missed a most important step!"

"What's that?" he asked, totally engrossed in our sharing.

Here's what I told Peter: What his mother and her architects missed was the needs and loves of the future owners— the people who were going to place their feet on the boards, make love in the beds, and dream of what they want their life to be day by day.

When I'm finished designing a home that's been created through the hearts of all the players, the essence of what they yearn for in their surroundings, I can literally hear a sound that I know is truth. Honestly! As I choose a fabric, create a color scheme, hang the pictures that combine my client's spirit and my knowledge, it is profound. It is my world and their world becoming one. It is the completion of a circle, their new consciousness and my openness to reflect them back to themselves. It all helps to create a perfect marriage of the internal and the external that will provide security, constancy, and joy. And it literally has a sound. It hums!

The Third Mind

I have a friend, Martin Weiner, who is a sculptor in Ojai, California. Before he ever begins sculptures for clients, he goes through a very introspective process that helps them discover the forms, the mass, the medium, and the type of expression that is going to make their hearts sing. This is magnificent. It is bringing together the soul of the sculptor and the souls of the seekers. Marty's sculptures are so alive and powerful. They're like that because they come from a "third mind," one that has been created from the combined minds of the sculptor and the seekers. As these sculptures live in the surroundings of their owners, they are a constant reflection of the owners themselves on a very high level.

As we see ourselves in the favorite things we choose, we feel a strong identification with them and a strong sense of our own identity. Abraham Maslow, a psychologist who identified the Hierarchy of Needs, claims this is a factor in feeling safe, feeling like we belong to life, feeling that we have a stable base. When this identity is not clear, it behooves us to do the connecting, the going within, to find out what will help us become secure. But I've already said this in so many ways throughout the book. I hope you don't need to hear it anymore, because now you *feel* it! So let's move right into the next exercise.

exercise 20
Savor the Moment Before You Design

What you'll need: your small spiral notebook and your pen.

In this moment, as you move from contemplating to acting, you may be feeling something. Possibly it is some revelation, some excitement about finishing, or some need for closure on this process. Whatever you're feeling, I invite you to journal it now, if only to complete the circle of this experience for yourself.

You have worked hard, you have found so much of *you,* and just that alone can cause emotions and feelings that deserve to be recognized and expressed. I will not lead you through this. It is your celebration to create. Here's a chance to honor who you are and what you've accomplished. No one may ever read it but you, but that's the most important reason to make sure you do it.

What to Do

Do your journaling and get ready to begin the design!

HINTS for a SUCCESSFUL REDESIGN

If you're redesigning an existing space, I suggest that you push your present furniture around, following the simple rules listed here. Hang the pictures that way also. Then you can replace pieces, knowing where they'll go and how they are going to be used. Placement is a huge part of the design work. The rest is you using your style. So here we go. Relax. Be patient. Remember your home design personality. Use your ability to visualize. Live with something for two weeks before deciding it is wrong.

the PRINCIPLES of DESIGN

Before I go on with the how-to formulas, I want to give you a list of the principles of design. Principles are *not* rules. They are what happens when you do particular things or use certain lines or shapes or colors. They tell you the outcome of your choices. I prefer principles to rules myself. They allow me to move away from stereotypes. Here is a simple short list for your information. Study it carefully.

Line

1. A horizontal line widens.

2. A vertical line heightens and lifts.

3. A variety of lines crossing and shapes repeating creates pattern and busyness.

4. A diagonal line enlarges or heightens, depending on how it is used.

5. A straight line can connect two areas or separate them, depending on where they stop.

6. A wiggly line creates activity and busyness.

7. A straight line points to something.

8. Romantic or feminine looks are achieved by curved lines, flowers, lightness, pastels, round shapes, sheer fabrics, and warmer colors.

9. Masculine or sophisticated looks are achieved by straighter lines, geometrics, bold stripes, a larger and heavier scale, bolder and stronger colors, and heavier fabrics.

ELEMENTS *of* DESIGN SUCCESS

*t*O CREATE a successful design, you need these elements to be present.

Beauty

Pleasing colors, a balanced color scheme

A variety of lines: horizontal, vertical, curved, straight

A variety of shapes: round, square, diamond, etc.

A variety of textures: bricks, shag, tapestry, etc.

Balance in placement

All of the above done to your design style

Function and Comfort

Good lighting

Comfortable seating

Easy passage through the area

Accessible tables

All of the above done to your design style

Imagination

The presence of some genius, surprise, whimsy, humor, and cleverness, compatible with your design style

Personality

The touches that show the spirit, the style, the essence of those who live there, which will come from all the data you've collected

Care

Attention to detail

Good maintenance

Please remember that the suggestions I've presented above form a skeleton list, a starting place. For the room to be successful for you, everything needs to reflect what you want and love. If you love curved lines more than straight, for example, you'll want to choose more furniture, paintings, and patterns with curves, but you will want to balance them with some straight lines, such as a very straight, tall vase or a grandfather clock. The opposite would apply for those who love straight lines.

Focal Points

1. A room sometimes has a focal point that is forced by the architecture.

2. Sometimes there is more than one focal point.

3. A room can have too many focal points or too few.

4. Every room has a center axis (see page 255 for more on this).

Color

1. A dark color takes the eye away and absorbs color. It diminishes size (makes things look farther away than they really are).

2. A light color comes toward you and reflects light. It enlarges an object (makes things look closer than they really are).

3. A cold color lowers body temperature, has lower vibration, and recedes.

4. A warm color raises body temperature, has higher vibration, and comes toward you.

5. A bright color pulls the eye, so it can be used to highlight something.

Pattern

1. When a shape is repeated, it forms a pattern. Repetition also emphasizes that particular shape.

2. A large repeating motif in a wallpaper or fabric pattern needs a large display area, since the repetition of the motif forms the pattern.

Relationship and Proportion

1. Everything in a space is in relationship to everything else. (This is an important one!)

2. Large-scale items need space to be shown off. They also absorb space.

3. Small-scale items need small spaces.

Texture

1. Soft texture warms a space.

2. A variety of different textures creates interest and fills space.

3. Texture can keep a space from appearing flat.

4. Texture deepens a color.

There are more principles, but if you've absorbed these, you have a lot to work with. Here's how to use them. First, decide what you want to accomplish (raise a ceiling, widen a room, draw attention, and so on). Then find the appropriate principle to assist you.

11 STEPS to a GREAT DESIGN

Your best sequence of steps for designing is:

1. Connect to your home design personality.

2. Choose one room as your first project.

3. Label your room by creating a description of what you want.

4. Decide on your starting point, such as a painting, your beloved object, or a color.

5. Arrange your furniture. This process can be done with your present furniture to see what works. Then you can purchase new furnishings as needed once you see what works in terms of size and shape.

6. Plan the placement of your wall treatments (pictures and other wall orna-

ments). You need to do this planning now, whether you're using wallpaper or just plain paint. You'll find out more later, but the key is that the pictures and other wall treatments relate to the furniture, a window, or a doorway—to *something* in the room. If you're stenciling, consider the stenciling as an object also.

7. Plan the selection of the actual pieces of furniture.

8. Plan the color scheme and where each color will occur. Include color decisions on walls, paint, stenciling, and so on.

9. Plan the lighting.

10. Plan the design of window treatments.

11. Plan the accessories.

Now, let's take these steps one by one.

Step 1: Connect to Your Home Design Personality

I assume you've done the process, so enough said—let's move to Step 2.

Step 2: Choose One Room to Start

Any room is fine. The steps are the same. But it's easier to work through these steps one room at a time rather than trying to tackle several (or, God forbid, *all*) rooms at once and bogging down.

Step 3: Label the Room

Before you do anything else, absolutely before you do *anything* else, it is paramount that you write out a simple statement of what you want this room to be, look like, feel like, and act like. You want to be sure it matches the template you established with your home design personality. Here are examples.

• "I want a cheerful room with lots of life and freshness, a crisp look that reminds me of a garden. I want people to have great conversations in here and feel carefree. I don't want any TV watching going on in here. This should be a great room for napping."

• "I want a soft, sophisticated, and elegant look, with low lighting and lots of comfortable seating near the fireplace. I want to use elegant fabrics, crystal, and lots of silver."

• "I want a room that is quaint, colorful, and country, with quilts, plants, lace, and many antiques. I want us to be able to play board games, talk on the telephone, work on the computer, and read."

• "I want a room that reminds me of a pub, with dark colors, a piano, a bar, low light, and comfortable chairs."

This is called thinking through the project. It's only a beginning, and what you want may expand, but it assists you in focusing, or centering. Once you've labeled the room and know exactly what you want it to be and do, you will be strongly self-directed.

Step 4: Choose a Starting Point

To choose a starting point, select one thing for the room that supports the label you've given it. You don't even have to buy it or use it. It can be anything, such as:

• A printed fabric that really catches you, or a powerful color

• A painting

• A china pattern

• A collection

• A favorite quilt

• A large accessory

Step 5: Arrange the Furniture

First, here are some things to consider when arranging furniture.

• Important information about conversation areas: People must face each other, be comfortable, and not have eye contact blocked by an object such as a lamp. They should have a table or other flat surface within reach, never face a blank wall, and never be too far apart.

• You can pull your furniture away from the wall, or you can put a piece of furniture on an angle. Often, in a small room, I'll angle everything, and it tends to push out the walls a bit and create a lot of interest and space.

• If you've been doing this process in a group, it really works to remain a group and assist each other in the arrangement of the rooms that you want to address. First, furniture is heavy, and there'll be more of you to move it around. Second, it means you can change it and change it until you get it right. Read the principles of design (pages 249 and 251) first and consider each person's design personality.

• A lot of your preferences from our process need to be honored here, such as how much you like space filled up, whether furniture that's angled bothers you, and whether you are symmetrical, which means you like things centered and balanced in pairs. Look at your picture journal to see how you prefer your furniture placed—open with lots of space or closed and cozy, uniquely angled or rigidly straight. If you look at the photos, you will be able to tell.

DID SOMEONE *say* BUDGET?

I AM CHOOSING not to address the budgeting issue. I believe a room can be beautiful on any budget. But I will say this: It is important for you to decide on a budget before you begin any new design or redesign, then stick to it so you finish the room. Remember that you can achieve the same look on any budget—just choose furniture and materials with the look you want (abstract, country, Victorian, and so on) that fall in the price range you've decided on.

Furniture Arrangement by the Numbers

Now let's get down to what you'll need to do to arrange your furniture.

1. Strip the room of all accessories, pictures, and small pieces of furniture. You need a clean canvas before you begin. When accessories and pictures have been moved away, you can see the bare architecture and use the space it creates more effectively.

2. Find your center axis (refer to the illustration below), which is usually di-

rectly in front of the focal point. If the room is rectangular, a fireplace or window can be the center point of the room. If a room is square, usually the center point is the center of the room.

3. Decide on your focal point—the place where the eye will go naturally because of the architecture. Look around the room and see if there is a place that naturally draws your attention, such as a fireplace, a view, or a strong wall. If there isn't, you get to choose. It could be that you'll decide to put a very striking rug on

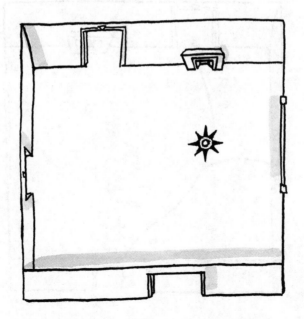

This room's center axis uses the fireplace as its focal point.

the floor (like a bright geometric), and that would become your focal point.

4. Establish the traffic lanes in the room. These are the paths that people naturally walk. Be sure you get them all. Remember that you can redirect traffic by rearranging the room. (Refer to the illustration below.)

5. Walk around and use the traffic lanes to decide whether there is enough space for one or two activity areas, or even more.

6. You've listed the activities in prior exercises; now assign them to the islands that exist between the traffic lanes. Prior-

ity activities (such as a conversation area) should occupy a large space in a living room. Bear in mind that one space can accommodate more than one activity. (Refer to the illustration on the opposite page.)

7. Decide how many people you wish to seat, then begin to place furniture to accommodate all the activities you've just listed, keeping traffic lanes open.

8. Identify your largest blank wall. That's where your most prominent piece of furniture belongs (an armoire, a large breakfront, a bookcase, a highboy, a very

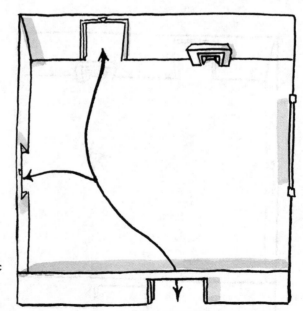

A room has its natural traffic lanes, which can be redirected with furniture.

large sofa, a bed, a grand piano, a large shelf unit). If you have few available walls, furniture may need to float.

9. Once you've placed the major pieces of furniture, add smaller pieces, such as end tables, ottomans, chairs, sofa tables, and so on.

Step 6: Decide on Placement of Wall Treatments

Here's a helpful designer secret: Things that are hung on the wall help the fur-niture "belong" to a room. Bear this in mind as you work through the fol-lowing list.

1. Consult your picture journal as to the type of art you prefer (pictures, tapes-tries, clocks, anything you're going to hang on the wall).

2. As you're pondering placement, re-member that everything that's hung on the wall must relate to something nearby. For example, it may be hung over a sofa or table, by a door, or near a window.

3. Look at all of your walls and decide

Group pictures and
other hanging objects
off-center above a
central piece of
furniture.

what spaces seem to need something. But don't fill *all* the space! Empty space helps balance the spaces that are filled. Check back with your home design personality here and ask, "What do I prefer?"

4. Hang all art within 14 inches of the object it relates to.

5. Never hang something too small on a very large wall. If you do, it will have too much space around it and therefore look lost. And never center something small over something large. Instead, try positioning it off-center.

6. Hanging things at eye level is a myth. Hang things high, low—wherever they look great and relate to something. A picture hung on the wall under a lampshade is fun.

7. If you like groupings, try this: (a) If all pieces are alike in size, hang them asymmetrically (or don't, if you prefer symmetry). Be different! (b) If all pieces are different sizes, start with the largest and place it off-center. Work down in size randomly, then scatter the smallest pieces within the framework of the larger ones. (Refer to the illustration above.)

8. Anything can be hung on the wall: rugs, paintings, photography, posters, musical instruments, objects. Once I hung a large puppet. I've even hung a chair on the wall! (Of course, it had to be the *right* chair.) It looked fabulous.

Step 7: Select Your Furniture

After working through Step 5, you know where to put your furniture. This step is about choosing the actual pieces of furniture for each room.

1. Look at all your preferences, your beloved object, your picture journal, and your storage needs. They'll all help you choose. Because you know where everything is going to be placed, it's time to decide what that furniture is going to look like—its style, whether it's upholstered, inlaid wood, trimmed with brass tacks, fancy, durable, leggy, overstuffed, useful for storage, and so on.

2. Decide what serves your style of living, comfort, durability needs, and so on.

3. Consider the size of your room to decide what scale is best for your furniture.

4. Consider the position of each piece. Will the chair be seen from the back? Does the back of the desk have to be finished? Will the table ever be opened?

5. Have a good variety of high and low pieces so everything isn't the same height.

6. Keep these design tips in mind:
- Dark woods need lots of light.
- Carving needs light to show it off.
- Decoration needs space around it.
- Conversation areas should be comfortable.
- Relate the shape of the dining table to the shape of the room.
- Put tables where they're needed, not randomly placed.

7. Use ingenuity when selecting pieces. Consider nontraditional options, such as:
- A sleigh for a bed
- A chest for a coffee table
- Chests as end tables
- Trunks as tables
- Ladders as shelves

8. Feel free to mix woods. Treat them as colors. One piece of painted furniture enhances all the other woods in the room.

Furniture selection is fabulous and painful. You're spending big bucks, and you have to wait for delivery. Plan some distractions so you don't run out of patience.

Step 8: Plan the Colors and Where They'll Go

My first premise with color is that if you arranged really well, color isn't as important as it would be if the inherent design were weak. But there is nothing more exciting than a great color scheme or an amazing accent that is a surprise. Experiment!

Check out your pictures and your preferences to see which color or colors you love. Did you tend toward lots of colors, a three-color scheme, or a monochromatic scheme (which means you like many shades of one color)? The monochromatic scheme needs an accent of a different color. Reread the principles of design regarding color on page 251. Then plunge in!

1. Choose a color.

2. Decide what other colors you'll use with that color.

3. Decide the proportions of each color. One color must predominate. The next is secondary, and so on. Never use the same proportions. This means that if you're decorating with blue and green, you must decide which is the main color and then (if it's blue) be sure you don't use as much green as you did blue! If you're using three or more colors, the same rule applies.

4. Decide where colors will be located, such as on particular pieces of furniture or on walls. Look at your picture journal. Where did you like color? Perhaps you liked it on the floor!

5. Did you choose pictures for your journal with high-contrasting colors or subtle contrasts? Choose the same for your home. If you chose lots of pictures to work with, then it will be very obvious to you. Favor the same colors, the same proportions, and the same amount of each color, and put the color where you prefer to see it. Be strong in sticking to your preferences.

6. When choosing colors, remember that they do not have to match. They are more interesting and prevent a flat look by giving dimension when they are slightly different. I always laugh (a kind laugh, of course) at people in fabric stores straining to see if the color is exactly the same. There's no need to do that!

7. When you want to lose (hide) something, make it the same color as the wall or whatever else is behind it. Furniture that's dark and large is great against a dark wall. It makes the room look bigger because the furniture's less prominent.

8. Be sure that color is balanced in the room. Strong color on just one side can put a room out of balance. Put a small amount of it across the room, too, unless where you placed it is close to the center of the room.

9. Be daring.

10. Always look at all colors in daylight in the room where they'll be used, and look at them together. When they look right to you, check them again at night in the same manner.

11. Deep textures make color seem more intense and give a warm, casual look.

12. Shinier surfaces are more formal, and they lighten color. So if you decide you are going to use light blue, and then you choose a shiny, light blue satin, the effect will be a really light blue and will look quite formal.

13. Flat colors (no sheen) are more casual.

Step 9: Plan the Lighting

Lighting is so important. When you have good lighting of the type you like, it can do everything to make a room work. I could write an entire book on lighting, but for now, I'll just give you a few tips.

1. Look at your picture journal. The photos you've chosen will show you the type of lighting you prefer. Some people love a totally lit room, corner to corner. Some prefer lamplight (a small pool of light). Some of you prefer a combination, and others love spotlighting or indirect lighting.

2. If you're using only lamps, use enough so you can eliminate dark corners.

3. When using lamps, you need at least three that form a triangle in your room. The triangle must cross the center of the room. (Refer to the illustration on page 262.)

4. Use a bulb with enough wattage to add sparkle to the room. A room with lighting that's too low can cause depression.

5. Attempt to place lighting so that you are not reading or talking in a shadow.

6. Lighting in the ceiling over a mirror must be placed carefully, or you'll look

Each room should contain three sources of
light, forming a triangle that passes
through the room's center.

like a raccoon. Holding a flashlight overhead at different distances from the wall
can tell you what works best. The one
that creates the big, dark eye shadows is
not the one you want! Two people are
better than one at figuring this out.

7. Avoid placing lights where you'll
look straight into them.

8. Never have a lamp between two
people who are talking.

9. Make sure a reading light is
placed so the light hits the book page.

Apothecary lamps are wonderful for this.

10. To decide the height of a lamp,
make sure that the height of the table
plus the height of the lamp equals between 50 and 56 inches.

11. A dining room fixture should be
about 30 inches above the dining table
surface. Often, they're hung too high.

12. Always be sure that lampshades are
clean and straight. A skewed, dirty, or torn
lampshade can kill the perfection of your
room. The eye goes right to the slight!

Step 10: Plan the Window Treatments

Window treatments—curtains, blinds, and the like—are so much a matter of taste. You again need to check with your personal picture journal. You may be surprised to find that you had *no* window treatments. Or perhaps you're a lover of fabric, so your windows are carefully covered with lots of full, gathered fabric. Today's trends have been to minimize window treatments. We seem to want our views preserved. But you have to decide what *you* want.

Windows are like people to me. You must think of the size of the window and dress it accordingly. Otherwise, it can look silly.

Here's another designer secret: The way you do your windows can be a key to making your room appear well finished. If you do not use a window treatment, be sure your woodwork is in mint condition.

My last piece of advice is to not skimp on fabric. If it comes down to a choice, I advise you to use a less expensive fabric and use lots of it, instead of the opposite. Too little fullness can kill a handsome fabric.

Important Window Treatment Footnotes

Here are seven last things to remember when you're choosing a window treatment.

1. Be very clear on the look you like.

2. Decide whether you've created a mood in your room that your window treatment should enhance, or whether it's the window treatment that will create the mood.

3. I always use three times the width of the window when I measure for yardage.

4. Window treatments are a great way to cover faults.

5. Measure and hang the drapery around rather than over your windows to make them appear larger.

6. When choosing a treatment, be sure that you take into account how the window needs to open and close.

7. Make sure treatments are made and installed well.

A well-dressed window can truly create an illusion. It is a place for creativity to excel. Try not to be too gimmicky. I've had many a laugh over some greatly overdone windows.

Step 11: Plan Your Design Accessories

Accessorizing is truly an art. It's fun. It can tell a story. It can draw the eye away from a problem. It can create the whole drama of a room. It can also be used with lighting to focus attention. It has a way of making your home look lived-in.

I feel that placement is as important as the accessory itself. I've seen many mediocre pieces placed in such an exciting way that you feel delight from the presentation. Here are some good rules.

1. Check out your photos in your personal picture journal and consult your beloved object.

2. Another designer secret: Always work with uneven numbers—three or five objects, not two or four, and so on. When you begin to arrange them, you'll see why: Even numbers invariably line up in regimental fashion. *Note: A* lamp does not count as one of the accessories.

3. Use a variety of sizes.

4. Use a variety of shapes.

5. Use different types of accessories to add visual interest.

6. When accessorizing bookshelves, use the same rules. Never line things up straight across or up and down.

7. When arranging your objects, stay with the rule I gave you about grouping pictures, where you begin with the largest one, never placing it in the center, and work down in size. Sprinkle smaller pieces within the framework of larger ones.

8. When you are grouping plants of the same species, bring them close together and let their fullness be the accent.

9. When including a flowering plant among green plants, place it off-center. Never place it dead center.

10. Collections are best displayed together. It gives them more impact.

11. Remember that when you're accessorizing, less is more. One striking accessory can do the job of many lesser ones.

12. Here's an idea for a fun surprise: Arrange a figurine or flower so it looks like it came out of a painting nearby.

I really encourage you to experiment with your accessories. They can create surprise, pattern, and fun.

It can be fun to take a cue from a picture and bring elements of it to "life."

your ACTION PLAN

This entire chapter is an exercise. It challenges you to bring together your personal preferences, a keen eye, an understanding of design principles, and careful consideration and creativity. Those are all tools for the job. You can have great success if you consider all the design principles carefully. Experiment, risk, listen to yourself, and promise yourself complete commitment until you're satisfied. If you're going to use a professional, remember your home design personality and communicate clearly. You'll have a wonderful time.

Incidentally, many designers will do single consultations to get someone started or turned around. It could be a great way to go. But however you do it, the operative word is *go*. Get going! It's time to make your dreams come true.

a LAST FEW DESIGN THOUGHTS

BEFORE WE LEAVE the subject of design, I have to share a few more of my design tips. (I just can't stop!) Think about them when you're creating your designs.

- I love a uniform carpet color throughout a home when it's wall to wall.

- I feel that plants should look very healthy.

- Live (or frequently dusted silk) flowers add so much.

- Unusual placement of pictures can show off creativity.

- A lived-in look can be accomplished with some clever organization.

- A piece of furniture used in an unusual way is exciting.

- And my favorite tip: A clever combination of colors or fabrics is best.

15

LIFE CHANGES, DESIGN CHANGES

This chapter may or may not fit your life right now. It's about
transition, such as when you change jobs or relationships,
or someone moves in or leaves. It's about change, and
I am convinced that change can be easier if you have
a wonderful, supportive home environment.

My friend Linda had an aunt who lived to a wonderful age—somewhere in her nineties. Linda reports that she remained beautiful, wise, and happy all through those years. She also remained fun to be with. These days, I think being happy is a great achievement. When Linda asked her aunt's secret, her answer was, "I kept on changing."

This is hard to do. Many of us want everything to stay the same, including ourselves. We want the familiar. It feels safe and comfortable. When change happens, we resist it by trying to stay the same ourselves. I know one person who went through a divorce and never changed her life, her home, or her routine. The only thing that changed was that her husband didn't come home after work. That gets you stuck, you go on living in denial, you feel resistant, you don't grow, flow doesn't happen, and you lose touch with yourself.

I remember when I was first divorced. I kept running home to be there to cook at dinnertime. It took a while to take on the new role. I needed to plan differently and set up space differently to remind myself that now I was single and

TIME *for a* CHANGE

*t*HERE IS A WONDERFUL movement therapist in California, Emily Conrad, whose primary premise is that we all need change for the body's sake. She says that our nervous systems and lives are stimulated by change. She endorses forcing changes into your days so that routines occur differently.

One way to change your routine would be to wear your wristwatch on the opposite arm. Or you could try a different sequence in your morning routine. This, Emily claims, moves the nerve impulses along new channels so they are used, and habit isn't carving deep ruts. If you accept her perspective and apply it to the concepts in this book, it would behoove you to move many of your things around in your home environment to keep you alive, alert, and responding differently.

could be creative in finding a new life.

Change is inevitable—the only sure thing there is. Because of this, you are smart to become more open to change and the ways you can transform yourself to flow with life. There are all kinds of change: The kind you want, the kind you don't want, the kind you're afraid of, and the kind that is full of surprise.

When change feels negative, you're disappointed, terrified, grief stricken. Those emotions are all important to feel and important to deal with. But when you're ready, it is valuable and important to ask those chaos questions again: Where are you going now, and what's going with you? Also, ask what's going to get you there.

If at any time you feel that you or your life is changing, go back to the beginning of this book and do some of the earlier exercises again. They'll allow you to actually see the changes that are happening in you relative to the changes and transitions you're going through.

LET your HOME HELP you

Your home environment can be a powerful tool to assist you through your life changes. Sometimes I get really stressed out on a daily basis. I'm dashing from one event to the next without feeling or experiencing anything. I become way out of touch with myself. At these times, I know that changing some things in my surroundings or routine will help me. I try to imagine what will slow me down. Perhaps it's to become a bit more efficient. Perhaps it's just to improve my basic living.

If I need more efficiency in my life, I pay some bills or make my system of bill payment better, clean the house or re-arrange it, or change a closet. If I need an upgrade in my living conditions, I get out the candles and the pretty napkins. Then I promise myself that I'll sit down to eat, I'll light the candle, I'll eat slowly enough to taste the food, I'll take the time to put my meal on a tray and walk out to the creek with it. There, I can really let nature do some of the repair work. I might place potpourri around to awaken my sense of smell. I'll buy some new CDs or dig out some old ones and be sure I play them as I dress or cook or work. These are all assists from the environment.

This is one way to approach it. You see that you're out of balance. You figure out how the environment can help by slowing you down or making you feel good, and after you've installed the means, you use them. In no time, you're back in balance. You might move some art piece to stimulate your visual sense or remember to open the windows when the breezes are blowing.

In the winter, blooming plants can lift your spirits. I have an orchid that stayed in bloom all the way from Christmas to July 25. Such a joy! But perhaps blooming plants don't do it for you. Instead, it might be the sorbet that's always in your freezer, the popcorn popper always on hold and ready, a nap on the deck, a new bath ritual, a kite hung on the wall. It's *your* pleasure that you need as your "upper." Get in touch with it.

What I like about this concept is the in-ternal/external focus. You have to go inside to search for what will make you feel good now. Sometimes it's just comfort: wrapping up in a blanket or cooking and eating mashed potatoes.

You can't expect that the same rituals will always work. Remember that you are changing internally, too. Even though you might be out of touch with what is happening, go inside to figure out what you want. Then install the "tools" into your surroundings. As it all unfolds, you'll be using your space and your objects in this sensitive way, and you'll be transported back inside through your senses. Muscles relax, vision clears, tension leaves the neck, life looks abundant, and you feel free. You're on the money.

DEALING with BIGGER TRANSITIONS

Perhaps the transition you're facing is really large—a change that involves grieving, moving, letting go, or reconstructing. Your home design personality needs to be tested again at those times to see if you are changing internally. Pick any of the earlier exercises and see if you come up with the same information as you did before. If not, use the new information to keep you going on the path of your truth, your new you.

Probably the clearest example I can give about how I consider this way of working with design as a therapy would be to share with you another one of my stories. The story represents a very experimental time, when I began to suspect that the home environment could be a medicine for healing.

A new client, Theresa, came to me and asked that I use her home environment to help her work through the tragedy of losing her husband. She had cared for him through a very long illness. Their marriage had been a strong one, and it was hard to see it end. Theresa yearned to be comfortable in the house alone, to see her identity in the house, and to have it be a spontaneous, vital, flexible space for her in her movement toward be-

coming a single woman with a new life.

Theresa did not feel ready to sell her house, but there were many memories screaming out from all corners. I knew we had to take the house apart and put it back together as if she were just moving in.

We began with conversations, the sharing of memories and dreams she had for her future. I had her collect pictures of her likes and dislikes. As I looked at her pictures, I saw that she had a very strong vertical element, so I decided to use this as a tool. We created many verticals in her home: pictures hung one on top of the other, paintings hung over doorways, pictures hung over pieces that were already tall. She felt supported by these lines. They literally pulled up her energy. I told her to experiment more with this. She did, and when I arrived the next week, her eyes were sparkling and she was excited and happy.

Later in our process, Theresa was feeling very out of touch with who she was—very fragile, harried, and confused. My take was that she needed grounding and a place to put her caring to work. She had a wonderful dog named Ponce. She loved caring for Ponce but was often too busy. We found a new space for her to groom him and arranged it so everything she needed was there. I suggested she take large chunks of time, put music on, talk to Ponce, and express affection.

Theresa also talked about loving to soak in the tub. Her bath area was less than perfect, so we designed it differently, with plants, perfume bottles, moisturizers, oils, sponges, candles, magazines, and music. We customized it so it was very personal to her. She benefited tremendously. She said it was wonderful to care for herself in this way. Her caring had been focused on her husband, and she had neglected herself.

Isolation was another dynamic going on. It is a natural feeling attached to loss and change. I suggested that Theresa keep a light on in any adjoining room to counter the feeling of being alone in the house. We also made sure she had many places to entertain friends. I suggested she bring in fresh flowers often. We put up window treatments that opened views and let in light. We pulled out objects that expressed her own identity more than her identity as part of a couple.

Through the entire process, Theresa kept healing and growing. When we were finished, she was comfortable at home and ready to move out into the world as a single person. I was ecstatic over the research that I had accomplished and the answers I'd gotten. Since that time, I have used this process over and over again. I am convinced it is a tool for change.

A New Slant on a Custody Case

Another time, I had an attorney friend, William Ehrich, call me in the interest of his client, who was arguing for custody of his children. The client owned his own home, but Bill felt that the father needed help reshaping the home space so it was child friendly. He also felt that doing this would support the father's case. Divorce is a big life change, and I was impressed that my attorney friend considered the home environment an important ingredient in this father's role. (Of course, he's heard me talk about it enough!)

I took on the father as a client, with no attachment to the outcome of the case. The courts and the family would resolve that. I cared more about the father, the children, and the goal. We were going to help two children in transition feel safe, secure, warm, sheltered, and connected in their father's home. I looked forward to assisting them.

Because of the ages of the children—5 and 7—making spaces safe for toddlers wasn't our issue. Locks on cabinets, sharp edges, and drafty windows didn't need our attention. One goal was to make a warm, cozy place to be with Dad. Another was to show the kids that they belonged. We were also going to have the surroundings reflect to the children how life can remain continuous, playful, happy, safe, and secure as it changes.

I found the father open and excited, and I found a house that needed change. The budget was small, but I knew the changes would not be costly. Creativity was the necessary ingredient here, as usual. The house lacked color, appointments, light at night, and imagination. Spaces had not been set up for activities.

We had a long question-and-answer session. Afterward, I felt that I knew who this father was and the personalities of the children. I rearranged a few pieces of furniture and art to start the process and help him see the energy beginning to change. Here are two quick fixes I showed them.

The dining room was square and housed a nice, old, round wooden table. There was also a glass-doored cabinet that was empty and looked lonely. I found a full set of very pretty dishes in the kitchen. We moved those into the cabinet. Now the children could set the table from the cabinet and share in meal preparations. The small kitchen had less to store, and the cabinet looked used and therefore far more attractive and warm.

The father's bedroom was large and housed his desk for home business, a large rug for yoga, and his bed. One wall was covered with lots of paintings done

by the children. He spoke of how these paintings filled his waking moments every morning. "God, I love this wall," he said. "The children's art feeds my excitement about the treasure of their lives. They are a comfort to me when the children aren't here." I asked if he usually joined the children in weekend art activities. "Oh, sure," he said.

"Well, why aren't *your* paintings from these sessions adorning *their* bedroom walls?" I asked. He had no answer. If their paintings were so important and inspiring to him, he could assume the same would be true for them. They would all get to know each other more. The next time I visited, his art had been hung!

We decided that the children should have something alive in their rooms. We put a fish aquarium in the son's room and African violet plants in the daughter's. Dad's caring for these when the kids are gone gives wonderful messages. All of this, plus warm paint colors and soft, cuddly places to be, gave this father his happy home. He even started bringing in fresh flowers weekly for the center of that lovely wood table. The home environment assisted this family's transition through divorce.

My Own Transition: Cabin Fever

My husband and I, after 31 years of marriage, came to a mutual decision to go our separate ways. The process of separation was painful. Acknowledgment of error, letting go of the familiar, aloneness, self-doubt, and the actual physical detachment demanded my attention. When the time came for our annual family vacation, I had a revelation that helped me personally.

For 27 years, Ray and I had taken the children on vacation to Canada. We stayed for two weeks in a funny, nondescript cottage on a lake, with a boat and water skis, and had lots of fun. Being a "home environmentalist," I always took nesting supplies to make the cottage a lovely space for the time we were there.

Sometimes it was posters, sometimes colorful pillows, but it was always something. One year, I wallpapered the cabin with the unending school pictures of all three children. It may have been the most successful "decorating scheme" ever!

Because of our new choices, our usual vacation wasn't possible. We both wanted Canada, so we split the two weeks between us, with my week coming second. The children still vacationed with us, so they were there for the whole stay. Ray made the decision to share his week with a new woman in his life. I had no problem with the decision—at least, not right away.

I joyfully arrived for my week but was not ready for the wave of emotion that hit me. Canada had always been a special time for us. Responsibilities drifted away, and the two of us managed to really be in touch and share our dreams. The memory of that, and the energy of Ray's new relationship in "our" space, all of a sudden came crashing down around me and created a real dilemma. I let the tears come, and another stage of my mourning began.

I needed to move on, deal fast, survive, and reverse this wave of turmoil. I raced back to the car, grabbing my objects so I could sweep the cabin free for the new me. I had invited a very close woman friend to come along, and in honor of her love of feminine, soft themes, I had brought along pretty bed linens, colorful posters, a few crystal objects, and some pastel throw rugs and towels.

For the next 2 hours, I literally swept out the old, the hurt, and the loss and ushered in the new. I cleaned. I lifted the plain white cotton curtains around the rods and fastened them in puffs. I dressed the beds and thumb-tacked the colorful posters onto the walls. I set the table with my crystal and the flowered dishes from the kitchen.

The space was transformed. It was bright, pretty, and different. It now held me, my new relationship with my children, and my friend with light and softness. The pain was leaving, and the week had begun. I felt such relief. Another let-

KNOCK DOWN *the* (MEMORY) WALL!

ONE COUPLE I was designing for were able to make significant emotional changes by changing their home environment. Their master bedroom adjoined the vacant room of their only child, now grown and gone. There was sincere sadness in their lives when this child went away. The family had been a threesome in living and in traveling.

As we talked about the design, I sensed a great hesitancy on the couple's part. They knew they wanted to move ahead because they needed to enlarge their space and get on with their lives, but they were finding it very difficult. Their bedroom had always been too small for them. Now their son was gone, but memories of him were holding them back from seeing his room as available space. They saw it only as a big, empty hole that reminded them of his absence. They already had a guest bedroom and study upstairs.

I made a suggestion: "Remove the wall between your room and your son's room, and use the space to enlarge both the master bedroom and the bath." I could see that

ting go had happened. I was dealing with a temporary environment, but it still had its impact.

Healing through Change

I have seen healing over and over again when the home environment is adjusted. The life change might be a child leaving for school, an in-law moving in, a death, a job change, illness, a new activity, or a temporary guest. It might be a parent redecorating a child's bedroom after the child has gone off to college or has moved into the other parent's new home after separation or divorce.

Creating new energy in a vacated space can move life forward, ease grief with hope, and creatively help us heal. The newly opened space might become something different than it had been: an office where a family member could write, a library for quiet reading, a meditation space, or a walk-in closet or dressing room. The process of moving out the old—cleansing—and bringing in the new—reappointing—is appropriate and

the particular way that the walls were aligned would make the transition wonderful. With the wall gone, more light would flow through the windows into the enlarged space. A much-desired king-size bed would now fit, and a large entertainment center, too!

They loved the idea. The symbolism that I saw was that "the cradle" would be gone, but the "cradle space" would now live within the new nest of a loving mother and father. My solution might have been a bit esoteric, but the empty room is no longer a reminder—instead, it has become a contributor to better living.

Walls are so pliable. Rearranging them can create all sorts of new possibilities and help with change. First talk about what you need now, in the present. Then move the walls of your home—the external walls—which will move the walls that you have built within you.

significant. It's almost as if cellular change were happening.

My premise is that the dynamic of changing the home environment symbolizes transformation and does indeed move you along. Change of one part of your life naturally fosters change in other parts. The newness of the changed space takes away the familiar that might cause pain. The new scene is unfamiliar at first, but if it's carefully formulated according to new needs, it helps encourage us to find new ways of being in the space.

At age 66, there's one thing I'm sure of. Life changes a lot! In fact, I feel like I've lived three or four lifetimes in one! I don't know if I'm getting better at this living thing, but I do know that changing the environment to serve the changes in life continues to be profound for me. When we change body size, we're forced into new duds, but somehow change in life or lifestyle relative to other change does not penetrate our thought processes where our homes are concerned. Our family sizes change (down or up), our jobs change, our relationships change,

what's important to us changes. Whatever the reality, it always needs to be addressed in terms of our priorities and setting up or resetting up of the home.

The adjustments to our home environments assist us in integrating the acceptance of change into our lives. A fresh design approach acknowledges the way life is and opens the door to new possibilities. I remember having the thought one time, when wild raspberries finished fruiting in my backyard, that I wished those raspberries would always be there. But then I realized if that happened, it would eliminate the seasons of corn and apples. It was a good lesson from nature that change holds great potential.

MOVING through LIFE CHANGES

Each of us faces innumerable life changes, big and small, week in and week out. We may not feel that we have much control over what's happening in our lives—or we may feel that a change has put us on top of the world. But through good and bad, one thing never changes: We still need a place to lay our heads every night, a place to wake up in every morning. It keeps reminding me that we have a powerful tool—our home space—to assist us not only in living but also in changing.

Baby Steps

Probably we're best at change when a new baby is on its way. It's such a positive change, and the excitement of new life is delicious. We contemplate which room will be the nursery. We picture the baby in the crib. We envision ourselves rocking and hugging. We imagine the greeting from the napping child as we open the door. This visualization of the living experience works powerfully in designing.

We continue by scanning the catalogs and stores for the right colors and patterns. We search for the newest means of diapering, settling, and amusing the new angel. We select accessories that teach and bring awareness. We plan for the environment to inspire our child to reach

HOW *to* BECOME *a* QUICK-CHANGE ARTIST

*O*NE WAY to help get through life's changes is to shift the position of objects or remove things that have vivid memories for us. You can redistribute these objects throughout your home. In the process, everything takes on a new look. Redesigning can reidentify a person. Reorienting space can make your home more practical and can raise your pleasure quotient immeasurably.

Just working on the closets in the face of change is helpful. I'll never forget a former classmate of mine telling me at an alumnae meeting how she felt so good going through all her closets and reorganizing. She did this as soon as the kids had all gone off to college. She felt lighter as she tossed away or stored things that were no longer needed for day-to-day living. This gave her the opportunity to keep her closets vital and not let them turn into the gravesites we've talked about. Purging and re-creating your closets will give you a feeling of dominance over your life *and* your home.

his or her greatest potential, and we work to set it up so that it does. We know what we want the home environment to do in this scenario, and we set it up to do it.

A smaller room is usually chosen for the nursery, so ordering the space efficiently is part of the process. We make sure the necessary diaper changes happen easily, along with cuddling, suckling, and telling stories. It's the best way possible to start building a room. If we used this thought process for the entire home, we couldn't miss.

a SECOND LOOK *at* DECOR

ETH AND HER ATTORNEY HUSBAND, Tim, had one child and lived in an adorable English cottage-style home. There was lots of wood, a deep walnut that was original to the house. The windows were small and quaint, as were the rooms. Their life and their house were charming.

Then Beth and Tim decided to have another baby. When a second babe comes along and childcare is not an option, Mom usually spends more time at home during the day, just because of the difficulty in traveling with two children who are very close in age. Well, Beth's next winter was excruciating. She was at home a lot.

Before marrying, Beth had been a professional. She continued to work until she and Tim decided to have children. Now she was at home most of the time and found that the darkness of the wood, which once added to the feeling of quaintness, now added to her feelings of depression.

The normal controversy about painting wood ensued. It went on and on between Beth and Tim, Beth and the painter, Tim and the painter, Beth and Tim and their friends, Beth and Tim and both sets of parents, and Beth and me. The bottom line was that this couple was not ready to move, and Beth truly needed more light. We worked very hard at finding white and eggshell shades that worked together to create dimension and depth. We ended up painting all the woodwork. The result was gorgeous. I got so many thank-you calls from that couple! It was tremendously gratifying.

Emptying the Nest

Dealing with the empty nest is difficult. These intense emotions keep many families from changing their space as the children leave. It's hard to let go of the past. Keeping the rooms as they were seems to hold emotions steady but also keeps us in denial. We try to be sure our children won't feel abandoned or removed. I'd suggest that all of this work involves conversations. Here particularly, let your children know that it is wonderful to have them moving on, but not easy. Communicate how you feel.

Perhaps involving departing children in what you plan to do with the space would help. We need their rooms for new parts of our lives. They need to understand this and not take it personally. Perhaps a guest bedroom designed with a child's return home in mind can prevent hurt. It could also help to keep some favorite clothes hanging in that closet. Transition can happen in stages. Many times, shared feelings are a prerequisite of this environmental step. Just saying, "You are not a candidate for being forgotten," may be all that's needed.

Job Changes

Job changes can produce the need for many adjustments. Sometimes the change creates the need for a home office, an area for storage of tools of the new trade, or catalogs. If this new priority is not addressed, it has huge potential for creating chaos. Items get stored anywhere and everywhere. Work gets done in someone else's space or in the family space, and all this creates loss or confusion or highly emotional arguments. Schedule changes can adjust the times of the day that spaces are used. That can lead to different needs in furniture and lighting. A change in schedule might mean just the purchase of a coffeepot with a timer so the new employee begins punctually and awake!

A new job might introduce the dynamic of travel, which calls for new ease in accessing suitcases. You might need to move them to a different storage space or even incorporate them into your clothes closet. New schedules of caring for clothing and purchasing travel supplies make this addition to life fun and easy.

One example of this is in the life of a designer friend who has lived in the Philadelphia area with his family for many, many years. Now he commutes to New York City, where he teaches at Par-sons School of Design, so he's home on weekends and in a city apartment during the week. Designing the apartment so it doesn't feel like a hotel room took great creativity. But it had to be done, so his life during the week didn't become only a matter of sleeping, eating, and working.

GROWING *and* CHANGING

*L*IFE KEEPS CHANGING. The kids grow up, and that brings new issues. Teenagers need more privacy—but they also need to respect Mom and Dad's privacy. I always ask parents where they spend their personal talking-together time. So often, they haven't turned the page and created separate spaces for everybody to start stretching and growing in new ways.

Parents really need a place to get away together for conversation, entertainment, or rest. But they usually have to create it. Remember, this shift in the family's growth challenges all the relationships. Kids are becoming individuals, and couples are struggling with new feelings. If the parents actively seek a space where they can be alone as a couple, it provides the kids with a model of healthy intimacy and the responsibility of taking care of a relationship.

One couple I knew had two chairs specifically identified as the chairs where necessary sorting and dialogue would happen. They were in the bedroom. The chairs swiveled so they could be face to face or not, as needed. Another couple created a space for Mom's "back to school" office from the sitting room off their bedroom, but they made sure that they turned another space into their "serious conversation area." I think it was a living room that had been unused for a long time. Those living rooms are hanging out all over town. Use them! They are begging to help you with change.

Getting Ready
for Retirement

Marge had worked all her life and now was facing retirement. She decided to bridge the jump from the structure of a job to no structure by taking up a hobby right away. But a hobby can't get off the ground or be appreciated until the space where it can happen is planned. Marge had always wanted to learn flower arranging, so that's what she chose. She had the best time creating a nest for her new activity. She was clear that she wanted an exclusive space, one where she could dawdle, play her music, and spread out. She also wanted to be able to store all the perfect tools: frogs, containers, potting soil, scissors, wire—everything she might possibly need. The room she chose had an eastern window, so she even incorporated space for growing seedlings and flowering houseplants.

This new focus and its creation took much of the angst out of leaving the "office family" for Marge, and the work prevented her from feeling unimportant. The amusing part of this story is that the hobby grew into a small business. When friends saw the fresh and formidable floral designs Marge created, they all wanted one in their home.

MOM and DAD are MOVING IN!

Change has so many faces. Borrowing a thought from John Lennon, my brother-in-law likes to point out that life is what happens when you had something else planned. Probably one of the most complex and hard adjustments comes when in-laws become a part of the household. It isn't only hard for the family; it's difficult for the in-laws, too.

This is a time when boundaries are really threatened. Everybody is afraid that they are going to lose their privacy or identity or peace. It's scary. Only the courageous should take it on, although I know of many situations where it has enriched life. They were the situations when everyone involved used creativity and acceptance to create the new household. Here again is where the open sharing of feelings can be a powerful tool.

There are many ingenious ways to keep everyone happy. Probably the biggest problem that comes out of this new family structure is that everybody is in each other's faces. No matter how much you love each other, if someone else is *always* in your face, you're in pain. Step one could be to make sure every individual who now makes up the family has a really nice private space. You also need to be sure the in-laws have spaces for their hobbies and dreams.

The use of space—and dedication of space to specific people and activities—needs to be talked about, and everybody needs to be aware of everyone else's needs. It's about boundaries, as we've discussed in other parts of this book. I had three clients who ran headlong into these challenges, and when I checked out their situations, I saw that their problems could have easily been prevented. Fortunately, they all proved easy to fix! Let's look at what happened.

Making Room for Mom

Alice's mother had come to visit for many different periods of time and had finally stayed. Alice told me, "It's so hard. She is never in her room."

I could totally understand the constant exits the mother made from her space when I saw the room. There were no pictures on the wall, and none of her "things" from her old home were present. Her suitcase was still on a suitcase stand, and she had no comfortable chair to sit in so she could read or daydream or gaze out the window.

I think Alice's family ended up in this stressful state because for a while, they were unsure whether Mom was in their home permanently or whether she was a guest. She didn't know and the family didn't know. The decision point sometimes never comes, and it prevents a positive move into the new lifestyle.

What steps do you need to take to make this situation work? Just deciding Mom's here to stay for a while is one. Then ask: Where is the best place for her to be? What colors would she love? What can we bring from Mom's to make her feel like this is now her home? What does she need in the practical sense? Which closets are going to be hers? Will she need a private phone? What else will make her feel good? Can there be two chairs in her room so she can have visitors? There are so many ways to soften or enhance changes in living situations. The changes will make the reality feel more comfortable and within control for everyone.

Making Dad Feel Welcome

Another client's father had the habit of getting up at night if he heard his daughter. He thought she needed company. Actually, she was getting up so she would have some time alone. In this instance, a conversation really needed to happen. Diane needed to say, clearly but lovingly, "Dad, I need some time alone." But there was more going on.

When I checked out the household layout, it turned out, again, that Dad's room was just a sterile box. I would have run out of it, too! It was boring, lacking in any kind of personal accessories, and had

no color. We changed that! We even brought a cherished butterfly bush from his old yard and planted it outside his window. This favorite plant sent a clear message of welcome.

Congregating in the Kitchen

A room that people often forget about when combining generations is the kitchen. I had one client, Cheryl, who was sure she had to put in a whole new kitchen. "We're always walking into each other!" she exclaimed. "When everyone is in the kitchen at one time, it's bedlam."

Gutting the kitchen wasn't necessary, yet something had to happen. You'll laugh when you hear how simple the solution turned out to be: Moving the spoons for cereal and repositioning the utensils closer to the stove made life in the kitchen run as smooth as silk.

Cheryl's mother and father both loved to help with the cooking. They ended up really *being* a help when the cutting board was moved out of the traffic pattern and they could slice and dice veggies for salad or soup without getting underfoot.

Kitchen organizing goes back to the rule I've talked about before—the one that says, "A place for everything and everything in its place." But a more important rule is the one that says, "Everything must be near where it's going to be used." In this case, plastic containers (but only a reasonable number of them!) placed at the end of the kitchen assisted Mom and Dad in helping with cleanup, too. I like the kind that nest inside each other!

Adjust Your Attitude as Well as Your Home

Changes like these make people feel that they belong—and that they're needed. Adjusting work areas, family areas, and TV areas to easily include everyone is necessary. If you're in this portion of life, make sure you use your home environment to help integrate everyone into the new family dynamic.

Willingness is the word that comes into my mind in this particular process. It's a willingness to change our perceptions about how we're going to live in our home space. If we approach it as an exciting challenge instead of with the fear that life is no longer going to be special, that's what we'll get. Be aware of the things that need to happen as you change and grow, and every bit of your life and the home will remain precious.

I am continually saddened by the way our culture deals with folks over age 65. Perhaps it's because I am now part of that age group. I hope we get better at it, and I intend to be as creative in my life as the situation allows.

WHEN ILLNESS brings CHANGE

When illness strikes, it is of the utmost importance to consider your home environment. Number one, if you have or are recovering from a long-term, debilitating illness, you're going to be in your home more, so you may need more stimulation, more interest, more color, and more comforts. You may have entirely different needs, and they need to be well thought out and provided.

I once worked with a young woman named Bonnie who had a brain tumor. She was very tall—6 feet at 14 years of age. I knew identity and comfort were essential for her to heal in any way. "Tall" became my focus. Her mirror was attached to her dresser so the top of her head was right at the top of the mirror. We detached it and hung it higher so there was space above her reflection. I raised the curtains to the ceiling and let them go all the way to the floor. I wanted to emphasize that long was beautiful.

We put interest on the ceiling by painting white, puffy clouds on a sky-blue background. We raised pictures higher, so Bonnie could see them comfortably. We rearranged the furniture so she felt spaciousness around her.

The solutions we devised in Bonnie's case were to reinforce her identity. That may work for you in the face of illness, or you may need to make things different in terms of beauty, softness, and ease. If you have to take your meals in bed, or if you're spending a lot of time in bed, be sure that your views and wall treatments are lovely and that your side tables and dressers hold beautiful, meaningful things that inspire you, comfort you, and remind you of how good life is.

I remember a story of a man dying of AIDS. It had been a long illness, and his mother had been a confidential companion in the journey. As he died, he was in an environment that he had orchestrated. He had curtains that were billowy and were actually blowing with the help of fans. He had colors and paintings in front of him that he adored. He had fabrics on his bed that were exquisite and of his choice. He had Beethoven's Fifth playing. He told his mother in those moments that he was happier than he had ever been in his life.

Who knows what caused this dying man to feel so happy? Was it because he now knew himself better than he ever had before? Or was it because he had cared for himself more carefully than ever before? Whatever it was, he had created his home environment to support him in his last journey—and it was the best journey yet. Bravo!

CHANGE for CHANGE'S SAKE

The one kind of change I haven't mentioned so far is change for change's sake. Life sometimes has a way of remaining the same for long periods of time. This can lull us into never addressing our environments or our lives, and then habit becomes the mother of apathy. I've been called into a designing job many times to lift the environment, which I know translates into lifting life. It, too, is important work.

I facilitate makeover classes where we go into someone's home and move things around by hanging pictures and accessorizing. These classes are really fun, and they present a concrete realization of the concept of change for the better. Seeing how different the space can be with some simple reshuffling is mind boggling. We always seem to leave the home we've

worked on with a sense of excitement and new potential. It looks different. It has new activity spaces. And old things have taken on a new look.

Remember, life needs to be full for everybody. When some changes happen, we treat them as though they are temporary and therefore give them little attention or affection. Or we forget that change affects everybody. Often, temporary changes become permanent silently, and habit sets in to prevent or camouflage the need for adjustment.

Temporary changes deserve attention. (Think back to my Canada vacation story on page 275.) I've even rearranged hotel rooms where I'm staying for just one night! Every moment of life is important, and the space where short amounts of time are lived need to be both functional and pleasing. Change your spaces, change your spaces, change your spaces. Especially when your life changes!

Some people find change exciting, but I know a lot of people find it intimidating instead. To help you embrace change, here's a final exercise.

exercise 21
Work with Change

What you'll need: your small spiral notebook and your pen.

Everything we've talked about earlier in this book applies to this chapter also. Use your preferences. It is essential. The only difference is to realize that your life has changed and your needs have shifted. To find out how, you'll need to ask yourself some questions.

Some Questions to Help

These questions can change with each project you choose, but reading them is helpful in seeing the process and how you can proceed. Just keep remembering that it's about making life better now. Remember, too, that change keeps you excited, youthful, and engaged with life.

1. What has changed? (It could be a mood, a partner, or your income.)

2. What could ease your adjustment? Take lots of time and discover what alterations to your home environment could help with the change you're experiencing. Once you've decided, define the project carefully.

3. What in your home will you change so that the transition happens easily?

4. What tools are needed for the project or activities?

5. When do you want to start the project?

6. How long will it take to set up the space?

7. How much money do you want to invest? (It's possible that no money is necessary, only shifting of objects or priorities.)

8. What feelings do you want to have in the space?

9. What arrangement of furnishings would be best?

10. Does there need to be an adjustment in lighting, or does the present lighting work?

11. What furniture will you need?

12. What colors do you want to use?

13. What special support systems are needed? (Like music, air fresheners, television, special storage, favorite themes in accessories)

14. What inspiration do you need? (Like books, sayings, pictures, fresh flowers, and so on.)

What to Do

Let your answers not only provide you with insights as to what you need to do or would enjoy doing next, but also provide some direction and motivation. Let your changes take you in a healthy direction and give you something worthwhile to show for them!

your ACTION PLAN

Whether you're young or old, rich or poor, busy or idle, married or single, you have a home. It might just be a room, but it's your home. Make it an adventure in authenticity, an experiment in creativity, a leap in sensuality. Fill it with your kind of inspiration so that when you walk into it, there's the same feeling of specialness that you encounter on a bright, sunny day when everything seems so right with the world. This is soul work you're doing. You'll make your home sweet, and it will make you free. And you'll know yourself better in the process.

I wrote this chapter with so much gratitude. Its stories come from the experience of my career. Each story has stretched me and grown my work. I placed this chapter at the end of the book to show you how the process I've presented will continually serve you and how a home continues to be a vessel for change. I hope you have enjoyed your journey through the discovery. I also hope your home is heaven for you. Bless it constantly with who you are.

I wish for you that your home, your living, and your loving be your best friends.

Index

Underscored page references indicate boxed text. **Boldface** references indicate illustrations.

D

Daily itinerary
  exploring, 161–62
  example, 170–75
Death of spouse, making adjustments after,
  271–72
Decluttering
  action plans for, 197, 219, 240
  of clothes closet, 209
  difficulties of, 200
  exercises for
    creating clutter-clearing checklist, 215–16
    creating organizing notebook, 217–18
    focusing on decluttering, 213–14
    uncovering reasons for chaos, 195–96
  how to start, 182–83
  lists for, 202, 208
  maintaining energy for, <u>201</u>
  meditation for, <u>210–12</u>
  notebook for, 202–4, 205
  permission needed for, 207–8
  questions to help with, 206–7
  reasons for, 213–14
  relocating items after, 209, 214
  steps in, 187
  stories about, 13–15, 202–6, 207–8
  storing items after, 208–9
Design
  author's philosophy of, 12
  budget for, <u>254</u>
  do-it-yourself, 245
  extra tips on, <u>265</u>
  with heart in mind, 246
  steps in
    arranging furniture, 254–57
    choosing room to start, 252–53
    choosing starting point, 253
    connecting to design personality, 252
    deciding on placement of wall treatments,
      257–59, **258**
    labeling room, 253

    planning colors, 260–61
    planning accessories, 264
    planning lighting, 261–62, **262**
    planning window treatments, 263
    selecting furniture, 259–60
Designers, professional
  using discovery process, <u>245</u>
  working with, 102–3, 244–45, <u>244–45</u>, 265
Design evolution, of author, 7–12
Design personality, 24–25
  of author, <u>104</u>
  connecting to, 252
  decluttering and, 182
  discovering, 17–19
    action plans for, 24–25, 32, 49, 65, 79, 93,
      115, 131, 143, 176
    alone or with others, 29–30
    creating workstation for, 30–31
    importance of, 4–5
    rewards of, <u>29</u>
    stories about, 20–24
    supplies for, 31–32
  revealing, 28, 29
    analyzing picture journal, 109–14
    choosing fabrics, 140–42
    choosing beloved object, 61–64
    creating fantasy day, 69–70
    creating picture journal, 106–8
    defining lifestyle, 41–43
    exploring daily itinerary, 161–62
    finding common ground, 129–30
    making happiness list, 91–92
    making household activity inventory,
      165–67
    making life list, 163–64
    selecting representative household object,
      37–40
    summarizing activity space needs,
      168–69
    visualizing feelings, 44–48
Design plan, discovery process for, 19–20